Literacies in Language Education

Related Works

Teaching World Languages for Specific Purposes: A Practical Guide
DIANA M. RUGGIERO

Online World Language Instruction Training and Assessment: An Ecological Approach
CARMEN KING RAMÍREZ, BARBARA A. LAFFORD, AND JAMES E. WERMERS

Teaching Languages in Blended Synchronous Learning Classrooms: A Practical Guide
ALBA GIRONS AND NICHOLAS SWINEHART

Integrating the Digital Humanities into the Second Language Classroom: A Practical Guide
MELINDA A. CRO

Community-Based Language Learning: A Framework for Educators
JOAN CLIFFORD AND DEBORAH S. REISINGER

Integrating Career Preparation into Language Courses
DARCY LEAR

LITERACIES IN LANGUAGE EDUCATION

A Guide for Teachers and Teacher Educators

Kate Paesani and Mandy Menke

Georgetown University Press
Washington, DC

CARLA

Library of Congress Cataloging-in-Publication Data

Names: Paesani, Kate, author. | Menke, Mandy R., author.
Title: Literacies in language education : a guide for teachers and teacher educators / Kate Paesani and Mandy Menke.
Description: Washington, DC : Georgetown University Press, 2023. | Includes bibliographical references and index.
Identifiers: LCCN 2022019948 (print) | LCCN 2022019949 (ebook) | ISBN 9781647123338 (hardcover) | ISBN 9781647123321 (paperback) | ISBN 9781647123314 (ebook)
Subjects: LCSH: Language and languages—Study and teaching (Higher) | Literacy—Study and teaching (Higher)
Classification: LCC P53.475 .P34 2023 (print) | LCC P53.475 (ebook) | DDC 407.1/1—dc23/eng/20220721
LC record available at https://lccn.loc.gov/2022019948
LC ebook record available at https://lccn.loc.gov/2022019949

∞ This paper meets the requirements of ANSI/NISO Z39.48-1992 (Permanence of Paper).

24 23 9 8 7 6 5 4 3 2 First printing

Printed in the United States of America

Cover design by Brad Norr
Interior design by Robert Kern, TIPS Publishing Services, Carrboro, NC

Contents

APPENDIXES

Illustrations

Figures

Tables

Preface

WE HAVE BEEN CARRYING out research and teacher professional development on literacies in language education for a combined twenty years, and the most important thing we have learned from this work is that a literacies orientation can be hard for teachers to understand and enact. This book thus attempts to demystify literacies in language education by addressing curriculum and instruction using teacher-friendly language, research-informed examples, and practical materials. The audience for this book is secondary and postsecondary teachers and teacher educators of all languages and proficiency levels.[1] Indeed, the principles and practices introduced within these pages are neither language nor level specific, and the examples come from a range of more- and less-commonly taught languages.

Two important events motivated this book. The first was our initial collaborative research project. When Kate arrived at the University of Minnesota in September 2016 to become the director of the Center for Advanced Research on Language Acquisition (CARLA), she approached Mandy about conducting a small study of the Spanish language program she directs. That program was transitioning from a curriculum solidly grounded in communicative language teaching to one more reflective of literacies principles. That study, which analyzed text-based materials that had been developed by the Spanish program's level coordinators (Menke and Paesani 2019), quickly developed into a larger-scale project investigating teachers' understanding and implementation of multiliteracies pedagogy in introductory and intermediate Spanish courses (Menke and Paesani 2021). Findings from this research revealed several implications for language teacher professional development, and these implications formed the basis of CARLA's Literacies in Language Education project (https://carla.umn.edu/literacies/). The second event motivating this book was an email message Kate received from Hope LeGro, the assistant director of the press at Georgetown University Press (GUP). Hope was interested in developing a partnership between CARLA and the press to highlight the center's work and increase the number of guidebook-style publications in GUP's catalog. When we met to discuss this idea at an academic conference, it was clear that the Literacies in Language Education project was a perfect fit.

The purpose of the Literacies in Language Education project is to "give teachers research-based tools, resources, and experiences that help them effectively apply multiliteracies pedagogy and engage students with authentic texts in secondary and postsecondary classrooms" (CARLA 2021a). As codirectors of the project, we have created the following resources, all of which are available on the CARLA website (https://carla.umn.edu/literacies/), linked from this book's companion website (http://carla.umn.edu/literacies/book/), and referenced throughout subsequent chapters:

- a glossary of key literacies terminology
- a bibliography of scholarly resources organized according to four topic areas (general resources; curriculum and instruction; student learning outcomes, perceptions, and experiences; teacher understanding and applications of multiliteracies pedagogy)
- target language text resources in over fourteen languages
- a lesson analysis checklist for evaluating existing text-based instructional materials
- an infographic comparing multiliteracies pedagogy with communicative language teaching

To share these resources, we teach an annual CARLA summer institute focused on equipping teachers with the conceptual and pedagogical knowledge essential to developing their students' foreign language literacies through engagement with target language texts. We also present regularly at national and international conferences and conduct workshops across the country with secondary and postsecondary teachers and teacher educators. This collective work has contributed to the ideas and resources presented in this book.

Before summarizing the book's contents, we'd like to explain its title: *Literacies in Language Education*. You may have been surprised to see the word "literacy" used in its plural form—"literacies"—when you picked up this book or saw it in the GUP catalog. One important goal of this book, as the definitions presented in chapter 1 will make clear, is to move away from the traditional notion of literacy as the ability to read and write. Instead, we embrace an expanded understanding of literacies as being multiple. This plural term captures the dynamism of language and its contexts of use; the importance of preparing students to interact with the range of text types they will encounter in their academic, workplace, and personal lives; and the multicultural and multilingual landscape of secondary and postsecondary language classrooms. You may have also wondered why we use the term "language education" rather than the more common terms "second," "foreign," or "world language education." As we mentioned regarding our intended audience, the scope of this book is broad and inclusive of a variety of teaching contexts, languages, and levels, and the title reflects this intent. We furthermore recognize that terminology around language education is always complex and sometimes fraught (e.g., Reagan and Osborn 2021). Distinctions between second and foreign languages, for example, can be ambiguous and exclusionary. By using "language education" in the book title, we aim to describe the teaching of languages other than one's first language(s) and to reflect our belief that all languages are valuable and worthy of consideration when adopting new teaching paradigms, including the literacies approach described herein. The one exception to this phrasing is the term "foreign language literacies," which we use to explicitly highlight adaptations of multiliteracies pedagogy, the framework undergirding this book, beyond its intended use for first language literacies development (New London Group 1996).

This book is organized into two main parts that are bookended by introductory and concluding chapters. To facilitate readers' conceptual understanding, the book also includes a glossary of key terms; these key terms are italicized when they are introduced and defined in relevant chapters to let you know that they also appear in the glossary. Each chapter, apart from the epilogue and chapters 2 and 6, follows the same general structure. Chapters begin with an overview of the topic, present research-informed principles and practices relevant to understanding and enacting the topic, and then highlight problems and solutions related to teacher professional development. Chapters conclude with three practical sections: questions to encourage reflective teaching practice, resources from CARLA's Literacies in Language Education project and other sources to support classroom implementation, and key publications for further reading and viewing to deepen conceptual understanding. These resources, as well as the sample unit and lesson plans, templates, and worksheets discussed throughout, are additionally available on the companion website (http://carla.umn.edu/literacies/book/).

The introductory chapter, "Understanding Literacies in Language Education," provides a research-based conceptual foundation to help you create and implement language curricula that are centered around target language texts. Working from the premise that language and content should be integrated at all curricular levels (secondary and postsecondary, introductory through advanced), chapter 1 overviews the concept of foreign language literacies, the knowledge processes of multiliteracies pedagogy (Cope and Kalantzis 2009; Kalantzis et al. 2016), and other key literacies principles that are revisited throughout the book.

With this conceptual understanding as a backdrop, part I focuses on constructing literacies-oriented language curricula. The three chapters in part I are each grounded in the backward design model (Wiggins and McTighe 2005) of curriculum construction, a recursive process that entails first identifying desired learning outcomes and content, then developing an assessment plan that provides evidence of student learning, and finally planning learning experiences to guide classroom activities. An overview of this model and its relationship to literacies principles is presented in chapter 2. To model the backward design approach, the first two planning stages are treated in chapters 3–5. Chapter 3, "Creating Learning Objectives," provides a general introduction to what learning objectives are, why they are important, and how they should be crafted. Research-based principles for designing literacies-based curricula (Bull and Anstey 2010; Kern 2003) are then considered in relation to learning objectives. The chapter concludes with a discussion of obstacles to attaining and strategies for encouraging teacher buy-in related to literacies-oriented language curricula. The aim of chapter 4, "Defining, Selecting, and Evaluating Target Language Texts," is to provide research-based tools to guide the selection of target language texts and to determine their salient features in a way consistent with literacies learning objectives. The chapter furthermore defines the concepts of target language text and genre and discusses challenges and solutions teachers face in working with target language texts in their original form. The final chapter of part I, "Developing an Assessment Plan," focuses on constructing an assessment plan that helps teachers determine whether students have met stated learning objectives and developed their foreign language literacies. In addition to defining key assessment terms, chapter 4 presents principles to guide the creation of a literacies-oriented assessment plan that includes both traditional and alternative assessments. The chapter concludes with a spotlight on professional development that offers strategies for honing language teachers' assessment knowledge and skills.

Part II of the book focuses on the third stage of the backward design model—planning learning experiences using the knowledge processes of multiliteracies pedagogy. These knowledge processes are introduced in chapter 6 and then detailed one by one in chapters 7–10. Chapter 7, "Experiencing: Building Textual Understanding," explains how to immerse students in target language texts through exploration of the familiar (e.g., known vocabulary, lived experiences), the unfamiliar (e.g., new perspectives, unknown cultural content), and thoughts, opinions, and feelings about textual content. We exemplify the knowledge process of experiencing with a detailed look at five activity types and then present a teacher professional development tool to help you identify and reflect on experiencing activities in your own teaching materials. The knowledge process of conceptualizing is the focus of chapter 8, which builds on the concept of textual features presented in chapter 4. "Conceptualizing: Connecting Form and Meaning" first defines conceptualizing and its role in students' literacies development and then examines form-focused activities that demonstrate these ideas. The chapter concludes with challenges language teachers face in relation to conceptualizing and how they can be addressed through professional development activities. The aim of chapter 9, "Analyzing: Exploring Cultural Practices and Perspectives," is to outline the process of creating activities that engage language learners in higher-order thinking and lead them to the critical analysis of target language texts. The chapter provides a rationale for integrating analyzing activities regardless of students' age or proficiency level, provides multiple examples, and addresses common barriers to successfully implementing analyzing activities. Part II concludes with chapter 10, "Applying: Assessing Student Learning." This chapter explains and exemplifies the specific characteristics of applying activities and considers their role in instructional and assessment practices. Key features of this chapter include differentiating applying activities from common communicative production activities, scaffolding applying activities to more effectively develop students' foreign language literacies, and overcoming the constraints of language textbooks.

The book concludes with an epilogue titled "Advancing Literacies in Language Education," the purpose of which is to consider questions and practical strategies for moving the field of language education toward literacies-oriented curriculum, assessment, and instruction. Topics addressed in the epilogue include the potential of a literacies orientation for enacting social justice in language education, the implementation of a literacies orientation at the secondary level, and the need for more and more accessible literacies-oriented materials (textbooks, lesson plans, activity examples, and the like).

This book is not the result of our work alone, and we wish to conclude this preface by acknowledging those who have contributed to this project. Although we have authored this book's chapters and created the resources for CARLA's Literacies in Language Education project, our thinking was influenced and advanced by numerous teachers and teacher educators at the University of Minnesota and beyond. We are grateful to the colleagues who provided feedback on book chapters and related materials prior to their publication: Lauren Goodspeed, Liz Lake, Jason Martel, and Helena Ruf. We also wish to acknowledge Heather Willis Allen, Kristen Michelson, and Chantelle Warner, who presented with us at a symposium on multiliteracies and language teacher education at the 11th International Language Teacher Education Conference, which CARLA hosted in May 2019. Their research and ideas continue to inspire us. The Spanish language program at the University of Minnesota has been not only an important research site but also a testing ground for many of the resources presented in this book. We are thus grateful to the coordinators and instructors in this program, in particular Stephanie Anderson, Cecily Brown, Sara Finney, Sara Mack, Frances Matos Schultz, and the participants in a professional learning circle on multiliteracies pedagogy. The changes made to the Spanish language curriculum came about in part because of findings from a multiyear proficiency project at the University of Minnesota. The Proficiency Assessment for Curricular Enhancement (PACE) project, funded by the Language Flagship, revealed that language students' listening proficiency developed more slowly than other modalities and led to the incorporation of more text-based interpretive listening activities in the Spanish curriculum. The PACE project was led by Dan Soneson from the College of Liberal Arts Language Center, and we are grateful for his support of curricular revisions grounded in target language texts and multiliteracies pedagogy. The CARLA summer institute we coteach also provided opportunities for feedback on the ideas and resources in these pages, and we are indebted to the teachers and teacher educators who have attended over the years, particularly the 2021 cohort with whom we piloted several chapters of this book. We would also like to thank the graduate research assistants—Marie Mangold, James Ramsburg, Carol Ready, Russell Simonsen, and Lauren Truman—who have worked with us to update bibliographies, format chapters, code learning activities, organize Canvas courses, sort data, and set up this book's companion website. At Georgetown University Press we owe our gratitude to Hope LeGro, without whom this book would not exist. Her enthusiasm and flexibility about the project motivated us to stick to our deadlines, even during the COVID-19 pandemic and the chaos it created in our working lives. Finally, this project would not have been possible without the steady support, extreme professionalism, and excellent sense of humor of the CARLA staff: Liz Hellebuyck, Marlene Johnshoy, and Karin Larson. Our most sincere thanks to all of you.

Note

1. We acknowledge that a literacies orientation can be and has been applied in elementary learning contexts (i.e., grades K–8), although very little scholarship demonstrates its application to language teaching at this level (see, e.g., Burke and Hardware 2015; Fterniati 2010; Reyes-Torres and Raga 2020). The combination of students' low linguistic proficiency and limited cognitive abilities in elementary contexts makes implementing this approach challenging and requires specialized skills and knowledge that are outside of our scope of expertise and experience. For these reasons, the discussions and examples in this book are specific to using a literacies approach with more cognitively mature learners at the secondary and postsecondary levels.

1

Understanding Literacies in Language Education

WHAT DOES IT MEAN to place texts at the center of language curricula? How does doing so diversify the language, voices, and perspectives we bring to our classrooms? How does it foster our students' agency and empowerment in the language learning process? These essential questions may seem daunting, but learning about literacies principles and their application to language education can help you answer them. The purpose of this introductory chapter is to help you build a conceptual foundation so that you may more effectively develop students' foreign language literacies through engagement with written, audio, audiovisual, visual, and digital texts. We define and deconstruct key literacies concepts, provide a rationale for foreign language literacies as a framing goal for language programs, introduce multiliteracies pedagogy as means for achieving that goal, and describe how teachers learn about and apply this approach. Throughout this chapter and the remainder of the book, we work from two key premises: (1) the study of language and texts should be integrated at all curricular levels—in introductory through advanced courses and in secondary and postsecondary contexts, and (2) the overarching goal of foreign language literacies development promotes students' communicative and critical thinking abilities, their cultural understanding, and their agency. These key premises are interrelated in that a literacies orientation to language education prioritizes the learning of language through textual content. To ensure that this book is both rigorous and practical, we adopt a praxis orientation to the presentation of literacies terminology, teaching practices, and pedagogical tools. That is, we consider how research-based evidence and theoretical concepts inform classroom instruction, experiences, and beliefs, and vice versa. We feel strongly that research, theory, and practice have equal value and that the only way to improve language teaching and learning and to develop students' literacies is for researchers and practitioners to learn with and from each other.

Understanding the Concept of Literacies

The multiliteracies framework (Cope and Kalantzis 2009; Kalantzis et al. 2016; New London Group 1996), which undergirds this book, is the perfect example of a praxis-oriented view of language education because it includes both a theoretical framework and a pedagogical approach. We talk more about the pedagogical approach later in this chapter, but for now, we focus on the most important theoretical concept within the multiliteracies framework: literacies. As you'll see from the definition in the next paragraph, this concept emphasizes the ability to interpret and transform target language texts and the interconnectedness of language, culture, and social context. We use the word "literacies" in the plural for two reasons. First, the concept of literacies is distinct from the concept of *literacy* in the singular because it entails much more than the ability to read and write. Second, talking about literacies in the plural captures the dynamism and diversity of language and literacy practices. For instance, an individual uses language differently in different contexts (e.g., work vs. home, speaking vs. writing, online vs. face-to-face), and groups of individuals use language differently from each other (e.g., based on age, gender, geographical location, social connection).

Although the multiliteracies framework arose in relation to first language literacies development, in this book we focus on how the framework has been applied in language education.[1] We thus begin with a research-based definition of *foreign language literacies* taken from Kern's seminal book, *Literacy and Language Teaching* (2000). For him, foreign language literacies

> is the use of socially-, historically-, and culturally-situated practices of creating and interpreting meaning through texts. It entails at least a tacit awareness of the relationships between textual conventions and their contexts of use, and ideally, the ability to reflect critically on these relationships. Because it is purpose-sensitive, literacy is dynamic—not static—and variable across and within discourse communities and cultures. It draws on a wide range of cognitive abilities, on knowledge of written and spoken language, on knowledge of genres, and on cultural knowledge. (16)

This definition may seem opaque to you, so let's break it down in more practical terms. Most importantly, foreign language literacies is about students' developing ability to interpret and create target language texts. The way we use the word "text" in this book may be different from your definition of this concept: we understand and define a *text* as being any concrete, observable product that communicates meaning. A text can thus be written, such as a poem; audio, such as a journalistic interview; audiovisual, such as a film trailer; visual, such as a painting; or digital, such as a blog post. A text can also be *multimodal*, or a combination of written, audio, visual, or digital modes. For instance, an article from npr.com includes written text, but it may also contain images, graphs, tables, embedded audio or video files, or hyperlinks to other articles. To *interpret* a text means understanding the gist or surface-level facts as well as critically examining cultural messages and viewpoints and the way language is used to express those messages and viewpoints. To *create* a text likewise means more than practicing grammar and vocabulary; it means applying the language forms and cultural knowledge learned from a text to create something new, be it a written text, a graphic representation, or a conversation. Foreign language literacies also involves different kinds of knowledge and abilities: knowledge of oral and written language; knowledge of cultural products, practices, and perspectives; and the use of strategies, self-reflection, problem-solving, inferencing, and other cognitive abilities (Kalantzis et al. 2016; Kern 2000; Menke and Paesani 2019). In a nutshell, foreign language literacies is about communication and critical engagement with texts.

We can also consider this definition of literacies in relation to individuals. As you might imagine, multiliterate individuals exhibit a range of knowledge and competencies, including the ability to draw on a repertoire of meaning-making resources (e.g., language forms, cultural knowledge in their first and second languages, understanding of genres), participate in a range of literacy practices, problem solve, and think critically. Armed with these abilities, individuals can better understand how social and cultural diversity affect and are reflected in texts and can more effectively communicate across modalities and technologies. As such, multiliterate individuals are empowered to be agents of their own learning and to participate in a range of social, academic, and professional contexts (Anstey and Bull 2018).

Literacies in Language Education

The definition of literacies outlined in the previous section is consistent with our earlier claim that the study of language and texts should be integrated at all levels. What is language-content integration and why is it important for understanding literacies in language education? The short answer to this question is that *language-content integration* "involves learning a second language through some form of content" (Martel 2013, 1142). Depending on the focus of your program, course, unit, or lesson, one may be emphasized more than the other. For instance, in immersion education or in cultures and languages across the curriculum (CLAC) programs, academic content (e.g., math, science, social studies) is often emphasized more than language learning, and courses are typically taught by content specialists. In secondary and postsecondary language programs, however, language learning is often emphasized more than academic or cultural content, and courses are typically taught by language specialists. Key to achieving language-content integration is "attributing complementary status to both language and content objectives in the . . . curriculum" (Tedick and Lyster 2020, 81), a goal referred to as counterbalance in the research (Lyster 2007). According to Tedick and Lyster, *counterbalance* does not imply "an equal or balanced focus on language and content"; rather, "counterbalance entails an ongoing shift in emphasis to prevent either language or content from taking on a disproportionate role in the . . . curriculum that eclipses the importance of the other" (2020, 81).

Language curricula grounded in the concept of foreign language literacies reflect this counterbalanced approach by always keeping the integration of language and content in focus through the interpretation and creation of target language texts. In fact, we argue that foreign language literacies should be the overarching principle guiding curriculum and instruction in secondary and postsecondary language programs. Why is this the case? Why prioritize literacies in language education as opposed to proficiency, intercultural understanding, or critical thinking? In what follows, we provide a rationale for literacies in language education that addresses these questions and demonstrates that prioritizing foreign language literacies development entails attention to students' language proficiency, intercultural understanding, and critical thinking.

Because of its focus on target language texts, many teachers and teacher educators worry that literacies pedagogy is incompatible with the proficiency- and communication-oriented approaches that predominate in twenty-first century language education. Rest assured that this is not the case! When we develop students' foreign language literacies, we cultivate their ability to engage not only in interpretive communication but also in interpersonal and presentational communication. You may already be familiar with these three communicative modes from the World-Readiness Standards (National Standards Collaborative Board [NSCB] 2015). The following definitions incorporate ideas from the World-Readiness Standards as well as from the multiliteracies framework (CARLA 2021a):

- *Interpretive communication* allows a reader, listener, or viewer to construct meaning (e.g., understand, interpret, analyze) from written, audio, audiovisual, digital, or visual texts. Engaging with texts in this way includes establishing literal understanding of basic information, making inferences, and analyzing cultural products, practices, and perspectives embedded in texts. Because this is a one-way communication mode, there is no possibility of meaning negotiation.
- *Interpersonal communication* involves interaction and meaning negotiation in spoken, written, or signed conversations. When students interact in this mode, they explore and negotiate relationships, shared assumptions, conventions, imagination, creativity, and emotions that are grounded in their understandings of the texts they interpret.
- *Presentational communication* entails sharing information and ideas to an (often) distant audience in order to inform, explain, persuade, or narrate on various topics. Learners also demonstrate awareness of communicative conventions relevant to the text type they are presenting. As with interpretive communication, there is no opportunity for meaning negotiation during oral and written presentational tasks.

With these definitions in mind, let's review some research evidence showing how a literacies orientation develops students' language proficiency. Although there are numerous studies demonstrating the impact of literacies pedagogy on language learning, we focus on only three here, one each related to the interpretive, interpersonal, and presentational modes of communication. First, a study of novice-level postsecondary German learners explored students' language learning when they spent half of each class period interpreting a full-length German romance novel and the other half carrying out form-focused communicative activities (Maxim 2002, 2006). Using a four-stage textually oriented pedagogy, interpretive activities included identifying major events in the romance novel, pinpointing textual details and the language that expressed them, reproducing textual language to demonstrate understanding, and connecting the text to real-world knowledge to identify implications. Study findings showed that students were able to read a novel after only four weeks of studying German. Moreover, development of students' reading proficiency did not compromise their language development: students in the romance novel group scored just as well on language-focused departmental exams as students who did not do extensive interpretive reading. A second study investigated intermediate-level postsecondary French learners who participated in a global simulation—a culturally grounded, fictitious scenario in which students take on roles that they enact through course activities—implemented using multiliteracies pedagogy (Michelson and Dupuy 2014). Findings revealed that through their participation in various activities, including those that developed proficiency in oral and written interpersonal communication, students expanded their meaning-making repertoires. That is, in addition to using grammar and vocabulary to express themselves in oral and written interpersonal tasks, students also saw the value of communicative resources such as gestures, facial expressions, and body language. Through their adoption of a specific character role, students were also more aware of the register and tone they used to communicate, thereby increasing the diversity of their linguistic repertoires. Finally, a third study investigated one fourth-grade Spanish learner's presentational writing development (Troyan 2016). The genre-based pedagogy adopted in the study reflects multiliteracies principles through its focus on language-content integration and reading and writing texts. Analyses of the student's writing before and after the pedagogy was implemented showed improvement in her ability to produce more cohesive, informative, and detailed texts. Furthermore, the student's writing, which possessed traits of oral interpersonal speech at the start of the study, was more reflective of the descriptive genre she had studied through the reading and analysis of target language texts.

In addition to developing students' proficiency and *communication* in interpretive, interpersonal, and presentational modes, prioritizing foreign language literacies creates opportunities to connect to the other Cs of the World-Readiness Standards (*cultures, connections, comparisons, communities*) (NSCB 2015). In fact, Kern (2003) proposed literacies-oriented definitions of the standards, highlighting how a literacies approach promotes complex thinking through conscious language use. These definitions are provided in table 1.1.

Several studies have used a literacies lens to study culture learning as defined in table 1.1. One study aimed to understand how postsecondary learners connect with Japanese language through a multiliteracies approach to anime (Fukunaga 2006). Based on the analysis of student interviews, the researcher found that to deepen their connection with Japanese culture, students became members of the anime community (e.g., through online gaming, anime clubs, conventions). Through participation in this community, students not only expanded their cultural knowledge but also gained insider perspectives of the anime subculture, learned more colloquial speech styles, and felt recognized and empowered by community members. Another study described an intercultural citizenship project between postsecondary English learners in Argentina and Spanish learners in the United Kingdom (Porto 2018). The project, focused on the 1978 World Cup, was designed to develop students' multimedia and digital literacies as well as their ability to engage in intercultural communication. Analysis of oral and written interactions, class artifacts, reflection logs, and course evaluations showed that students learned to communicate across

Table 1.1. World-Readiness Standards: Literacies-Based Definitions

Standard	Definition
Communication	Understanding and *interpreting* written and spoken language on varied topics, communicating in meaningful and *appropriate* ways, taking *audience* and *context* into account (i.e., rhetorical demands—this requires being able to shift frames of reference, norms, assumptions of what can and can't be said, and so forth).
Cultures	Understanding *relationships* between the *social practices, cultural products, and perspectives* (beliefs, values, attitudes, ideas) of people in the foreign culture (i.e., reading a cultural "code" through texts).
Connections	Strengthening *knowledge* of other disciplines through language study—art, music, film studies, history, etc.; acquiring information and *recognizing viewpoints* available through the language and its cultures (i.e., seeing how different rules of interpretation operate in a different disciplinary and/or cultural system).
Comparisons	Understanding the nature of language/culture through *comparisons* of the language/culture studied and their own (i.e., thinking critically about cultural systems and about how languages work).
Communities	*Participating* in multilingual *communities* at home and around the world for personal enjoyment and enrichment; relating to past and present worlds outside of our immediate community through textual interaction; examining the ways that language is used to capture and express ideas and experiences within those communities.

Source: Kern (2003, 8; italics in original).

their respective cultures to reach consensus, collaborate, support each other, and show solidarity. In addition, the focus on intercultural citizenship and communication facilitated students' ability to notice and reflect on language, negotiate meaning, and experiment with new language forms. Finally, based on observations of culture teaching and learning in preschool, secondary, and postsecondary contexts, Kearney (2014) concluded that regardless of age or proficiency level, culture teaching that is grounded in awareness raising (e.g., modeling openness and curiosity toward cultural and linguistic differences) results in more complex meaning making and perspective taking on the part of students, ideas embedded in our definition of foreign language literacies. For instance, in an interaction about Korean and English writing systems, one preschool teacher and her four-year-old student were able to discuss what normal writing entails and to consider both writing systems as equally valuable for writing one's name (Kearney and Ahn 2013a, 2013b).

As this brief review of studies grounded in literacies principles demonstrates, regardless of language or level, prioritizing foreign language literacies develops students' language proficiency and cultural understanding. Moreover, engaging deeply with the cultural content and language forms in target language texts has the added benefit of developing students' critical thinking abilities. Critical thinking is often posited as one of the most important benefits of the discipline of the humanities, including language study (Dumitru 2019). Within a literacies orientation, communication about texts is closely tied to critical thinking: it enables increasingly complex and diverse thinking and language use as well as increased agency and empathy. Indeed, "there is little point in teaching a student to talk about a literary style or a cultural feature in a foreign language unless that student can reflect on what is at stake historically, professionally, or cognitively" (Swaffar 2006, 249). Developing students' foreign language literacies is therefore at the core of language learning, an idea that challenges decades-long thinking that language—and by extension, proficiency—is at the core, with literacies development on the periphery (Warford and White 2012). Yet as we have demonstrated, a literacies orientation supports language acquisition, proficiency development, and more importantly, multimodal communication about culture through another language.

Key Literacies Concepts

Now that we've discussed the concept of literacies; why it should serve as a framing principle for language curriculum and instruction; and how it develops students' language proficiency, cultural understanding, and critical thinking abilities, we can explore additional literacies concepts that support subsequent chapters in this book. We start this section with a caveat: based on our experience working with teachers, we know that some of these concepts are abstract and that some teachers struggle to see how multiliteracies pedagogy is distinct from other approaches they use in the classroom. To help overcome these challenges, we invite you to reflect on pedagogical concepts and approaches you are familiar with:

- What approach (or approaches) do you use in instruction?
- What concepts, ideas, or practices form the basis of this approach?
- How did you learn about this approach and its related concepts?
- How long did it take you to feel comfortable implementing this approach?
- What challenges did you face in your learning?

Identifying your current state of understanding related to language teaching and learning and recalling your experiences learning the approach you currently use can help ease the transition to new approaches and encourage critical reflection about how they fit within your existing knowledge base and classroom experiences.

To facilitate this praxis-based work, we begin this section by positioning literacies and multiliteracies pedagogy in relation to an approach we suspect is already familiar to you: *communicative language teaching* (CLT). CLT, like multiliteracies pedagogy, places meaningful communication at the center of language instruction. CLT aims to build students' *communicative competence*, or the ability to use language appropriately to carry out specific functions in different social situations, such as narrating in the past to describe last summer's vacation to a friend. Functions, such as narrating in the past, are connected to specific language forms, such as the preterit and imperfect, and CLT activities help students acquire these forms and use them to carry out communicative tasks. These activities often follow a sequence of teacher presentation of new material, form- and meaning-focused (i.e., controlled) practice of that material, and oral and written communicative (i.e., free) production tasks.

Through this sequence, learners have opportunities to hear and create language (i.e., receive input and produce output) and to negotiate meaning to successfully communicate with others (Ellis and Shintani 2013; Richards and Rodgers 2014).[2]

Whereas CLT prioritizes functional, and most often oral, communication, *multiliteracies pedagogy* prioritizes meaningful communication around target language texts and the language forms and conventions used to express ideas within those texts. For instance, in multiliteracies pedagogy, instead of focusing on learning past tense forms to carry out the function of narrating, the focus might be on learning how past tense forms shape the chronology of a story and its related historical events. A crucial difference between these two uses of past tense forms is context. In the CLT example, the function of narrating can be carried out when hanging out with friends or relating an experience during a job interview, but it can also be devoid of context, carried out simply to demonstrate that one is able to use past tense forms accurately. In the multiliteracies example, however, this same language function is studied within the context of a target language text to understand its purpose, use, and meaning and to build students' linguistic knowledge en route to creative language production. The aim of multiliteracies pedagogy is thus not only to build students' communicative competence—although communicating appropriately in different social contexts is an important goal—but also to cultivate their ability to design meaning. *Meaning design* involves identifying, understanding, and analyzing patterns in the ways ideas are presented in texts and incorporating those patterns into one's linguistic and communicative repertoires. More specifically, meaning design has linguistic, sociocultural, and cognitive dimensions that involve

- making connections between language forms and the meanings they express in texts (linguistic dimension);
- attending to the social context, background knowledge, and lived experiences that inform ideas expressed in texts and how we interpret those ideas (sociocultural dimension); and
- engaging in higher-order thinking through learning processes such as interpretation, problem-solving, and reflection about the world and one's place within it (cognitive dimension).

If the concept of meaning design feels abstract to you, it may be helpful to think of it in relation to the definition of literacies we've developed throughout this chapter. First, meaning design is a means to an end: it is what learners must do to develop their foreign language literacies (Kern 2000). In doing so, students learn new language forms, conventions, and cultural content and incorporate this new knowledge into what they already know about both their first language(s) and the target language. Second, students design meaning by engaging in textual *interpretation* and *creation*, two concepts introduced earlier in this chapter. Students interpret target language texts to understand and analyze language forms, conventions, and cultural content; they create texts by using that understanding to express themselves in new ways. Finally, meaning design encourages critical thinking as students analyze and use language to carry out interpersonal, interpretive, and presentational communication tasks around the content of texts.

As we argued earlier, foreign language literacies should be the overarching goal for secondary and postsecondary language programs. Meaning design, interpretation, and creation are interrelated concepts that describe what students do to build and demonstrate their foreign language literacies. Together these concepts define the what of multiliteracies pedagogy in language education. To realize our goal and put the what into practice in the classroom, multiliteracies pedagogy includes four activity types, or knowledge processes: experiencing, conceptualizing, analyzing, and applying. These knowledge processes, or the how of multiliteracies pedagogy, promote students' foreign language literacies development and engage them in meaning design by tapping into the different ways that humans learn and create knowledge (Cope and Kalantzis 2009; Kalantzis et al. 2016; New London Group 1996).

The four knowledge processes will be treated in detail in chapters 6–10. For now, we present a brief definition of each to illustrate how these activity types develop students' foreign language literacies. *Experiencing* activities help students build knowledge by reflecting on what they already know and have experienced and by immersing themselves in new situations and experiences. In these types of activities, students do not carry out deep analysis of target language texts but rather build literal understanding of textual information and express their thoughts, opinions, and feelings about that information. *Conceptualizing* activities home in on the language, organizational, and genre features of target language texts so that students can see how these features work in context to express ideas. Students therefore unpack texts in conceptualizing activities and develop their explicit knowledge of the tools that will help them communicate appropriately, effectively, and accurately in the target language. In *analyzing* activities, learners question the meaning, importance, and consequences of what they have learned from target language texts. These activities encourage a big-picture view of textual meaning that includes relating what is learned to social, historical, cultural, or political contexts and purposes. Finally, *applying* activities allow students to demonstrate the skills and understandings gained through working with target language texts by producing language in new and creative ways. Table 1.2 provides a summary of the four knowledge processes, including definitions from the glossary that forms part of CARLA's Literacies in Language Education project (CARLA 2021a). The table also includes example activities and a mantra that you can use to remind yourself of the purpose of each knowledge process as you design multiliteracies lessons. For example, a common experiencing activity is brainstorming vocabulary based on themes students will encounter in a target language text. This activity reflects the mantra "explore familiar and new ideas" because it allows students to draw on their previous language knowledge to help them understand new information they will encounter when they read, view, or listen to a text for the first time.

Although we provide numerous examples of this pedagogy in subsequent chapters, a quick illustration of what the knowledge processes look like in context is likely useful to you at this point. The following lesson is based on a Grumpy Cat meme (Ladage 2015) in which Grumpy Cat's frowning face is pictured resting against a white pillow. Above Grumpy Cat's head is the phrase "Good morning?" and below her is the phrase "No such thing." The lesson in table 1.3 shows how each knowledge

Table 1.2. The Knowledge Processes of Multiliteracies Pedagogy

Knowledge process	Definition	Example activities	Mantra
Experiencing	Learning through immersion in texts, activities, and social situations. Expressing thoughts, reactions, opinions, and feelings and gaining global comprehension about familiar or new experiences, objects, ideas, situations, perspectives, and ways of communicating. Does not involve deep reflection or analysis.	• Brainstorming • Think-Pair-Share • True/False Questions	Explore familiar and new ideas
Conceptualizing	Learning how language forms, conventions, organization, and other features of texts work to convey meaning. Unpacking texts, practicing skills and knowledge, and explicit learning about textual features helps learners participate more fully in communication.	• Concept Map • Synonym Substitution • Text Annotation	Connect language and meaning through texts
Analyzing	Learning by connecting the content of texts to social, cultural, and historical contexts. Questioning the meaning, importance, and consequences of textual content. Critically reflecting on textual content and its relationship to one's own culture, perspectives, and learning.	• 3-2-1 Summary • Debate • Self-Assessment of Learning	Question the complexity of culture, language, and ideas
Applying	Learning by using new knowledge, skills, and understandings and by producing language in creative ways.	• Genre Reformulation • Personal Action Plan • Story Retelling	Create texts and showcase new knowledge

Source: CARLA (2021a).

process can be used to help novice English learners design meaning as they interpret this text and create their own meme using greeting and leave-taking expressions. This short lesson engages students in interpretive, interpersonal, and presentational communication and can be carried out after students have learned basic greeting and leave-taking expressions, as well as phrases such as "I like" and "I don't like." All activities are carried out in the target language.

The order of activities in table 1.3 suggests that the four knowledge processes are sequential, but this is not the case. As you'll see in later chapters, you can choose and mix the order of the knowledge processes in ways that most effectively meet students' needs, achieve stated learning objectives, and provide a balanced approach

Table 1.3. The Knowledge Processes: Example Lesson for Novice English Learners

Activity	Knowledge process
1. Students brainstorm words they associate with the morning (e.g., early, sun, coffee). They then indicate whether they are a morning person and provide one reason why using the phrases "I like" and "I don't like." The teacher projects the meme without the words and asks students to decide if Grumpy Cat is a morning person based on her appearance.	Experiencing
2. Students are asked to provide appropriate responses to the phrase "Good morning." Students then read the meme and discuss the response "No such thing": Is this a response you learned in your textbook? Is it an appropriate or expected response to "Good morning"? Finally, students are asked to identify linguistic and visual features of the meme indicating that Grumpy Cat doesn't like mornings (e.g., her frown, the question mark after "Good morning," the use of a negative response).	Conceptualizing
3. Students then consider the intent of the meme: What message was the author trying to convey? Why is the meme funny? Do you think some people won't find the meme funny? Why not? To facilitate target language use, the teacher can provide a list of possible answers for each question that are then compared in small groups.	Analyzing
4. Students work in pairs to create their own Grumpy Cat meme using the same photo but a different greeting or leave-taking expression they've learned in class (e.g., How's it going? See you later!). The class then votes on the funniest meme and discusses the features that made it funny.	Applying

to learning through all four activity types. For instance, prior to the experiencing activity at the start of the example lesson in table 1.3, the teacher might lead an instructional conversation—an analyzing activity—that introduces the Grumpy Cat character, explains its sociocultural context, and describes features of the meme genre. Likewise, to scaffold the lesson-ending applying activity more fully, the teacher might lead an experiencing activity in which students brainstorm vocabulary words they associate with different greeting and leave-taking expressions they know. These adaptations to the example lesson demonstrate that the knowledge processes are a flexible pedagogical framework that is easily adaptable across levels, languages, and instructional contexts. This flexibility is a departure from CLT activity sequencing, which often moves from mechanical (i.e., controlled practice of language forms, one correct answer) to meaningful (i.e., controlled practice with meaning-based options, limited number of correct answers) to communicative (i.e., open-ended, meaningful language use, unpredictable answers) activities (Richards 2006). Where the knowledge processes and CLT activities are similar is in the general organizational structure of text-based lessons: both incorporate preparatory activities (e.g., activity 1 in table 1.3), textual engagement activities (e.g., activities 2 and 3), and follow-up activities (e.g., activity 4). In other words, both approaches organize text-based lessons using a pre-, while-, and postreading, viewing, or listening structure.

To conclude this section on key multiliteracies concepts, we point you to two resources that will help solidify your understanding and help you think about multiliteracies concepts in relation to what you already know about language teaching and learning. The first is table 1.4, which summarizes the concept of literacies—our proposed overarching goal for secondary and postsecondary language programs—and its relationship to multiliteracies pedagogy and the four knowledge processes.

The second is a resource from CARLA's Literacies in Language Education project and linked on the companion website (http://carla.umn.edu/literacies/book/): an infographic comparing multiliteracies pedagogy with CLT (CARLA 2021b). This infographic presents key concepts from both approaches in relation to their purpose, foundational concepts, and pedagogical principles. As you interact with this infographic and digest the concepts presented in this chapter, we remind you that key strategies for incorporating new approaches into your teaching repertoire are (1) starting from what you already know, (2) thinking critically about how new concepts and practices are similar to or different from your existing knowledge base and experiences, and (3) reflecting on needed changes in your thinking to expand your teaching repertoire in ways that reflect the new approach.

Spotlight on Teacher Professional Development

As outlined in the preface, we conclude each chapter of this book with a look at how teachers learn about and apply multiliteracies pedagogy and how professional development can support these processes. In this first chapter, we overview key findings from teacher development research related to literacies in language education;

Table 1.4. Foreign Language Literacies and Multiliteracies Pedagogy: Summary

The goal: foreign language literacies	**The means to the goal: multiliteracies pedagogy**
A program focused on foreign language literacies development emphasizes • students' ability to design meaning through the interpretation and creation of texts • engagement with texts of different modalities and genres • the interconnectedness of language and culture • the centrality of language in understanding diverse societies and perspectives	A nonsequential, nonhierarchical set of activity types that develop students' foreign language literacies through • experiencing known and new information in a text through the expression of thoughts and opinions • conceptualizing form-meaning relationships expressed in a text • analyzing the sociocultural messages in a text • applying knowledge learned from a text

Sources: Kalantzis et al. (2016), Kern (2000), and Menke and Paesani (2019).

in subsequent chapters we home in on details as they pertain to each chapter's main themes.

Studies on how teachers learn about and apply literacies in language education represent a range of contexts and languages (K–12, postsecondary, world languages, English as a second or foreign language). This research points to six key findings that inform the ways in which we can support teachers as they apply multiliteracies pedagogy in their programs:

1. Teachers recognize that multiliteracies pedagogy can have a positive impact on student learning and the ability to engage in higher-order thinking (Kim and Xing 2019; Menke 2018; Menke and Paesani 2021).
2. Teachers' understanding and application of literacies concepts are influenced by their previous experiences and beliefs as teachers and learners (Allen and Paesani, 2022; Menke 2018; Menke and Paesani 2021).
3. Teachers' knowledge of literacies and their related concepts develops gradually toward more theoretically grounded and nuanced understandings (Allen 2011; Allen and Dupuy 2013; Dupuy and Allen 2012; Nauman 2011, 2014).
4. Teachers find it challenging to apply their knowledge about literacies concepts in their classroom practices (Allen 2011; Dupuy and Allen 2012; Menke 2018; Paesani 2013).
5. Teachers have difficulty seeing the connection between the interpretation of target language texts and the study of language forms (Menke 2018; Menke and Paesani 2019, 2021).
6. Teacher-created instructional materials emphasize some knowledge processes—particularly experiencing—over others (Kim and Xing 2019; Menke and Paesani 2019; Rowland et al. 2014).

What do these research findings mean for teacher professional development? How can you use these findings to support your own learning or that of teachers you supervise or mentor? The preceding list underscores the importance of crafting a long-term and holistic approach to professional development that encourages deep understanding of literacies concepts and the application of those concepts in instruction. This means that professional development experiences should build on one another, be grounded in the overarching concept of foreign language literacies, provide opportunities for guided practice, and encourage language teachers to identify and question their previous experiences and beliefs. One way to enact this long-term, holistic professional development in teacher education programs or postsecondary language departments is by introducing literacies concepts in the initial methods course and then infusing those concepts into subsequent professional development experiences such as additional methods courses, follow-up workshops, classroom observation feedback sessions, collaborative lesson planning sessions, and the like. In addition, these concepts should also be reflected in the materials teachers work with in their programs such as student learning outcomes, course syllabi, assessments, lesson plans, and grading rubrics. Throughout this book, we address each of these research findings by providing resources to maximize the benefits of implementing literacies in language education and overcome its challenges.

Conclusion

In this chapter, we argued that foreign language literacies should be the overarching goal of secondary and postsecondary language programs and provided a rationale for this approach. We also defined key literacies concepts, including foreign language literacies, meaning design, and the four knowledge processes of multiliteracies pedagogy, and exemplified them with a short (and adaptable) lesson plan. Finally, we provided a general overview of research findings related to teachers' understandings and applications of multiliteracies pedagogy in language education. This chapter serves as a conceptual foundation for the remainder of this book, which is organized into two parts: constructing multiliteracies curricula and assessments and teaching through multiliteracies pedagogy. The concepts, ideas, and pedagogical practices we discuss in these parts of the book build upon what you've learned in this chapter and will support you as you begin implementing multiliteracies principles in your own language courses and teacher development programs.

Reflecting on Research and Practice

1. What concepts from this chapter are the clearest to you? What concepts are the least clear? What resources and readings from the following lists will you consult to further your understanding?
2. How does your understanding of communicative language teaching and other pedagogical approaches help you understand multiliteracies pedagogy and its related concepts, if at all?
3. Look at the infographic "Making Multiliteracies Real: Comparing Multiliteracies Pedagogy & Communicative Language Teaching" linked on the companion website (http://carla.umn.edu/literacies/book/). What clarifications does this infographic provide? What questions does it raise?
4. What additional strategies can you use to facilitate your understanding of multiliteracies concepts?

Resources

1. CARLA's Literacies in Language Education Project (https://carla.umn.edu/literacies/)

   The homepage for this project provides a jumping off point for deepening your understanding of the ideas presented in this chapter. In particular, the Literacies Glossary and general resources tab in the Literacies Bibliography touch upon the main concepts you've just read about.

2. "Making Multiliteracies Real: Comparing Multiliteracies Pedagogy & Communicative Language Teaching"

This infographic, linked on the companion website (http://carla.umn.edu/literacies/book/), aims to deepen teachers' understanding of multiliteracies pedagogy by comparing it with communicative language teaching. The infographic presents key concepts from both approaches in relation to their purpose, foundational ideas, and pedagogical principles.

3. *Literacies* Companion Website (https://newlearningonline.com/literacies)

   This website provides links to minilectures and supporting materials for each chapter in the book *Literacies*, referenced in the Further Reading section. We suggest watching the video "Why Literacy?" (chapter 2) for a more in-depth rationale of the literacies orientation discussed in this chapter.

Further Reading

1. "Introduction: The Work of Learning and Teaching Literacies" in *Literacies* (Kalantzis et al. 2016, 1–16)

   In this chapter, the authors contrast traditional definitions of literacy with contemporary communication patterns and demands. They highlight the multimodal nature of communication in contemporary society and argue for addressing literacies to prepare learners to participate in an increasingly diverse world.

2. "Notions of Literacy" in *Literacy and Language Teaching* (Kern 2000, 13–41)

   In chapter 1 of this seminal book, Kern articulates the definition and principles of literacies as applied to language learning. This foundational chapter also reviews various conceptualizations of literacy and argues for a shift in instructional practices that align with a more robust, integrated view of foreign language literacies.

3. "A Multidimensional View of Reading and Writing" in *Dimensions of Literacy: A Conceptual Base for Teaching Reading and Writing in School Settings* (Kucer 2014, 3–18)

   This introductory chapter traces historical developments in definitions of literacy and what distinct disciplinary perspectives contribute to notions of literacy. Kucer proposes a "dynamic, interconnected, and multidimensional" definition of literacy and overviews the social, linguistic, and cognitive perspectives that underlie literacy (5).

4. "Moving to Multiliteracies in Foreign Language Teaching: Past and Present Perspectives . . . and Beyond" (Warner and Dupuy 2018)

   This article in *Foreign Language Annals* reflects on the literacy turn in language education from historical and contemporary perspectives, including discussion of emergent topics in foreign language literacies and research questions to address moving forward.

Notes

1. As explained in the preface, apart from the term "foreign language literacies," we use the neutral and general terms "language education" and "language" throughout this book (rather than the more common but less neutral terms "second language," "foreign language," or "world language") to indicate the study of languages other than one's first or native language(s).
2. Multiple versions of CLT exist, and we recognize that not all adherents to this approach use the presentation-practice-production sequence outlined here. For the purposes of this discussion, we describe what is referred to as "weak CLT," which espouses explicit, meaning-focused instruction of language forms; prioritizes oral, functional language use; and draws from a set of broad, generally agreed upon principles that teachers apply based on their specific needs (Richards 2006; Swaffar 2006).

Part I
Constructing Literacies-Oriented Curricula

2

◆ Introduction to Literacies Curriculum Design

WHAT IS A LITERACIES-ORIENTED curriculum? What are key considerations when constructing literacies-oriented curricula? These are the questions we address in the chapters composing part I of this book. To do so, we take the overarching goal of foreign language literacies development as a starting point and discuss how to achieve this goal as you craft learning objectives, select texts, and design an assessment plan. Throughout, we emphasize that target language texts are not an add-on but rather an integral part of the curriculum that must be considered at every design stage. Part I thus encourages you to think differently about how you structure courses, units, and lessons and also about how you make use of your textbook and other support materials.

By *curriculum* we mean "a sequence of educational opportunities for learners that builds on internal interrelations and continuities among the major units of instruction . . . to enhance learning" (Byrnes 1998, 265). These "major units of instruction" can be a series of courses (e.g., the four-year undergraduate curriculum) or thematic course segments (e.g., immigration, identity, the environment). Curriculum furthermore refers to learning objectives, the content to be covered, assessment practices, and delivery method or instructional approach (Nunan 2017). The process of curriculum construction is thus deliberate and entails more than your textbook or pedagogical approach. Indeed, the various components that make up a curriculum are closely interrelated rather than stand-alone pieces.

To help you understand and implement literacies-oriented language curricula, we have organized this book according to the three stages of backward design (Wiggins and McTighe 2005), and in part I we focus on the first two stages of this model by addressing learning objectives (chapter 3), target language texts (chapter 4), and assessment (chapter 5). This brief overview chapter provides an explanation of the backward design model and how it connects to literacies concepts. We also discuss challenges and tips for designing literacies-oriented curricula and describe a model curricular unit, which exemplifies ideas presented throughout part I. Given the brief nature of this overview, we do not conclude this chapter with a list of reflective questions, resources, or further reading; you will, however, find each of these sections at the conclusion of chapters 3–5.

Understanding Backward Design

There are many schools of thought regarding how language curricula should be constructed. For instance, a forward design model begins with syllabus planning, then moves to instructional planning, and finally to assessment of learning outcomes, whereas a central design model begins with instructional planning followed by syllabus, assessment, and learning outcomes planning as the curriculum is implemented (Richards 2013). In this book, we adopt a backward design approach to curriculum construction, called such because planning begins with the end (i.e., student learning objectives) in mind (Wiggins and McTighe 2005). The rationale behind this approach is that determining learning objectives at the outset provides a clear roadmap for teachers and students; that is, all participants know what the final destination is, and other elements of the curriculum—namely, course content, assessments, and instructional activities—are the vehicles for getting there. Moreover, backward design is reflected in numerous twenty-first century pedagogical materials and professional guidelines for language learning—including the American Council on the Teaching of Foreign Languages Proficiency Guidelines (ACTFL 2012) and World-Readiness Standards (NSCB 2015)—which consistently keep desired outcomes in focus (Glisan and Donato 2021).

Backward design includes three stages, illustrated in figure 2.1. The chapters in part I of this book will equip you with knowledge and tools to help you implement stages 1 and 2 of this model, whereas the chapters in part II focus on stage 3. For now, we briefly define each stage before putting them into dialogue with literacies concepts. Stage 1, Identify Desired Results, is where curriculum developers determine the essential questions and learning objectives that frame a course, unit, or lesson plan. These questions and objectives should be connected to overall goals (e.g., foreign language literacies development), to course content and themes, and to relevant local or national standards. During this stage, ask yourself these questions:

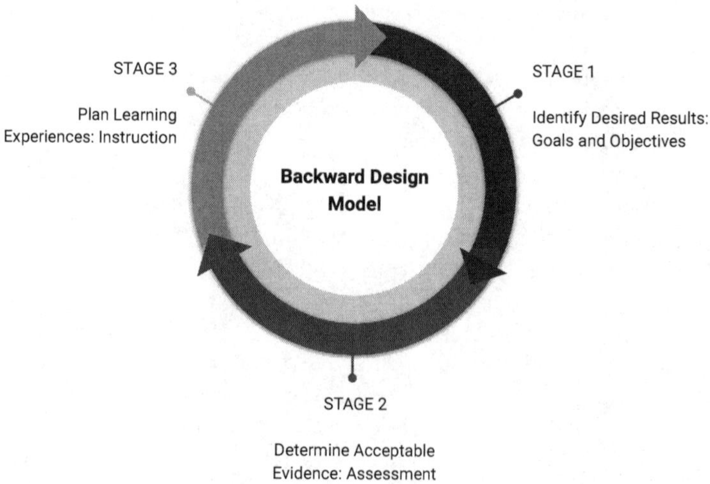

◆ **Figure 2.1.** Backward design model (Wiggins and McTighe 2005)

What should students know, understand, and be able to do? What content is worthy of understanding? In stage 2 of backward design, curriculum developers determine acceptable evidence of having met learning objectives. It is at this point that an assessment plan is developed to help gather information about students' progress toward meeting learning objectives that can subsequently inform instructional activities. During this stage, ask yourself these questions: How will I know if students have achieved desired results? What evidence shows student understanding or proficiency? Finally, stage 3 focuses on planning learning experiences. It is at this point that curriculum developers plan instruction in line with learning objectives and with an eye toward how learners will be assessed. During this stage, ask yourself these questions: What must be taught and how should it be taught considering goals and objectives? What activities will equip students with needed knowledge and skills? (Wiggins and McTighe 2005).

Although often presented as linear, the cycle depicted in figure 2.1 suggests that the three backward design stages are iterative and interrelated (Glisan and Donato 2021; Paesani 2017). This is because curriculum construction is an ongoing process and, at times, the work you carry out in one stage will impact work you have already completed in another stage. For instance, information gathered during various course, unit, or lesson assessments can help determine how and whether students are meeting learning objectives. Based on this information, you might adjust instructional practices to better prepare students for assessments or you might adjust your assessments to better align with learning objectives. Regardless of whether you follow a linear or nonlinear path when backward designing curriculum, it is essential that the three stages are aligned with one another. In other words, assessments must measure stated learning objectives and reflect classroom learning, and instructional activities must inform and be informed by learning objectives and assessments.

Literacies-Oriented Language Curriculum Design

Now that you have a basic understanding of what backward design is, we briefly explain how literacies principles map onto the three stages of this model. As you read this section, keep in mind that many ideas will be further developed in chapters 3–5. As we mentioned previously, when constructing literacies-oriented language curricula, it is essential to keep in mind the overarching goal of foreign language literacies development and its enactment through meaning design. Several guiding principles for curriculum construction can be gleaned from the definition of foreign language literacies and meaning design presented in chapter 1 and can be mapped onto the first stage of the backward design model: Identify Desired Results. In particular, to determine what students should know, understand, and be able to do, literacies-oriented learning objectives should target students' developing ability to

- interpret multiple forms of language in various genres and communicative modes;
- communicate about, analyze, and transform discourse;
- understand how communication and literacy practices operate in a variety of social contexts;

- take an active, critical stance toward language and texts;
- understand and use language, conventions, and cultural products, practices, and perspectives to make meaning; and
- identify and understand form-meaning relationships in texts (Bull and Anstey 2010; Kern 2003).

These guiding principles address the following aspects of the definition of foreign language literacies: interpreting and creating target language texts; understanding and thinking critically about relationships in texts; and developing linguistic, cognitive, and sociocultural knowledge through interacting with texts. The definition of foreign language literacies is also relevant for answering the second question framing the first stage of the backward design model: What content is worthy of understanding? First and foremost, literacies-oriented curricula should be grounded in target language texts, the bedrock of instruction in this approach. Consequently, the language features; conventions; and cultural products, practices, and perspectives represented in texts also comprise important instructional content. To bring these two ideas together, literacies-oriented curricula should prioritize language-content integration or language learning through textual content. This integrated approach ensures that neither language nor content takes on a disproportionate role in the curriculum and allows for the simultaneous exploration of language features, conventions, and cultural content and how these are manifested in target language texts. Language-content integration is thus crucial for ensuring that the study of language forms, conventions, and culture does not occur in isolation and that study of texts includes consideration of how their component parts make meaning and reflect cultural practices and perspectives (Bull and Anstey 2010; Kern 2003).

Multiliteracies principles also map onto stage 2 of the backward design model (Determine Acceptable Evidence) and help shape the design of both course or unit assessment plans and individual assessment tools. To provide acceptable evidence of students' foreign language literacies development, it is crucial to assess their learning at multiple points in a course or unit and to use a variety of assessment types and tools to do so. This means including formative and summative assessments as well as traditional (e.g., exams, homework) and performance-based (e.g., reflective journal, writing portfolio) assessments in your assessment plan. These individual assessments, as well as their place in the overall assessment plan, should also reflect the four knowledge processes of multiliteracies pedagogy, which we defined in chapter 1 and which will be addressed in detail in part II of this book (Kern 2000; Paesani, Allen, and Dupuy 2016).

Finally, planning learning experiences in the third stage of the backward design model involves the application of literacies principles through pedagogical tools. To develop students' foreign language literacies through instructional practices, they must have opportunities to interpret target language texts, apply what they learn through textual interpretation, solve problems related to language use in texts, and reflect on their learning and its connection to larger sociocultural contexts. In addition, as is the case with assessment, instructional activities should reflect the four knowledge processes of multiliteracies pedagogy: experiencing known and new information through the expression of thoughts, opinions, and facts; conceptualizing form-meaning relationships; analyzing sociocultural messages and their consequences; and applying knowledge learned in new and creative ways (Kalantzis et al. 2016; Kern 2000; Menke and Paesani 2019). Multiliteracies pedagogy and the third stage of the backward design model are the focus of part II of this book.

The model curricular unit in appendix A exemplifies how the first two stages of backward design—the focus of part I of this book—and related literacies principles are put into practice. This unit is intended for intermediate-level high school learners of English as a second language (ESL). The essential question guiding the unit is "What is the immigrant experience in the United States?" and the learning objectives reflect this question as well as the literacies principles discussed here. Specifically, learning objectives develop students' ability to interpret and create target language texts through behaviors such as describing, analyzing, explaining, critiquing, and producing. Learning objectives also build students' knowledge about immigration in the United States and the various experiences and perspectives individuals have in relation to US immigration. The content of the unit includes fact-oriented infographics, maps, images, and personal narratives about immigration and immigrant experiences. These target language texts help students build the linguistic, genre-based, and cultural knowledge they need to successfully meet the unit's learning objectives. Finally, the assessment plan includes formative and summative assessment tools that provide evidence of student learning in relation to the unit's learning objectives. For instance, homework and quizzes evaluate students' factual knowledge about immigration and their comprehension of target language texts, whereas creating a digital story evaluates students' ability to create a new text and communicate their personal experiences and perspectives related to immigration in the United States.

We reference this curricular unit at multiple points in part I of the book, and we encourage you to use it as a model for the creation of your own literacies-oriented units. A blank copy of the curricular unit template is also provided on the companion website (http://carla.umn.edu/literacies/book/). You may choose to use it in its current form or to refine and adapt it based on your own instructional context and student demographics. As you work with this template, however, keep in mind the principles presented here and the importance of aligning all three stages of the backward design model.

Conclusion

Language curriculum construction, be it literacies based or grounded in another approach, can be challenging work. We therefore conclude with some general tips for designing literacies-oriented curricula; keep them in mind as you read about creating learning objectives, selecting texts, and developing an assessment plan in chapters 3, 4, and 5, respectively. First, review successful literacies-oriented curricula for examples of learning objectives and curricular alignment (see, e.g., the German department at Georgetown University, the German program at Emory University, the lower-level French program at the University of Wisconsin-Madison). Next, take your time with curriculum design. Creating course and unit curricula is a time-consuming process, and it is important to recognize it as such. Start planning well in advance of implementing a new curriculum and acknowledge that making curricular change is a gradual and iterative process. Third, if you work in a multisection program at the postsecondary level or with a team of teachers at the secondary level, involve your entire team in the curriculum design process. Communicate with your colleagues, your chair or principal, the director of undergraduate studies, and so on to discuss how the curriculum fits with overall programmatic goals and meets your students' needs. Finally, once you have designed a new curriculum, remember that your work isn't done. It is important to gather information about how the curriculum rollout is going and to use that information to revise and refine learning objectives, assessments, and instruction to ensure that your curriculum is effectively developing students' foreign language literacies.

3

Creating Learning Objectives

THE OPENING LYRICS OF the Diana Ross classic from the film *Mahogany* (1975) help to introduce this chapter's topic of creating learning objectives:

> Do you know where you're going to?
>
> Do you like the things that life is showing you?
>
> Where are you going to?
>
> Do you know?

Learning objectives tell you and your students "where you're going to," or the final destination of a language lesson, unit, course, or program. Course content, assessments, and instructional activities indicate how and how well you are meeting those objectives and help determine whether "you like the things that life is showing you." These three curricular components thus work in concert, yet they are ineffective if you don't know where you're going, making learning objectives key.

Identifying the desired results of a lesson, unit, course, or program is the first stage of the backward design model of curriculum construction (Wiggins and McTighe 2005), and in this chapter we address one of the questions that must be answered at this stage: What should students know, understand, and be able to do? In chapter 2, we likened the backward design approach to a roadmap: learning objectives indicate the final destination on the map, course content (stage 1; see chapter 4) specifies what is interesting to see and do, and assessments (stage 2; see chapter 5) and learning experiences (stage 3; see part II) provide the stops and activities along the way. For example, if you are planning a road trip to Atlanta, you must first determine your route, plan the activities you will partake in, make restaurant reservations, and pack your bags. During the trip, you must also refuel your car, make comfort stops, and ensure you are adequately hydrated and nourished. Planning a curriculum works in much the same way. If your goal is to develop students' foreign language literacies, you must first select interesting and accessible content; then build an assessment plan that measures students' linguistic, cultural, and communicative growth;

and finally create and implement engaging lessons using the knowledge processes of multiliteracies pedagogy.

To help you create literacies-oriented learning objectives, this chapter begins with an in-depth look at the first stage of the backward design model. We begin by providing a general introduction to what learning objectives are, why they are important, and how they should be crafted. Next, we explain how literacies principles can be woven into learning objectives. Finally, we spotlight teacher professional development by addressing issues of buy-in related to literacies-oriented language curricula.

Identifying Desired Results: The What, Why, and How of Learning Objectives

Learning objectives are brief statements articulating what students will know and be able to do at the end of a learning sequence, be it a lesson, unit, course, or program (Clementi and Terrill 2013; Graves 1999).[1] These learning objectives articulate how students will reach a curriculum's overarching goals, including the goal of foreign language literacies development that we defined in chapter 1. Why is it important to articulate learning objectives? Learning objectives provide a roadmap for you and your students. They therefore indicate what is important to learn and be able to do in a lesson, unit, or course and guide decision-making about the instructional activities and assessments you are using. This decision-making has implications for other courses in your program; therefore, learning objectives contribute to both horizontal (i.e., across courses at the same level) and vertical (i.e., between courses at different levels) articulation to ensure that students have a coherent experience throughout their program of study. Learning objectives are also a tool to help explain why you teach language classes the way that you do to stakeholders outside of your classroom, such as colleagues, parents, and administrators. Finally, with clear learning objectives you can make informed choices about how and when to use your textbook and other course materials—including target language texts—to support learning, rather than allowing your textbook to be the curriculum by default (Byrnes 1998).

Key characteristics of learning objectives include the following (Anderson and Krathwohl 2001; Bloom 1956; Hall 2001; Tedick and Lyster 2020; Wiggins and McTighe 2005):

1. They are student centered, providing information about what students can expect from a curriculum and written in jargon-free language.
2. They articulate observable behaviors your students will be able to carry out (e.g., explain, identify, compare, justify, build) rather than unobservable behaviors (e.g., learn, think, read, appreciate) or instruction performed by the teacher.
3. Because learning objectives focus on observable behaviors, they are also measurable through formative and summative assessments.
4. They focus on both *declarative knowledge*, or knowing the facts of the curriculum, and *procedural knowledge*, or knowing how to apply what is learned through the curriculum.

5. They are specific and focused. That is, they clearly identify an expected outcome and do not identify multiple outcomes in one objective.
6. Importantly, objectives are not a list of instructional activities or textbook exercises, and they are not a list of language forms to be mastered. Instead, activities and language forms are tools that support students in carrying out the behaviors described in learning objectives.

In addition to defining what students should know and be able to do, learning objectives should also take into consideration any department, school, state, or national standards that inform your curriculum, as well as the topics and themes that your curriculum addresses. In other words, they should clearly connect to the overarching goals of your curriculum (e.g., foreign language literacies development, World-Readiness Standards) and address the essential questions you want students to consider in relation to course content.

How are learning objectives written to incorporate these different characteristics? To effectively articulate what students will know and be able to do as a result of completing instructional activities and assessments, learning objectives should include the following two component parts (Hall 2001):

1. A description of observable behaviors demonstrating student learning
2. The context and conditions of expected performance of those behaviors

To address the first component, learning objectives should begin with a statement such as "Students will be able to" or "Students can" followed by an appropriate action verb. The action verb you choose should be measurable, such that you can observe the behavior and use assessments to determine whether and to what degree students have met the learning objective. To address the second component, it is important to specify how and how well students will carry out the behavior. To do this, objectives might specify the mode of communication (e.g., orally, in writing), the type of content students are interacting with (e.g., informational texts), the strategies students apply to carry out the objective (e.g., skimming, scanning, inferencing), the language forms students will use (e.g., descriptive adjectives, the conditional, transition words), or the quality of students' performance (e.g., with a high degree of accuracy).

To help you better understand these component parts, read the list of language learning objectives provided in table 3.1 and consider why the examples in the left-hand column are not well formed and why those in the right-hand column are (Glisan and Donato 2021; Paesani, Allen, and Dupuy 2016).

Examples 1a and 1b both use action verbs—conjugate and describe—to articulate learning objectives. These actions are measurable behaviors that can be observed through oral and written learning activities. Moreover, both learning objectives specify the context or conditions of performance of these behaviors: conjugating in the future tense and describing in brief oral exchanges. Why, then, is 1a considered a poorly formed objective? If you go back to the characteristics of learning objectives outlined earlier, you will see that 1a targets declarative knowledge (i.e., the facts of the curriculum) only; it does not focus on how students apply that knowledge. In other words, 1a focuses on grammatical mastery without considering cultural

Table 3.1. Poorly and Well-Formed Learning Objectives

Poorly formed objectives	Well-formed objectives
1a. Students will be able to conjugate verbs in the future tense.	1b. Students will be able to describe their postgraduation plans in brief oral exchanges using the future tense.
2a. Students will be able to read travel brochures.	2b. Students will be able to interpret different perspectives on foreign travel presented in interviews and informational texts.
3a. Students will be exposed to and answer true/false questions about cultural artifacts.	3b. Students will be able to identify facts about housing learned from cultural artifacts such as print advertisements, photographs, and real estate pages.

content or communicative function. Alternatively, learning objective 1b specifies the procedural knowledge (i.e., application of what is learned) students will gain through instructional activities by indicating the communicative function students will carry out using descriptive language, vocabulary, and future tense verbs related to the cultural phenomenon of life after graduation.

Consider now learning objectives 2a and 2b, which focus on students' interaction with target language texts. Although both objectives include action verbs, the behavior of interpreting is observable and measurable, whereas the behavior of reading is not. Reading is an internal mental process that is hard to define and measure through instructional activities and assessments. Furthermore, in learning objective 2a, what students are supposed to learn through reading is not specified. Interpretation also involves internal mental processing, but it can be defined and measured. As you read in chapter 1, interpretation entails understanding the gist or surface-level facts of a target language text as well as critically examining its cultural messages and viewpoints and the way language is used to express those messages and viewpoints. Learning objective 2b specifies that learners are to interpret texts with a focus on differing perspectives; answering comprehension questions or relating perspectives in a text to one's worldview are examples of instructional activities that allow teachers to observe and measure this behavior.

Finally, the third set of learning objectives illustrates the difference between describing instructional activities (3a) and articulating an observable behavior (3b). Exposing students to cultural artifacts is something that a teacher does; it is not a behavior that students carry out. Likewise, answering true/false questions is a specific type of instructional activity rather than a description of what students know or are able to do as a result of completing that activity. The action verb "identify" in learning objective 3b shifts the focus away from the teacher and the activities learners complete toward the behaviors that students will carry out while working with cultural artifacts. In addition, this learning objective describes the context and conditions of expected performance by specifying the types of cultural artifacts from which students will identify facts about housing.

Examples 2a and 3a in table 3.1 highlight a common challenge teachers encounter when writing learning objectives: choosing appropriate action verbs. It is easy to fall into the trap of using vague language to articulate learning objectives with verbs such as read, understand, use, write, learn, think, or appreciate (Shrum and Glisan 2016). To avoid using verbs that are neither observable nor measurable, we recommend consulting Bloom's Taxonomy of Educational Objectives (Anderson and Krathwohl 2001; Bloom 1956). Bloom's taxonomy describes the cognitive processes that individuals engage in when building knowledge. These processes are articulated along a hierarchy that moves from lower-order to higher-order thinking. Table 3.2 presents the six categories in Bloom's taxonomy as well as possible action verbs for each.

To develop students' foreign language literacies, learning objectives should address multiple categories from Bloom's taxonomy, not just those describing lower-order thinking (e.g., remember, understand). We talk more about connections between Bloom's taxonomy and literacies-oriented curricula in a later section of this chapter. For now, let's turn to some tools that can help you craft effective learning objectives and that take into account the what, why, and how of learning objectives outlined here.

Tools for Creating Effective Learning Objectives

Three interrelated tools—beyond the characteristics and component parts presented in the previous section—can support you in creating effective learning

Table 3.2. Bloom's Taxonomy: Categories and Action Verbs

Category	Definition	Action verbs
Remember	Retrieve, recall, and reorganize information from long-term memory	define, list, memorize, repeat
Understand	Demonstrate comprehension and determine the meaning of instructional messages	describe, discuss, explain, identify, report
Apply	Use information or skills in a new situation	demonstrate, execute, implement, solve
Analyze	Break down information into its constituent parts and determine how the parts are related to one another or to an overall purpose or structure	compare, differentiate, examine, question, relate
Evaluate	Make judgments based on criteria or standards	argue, critique, defend, judge, support
Create	Put elements or information together to create a new, coherent whole or a new pattern or structure	assemble, construct, design, formulate

Sources: Anderson and Krathwohl (2001), Armstrong (2010), and Yale University (2017).

objectives. These include determining the topic or theme of the lesson, unit, or course for which you are writing objectives; identifying essential questions related to the topic or theme; and specifying the language, conventions, cultural content, and communicative functions to be developed.

Determine the Topic or Theme

Before you can begin writing learning objectives, you must first determine what you will be teaching. What themes are you addressing in your course? What is the topic of your lesson or unit? Establishing a content focus creates a context for a lesson, unit, or course; doing so not only provides framing for your learning objectives but also guides the selection of target language texts (see chapter 4). Indeed, according to Glisan and Donato (2021), the topic or theme you choose is a foundation for identifying learning objectives and "for establishing all other aspects of the lesson, such as the presentation of new grammatical structures and vocabulary, interpersonal pair work tasks, oral and written presentational communication tasks, selection of print texts and media, and out-of-class projects" (22). The theme or topic you select can be determined by your textbook or by your overarching goals for a lesson, unit, or course. For example, your beginning-level textbook may include chapters on topics such as education, travel, or social media, or your cultural studies course may address the theme of identity and include topics such as family, immigration, and professions. These themes or topics should play a prominent role in the learning objectives you craft.

Identify Essential Questions

Essential questions are the second tool that can assist you in writing effective learning objectives. Essential questions, which are a key component of the first stage of backward design, "foster inquiry, understanding, and transfer of learning" to other contexts (Wiggins and McTighe 2005, 22). They are not questions that can be answered with a brief sentence or yes/no response; instead, they are broad questions around a topic or theme that are formulated to "stimulate thought, to provoke inquiry, and to spark more questions—including thoughtful student questions—not just answers" (106). For a question to be essential it must not only provoke inquiry and deep thought but also encourage students to consider multiple viewpoints that are supported by the content they are studying, question assumptions, and connect to prior learning and experiences. For example, the question "What are the most common professions in the United States?" is not an essential question because it can be answered with a brief sentence and does not provoke deep thought. More appropriate essential questions include "What do professions tell us about a person's identity?" or "What determines the profession we choose?" These questions highlight the topic of a lesson, course, or unit and "encourage [curriculum] designers to avoid coverage and commit to genuine inquiry—the discussion, reflection, problem-solving, research, and debate that are the requisite for developing deep understanding" of that topic (Wiggins and McTighe 2005, 58). The learning objectives you write should lead students to answer essential questions about the selected topics or themes.

Specify Targeted Language, Conventions, Cultural Content, and Communicative Functions

Once you have decided on the topic or theme of your lesson, unit, or course and asked essential questions related to that topic or theme, a third tool for crafting learning objectives is determining the language, conventions, cultural content, and communicative functions you want students to learn (Glisan and Donato 2021; Tedick and Lyster 2020).[2] Doing so allows you to pinpoint the declarative and procedural knowledge students will develop: language, conventions, and cultural content are related to declarative knowledge, or knowing the facts of the curriculum; communicative functions are related to procedural knowledge, or what students will be able to do with the facts they are learning. These types of knowledge are thus interrelated and are essential to foreign language literacies development. For instance, if students learn past tense verb forms, they must also learn to use those forms to understand and express the chronology of a story. They likewise need to identify and use conventions associated with chronological narratives such as transition words and temporal adverbs. Doing so will help students both interpret and create narrative texts in the past. As you consider which language, conventions, cultural content, and communicative functions will play a role in your learning objectives, consider as well how they connect to the topic or theme of your lesson, unit, or course and how they will help students answer the essential questions you are asking.

An Example: Immigration in the United States

The three tools outlined thus far were used to create the learning objectives in the curricular unit presented in appendix A. The topic of this unit is immigration in the United States, and it was selected to meet the needs and interests of the unit's audience: intermediate-level high school ESL students who are likely immigrants themselves or children of immigrant families. This topic is reflected in the information presented in the unit overview, starting with the essential questions "What is the immigrant experience in the United States?" and "How do immigrant experiences differ across individuals?" These questions are open-ended and thought provoking, and they challenge students to question their assumptions, consider multiple perspectives, connect to their personal experiences, and transfer their learning to other disciplines (e.g., history, economics, sociology) and situations (e.g., family discussions, workplace encounters, travel). The curricular unit's learning objectives, repeated here, are closely tied to the topic and essential questions:

At the end of this unit, in oral and written communicative modes students will be able to . . .

1. discuss facts about immigration in the United States presented in narrative, visual, and audiovisual texts;
2. describe and analyze narrative, visual, and audiovisual texts presenting different perspectives on the immigrant experience in the United States;
3. explain and critique definitions of the American dream presented in narrative, visual, and audiovisual texts and relate them to different immigrant experiences; and

4. plan and produce a multimodal narrative of their own experience as immigrants or children of immigrants in the United States.

These learning objectives focus students on the immigrant experience as they gather facts, analyze different immigrant perspectives, deconstruct the concept of the American dream, and relate their own immigrant experience. These learning objectives also connect to the language, conventions, cultural content, and communicative functions that students will learn throughout the unit: understanding facts and figures related to immigration; expressing opinions, hopes, and feelings; and identifying and using features of multimodal narratives. Students carry out these communicative functions (i.e., procedural knowledge) based on their declarative knowledge of grammatical forms such as first-person verb conjugations, present and past tense, and infinitival clauses; vocabulary related to immigration history, the American dream, sacrifice, equality, and the like; textual conventions including page layout and use of titles, captions, images, and informal language; and the cultural topics of immigration in the United States, Ellis Island, the American dream, and immigrant voices.

Creating Literacies-Oriented Learning Objectives

Up to this point, our focus on learning objectives has been general in nature. In this section, we focus on the what, why, and how of creating learning objectives that effectively target students' foreign language literacies development. Key to creating literacies-oriented learning objectives is connecting them to our definition of foreign language literacies, which emphasizes

- the ability to interpret and create multimodal target language texts;
- the interconnectedness of language, culture, and social context;
- knowledge of oral and written language and of cultural products, practices, and perspectives; and
- development of cognitive abilities such as strategy use, problem-solving, and reflection.

To develop their foreign language literacies, students must engage in meaning design, or the identification, comprehension, and analysis of patterns of meaning in texts and the incorporation of these patterns into their linguistic and communicative repertoires (Kalantzis et al. 2016; Kern 2000; Menke and Paesani 2019). Chapter 2 presented guiding principles arising from these concepts, which we repeat here. To determine what students should know, understand, and be able to do, literacies-oriented learning objectives should target students' developing ability to

- interpret multiple forms of language in various genres and communicative modes;
- communicate about, analyze, and transform discourse;
- understand how communication and literacy practices operate in a variety of social contexts;
- take an active, critical stance toward language and texts;

- understand and use language, conventions, and cultural products, practices, and perspectives to make meaning; and
- identify and understand form-meaning relationships in texts (Bull and Anstey 2010; Kern 2003).

To illustrate how these literacies principles are translated into learning objectives, we return to the curricular unit on immigration (see appendix A). Learning objective 3—Students will be able to explain and critique definitions of the American dream presented in narrative, visual, and audiovisual texts and relate them to different immigrant experiences—reflects many of these principles. First, to realize this objective, students engage with various multimodal texts, including websites, video testimonials, infographics, and personal narratives, all of which touch upon the concept of the American dream. In so doing, they communicate about definitions of the American dream and how they are represented in these texts. As they move from defining the American dream to critiquing it, students learn to take an active, critical stance toward language and how it is used to express the American dream and toward a range of cultural practices and perspectives. Thus, learning objective 3 addresses the linguistic dimension of literacies development through exploration of vocabulary and grammar related to the American dream. It also addresses the cognitive and sociocultural dimensions of literacies development through skills such as inferencing and reflection and through the consideration of multiple cultural perspectives. Finally, in addition to aligning with the specific literacies principles outlined here, learning objective 3 also weaves together two general goals of language education that are often considered distinct: the ability to use language to communicate and to engage in textual analysis (Kern 2000; Paesani, Allen, and Dupuy 2016). This learning objective and the others in the curricular unit thus reinforce the key premises that undergird this book: foreign language literacies development and language-content integration.

One tool for helping you articulate this literacies-oriented view of communication as language-content integration is the five Cs of the World-Readiness Standards (NSCB 2015), a framework you may already use to construct language curricula. In chapter 1, we presented a retooled version of the standards that incorporates literacies principles, including meaning design, interpretation, perspective taking, critical thinking, multimodality, and multiculturalism. Returning to the list of objectives for the curricular unit on immigration, several of these retooled standards are evident. For instance, the communication standard is addressed through students' ability to describe and analyze target language texts and to plan and produce their own multimodal narrative, the cultures and comparisons standards are developed as students discuss immigration facts and phenomena and then relate them to different perspectives and experiences, and the connections standard is reflected in objectives emphasizing contemporary and historical knowledge of immigration and exploring definitions of the American dream and its different manifestations across individuals and cultures.

Much like literacies-oriented language education, the World-Readiness Standards also present an integrated view of communication (interpersonal, interpretive, presentational), rather than one oriented toward the distinct skills of speaking, listening, reading, and writing. Thus, the standards "provide concepts to articulate areas of student learning not based [solely] on linguistic skills but on specific, contextualized uses of language" (Paesani, Allen, and Dupuy 2016, 63). These ideas are also reflected in the unit learning objectives presented earlier: students engage in interpretive communication as they read, listen to, and view texts on immigration; they engage in presentational communication as they produce their own multimodal narrative; and they engage in interpersonal communication as they discuss, describe, explain, critique, and analyze texts and the cultural products, practices, and perspectives presented within them.

A second tool for helping to articulate literacies principles in learning objectives is Bloom's taxonomy, summarized in table 3.2. These different cognitive processes can be connected to the four knowledge processes of multiliteracies pedagogy (Kalantzis et al. 2016; introduced in chapter 1 and detailed in part II of the book), as reflected in table 3.3.

The *knowledge processes* framework is used to define the types of instructional activities you create around target language texts, but it also describes the cognitive processes students engage in as they carry out these activities. Connecting this framework to Bloom's taxonomy can thus help ensure that your learners engage

Table 3.3. The Knowledge Processes and Bloom's Taxonomy

Knowledge process	Definition	Bloom's taxonomy categories
Experiencing	Learning through immersion in texts, activities, and social situations. Expressing thoughts, reactions, opinions, and feelings and gaining global comprehension about familiar or new experiences, objects, ideas, situations, perspectives, and ways of communicating. Does not involve deep reflection or analysis.	Remember Understand
Conceptualizing	Learning how language, conventions, organization, and other features of texts work to convey meaning. Unpacking texts, practicing skills and knowledge, and explicit learning about textual features helps learners participate more fully in communication.	Understand Analyze
Analyzing	Learning by connecting the content of texts to social, cultural, and historical contexts. Questioning the meaning, importance, and consequences of textual content. Critically reflecting on textual content and its relationship to one's own culture, perspectives, and learning.	Analyze Evaluate
Applying	Learning by using new knowledge, skills, and understandings and by producing language in creative ways.	Apply Create

in different types of thinking as they work to realize literacies-oriented learning objectives. In other words, "when objectives place equal emphasis on the various components of [foreign language literacies], classroom practices should reflect this through a range of knowledge processes" (Menke and Paesani 2019, 44). To craft learning objectives that develop students' foreign language literacies through the act of meaning design, we recommend articulating objectives that touch upon multiple categories of Bloom's taxonomy. If you have lower proficiency or younger learners, it might be tempting to focus only on objectives that develop the ability to remember and understand; however, doing so does not engage students in textual interpretation and creation. The learning objectives in the instructional unit on immigration for intermediate-level ESL learners exemplify this recommendation, as shown in table 3.4.

To summarize, literacies-oriented learning objectives should integrate the concepts and principles outlined previously. In addition, they should reflect a broad understanding of communication that integrates language and content, addresses one or more of the five Cs of the World-Readiness Standards, and is interpersonal, interpretive, and presentational in nature. Finally, literacies-oriented learning objectives, whether they are developed for a lesson, unit, or course, should engage students in multiple types of thinking in line with the six categories of Bloom's taxonomy and the four knowledge processes of multiliteracies pedagogy. To help you integrate these ideas and address the what, why, and how of learning objectives outlined in this chapter, ask yourself the following reflective questions as you write and revise literacies-oriented learning objectives:

1. Why are students completing this lesson, unit, or course?
2. What skills or knowledge will they gain from working with this text?
3. Are language and content integrated or distinct in this lesson, unit, or course?
4. How will the lesson, unit, or course contribute to students' foreign language literacies development?

Table 3.4. Curricular Unit Learning Objectives and Bloom's Taxonomy

Students will be able to . . .	Bloom's taxonomy categories
1. Discuss facts about immigration in the United States presented in narrative, visual, and audiovisual texts	Remember Understand
2. Describe and analyze narrative, visual, and audiovisual texts presenting different perspectives on the immigrant experience in the United States	Understand Analyze
3. Explain and critique definitions of the American dream presented in narrative, visual, and audiovisual texts and relate them to different immigrant experiences	Understand Evaluate
4. Plan and produce a multimodal narrative of their own experience as immigrants or children of immigrants in the United States	Create

Spotlight on Teacher Professional Development

Even when teachers have access to strategies and tools for designing literacies-oriented curricula, including those presented in this chapter, they may feel reticent or ill-equipped to do so. A number of reasons contribute to this reticence, some of which were highlighted in chapter 1. For example, teachers' understanding and application of literacies concepts are influenced by their previous experiences and beliefs (Allen and Paesani, 2022; Menke 2018; Menke and Paesani 2021). Indeed, long-held beliefs about how languages should or should not be taught can make teachers reluctant to try new approaches. Literacies concepts may also conflict with teachers' existing understandings or with the approaches they currently use, such as communicative language teaching. In addition, teachers' knowledge of literacies concepts develops slowly, and applying that knowledge to curriculum and instruction can be challenging (e.g., Allen and Dupuy 2013; Menke 2018; Menke and Paesani 2019). For instance, Allen and Dupuy (2013) found that even after two teaching methods courses, graduate student instructors struggled to articulate learning objectives grounded in literacies concepts. Similarly, Menke and Paesani (2019) found that postsecondary teachers were hesitant about implementing literacies-oriented learning objectives in lower-level language courses because they believed that "lower proficiency impeded engagement in cognitively-demanding tasks" (44). Finally, based on our experience working with secondary and postsecondary teachers, a common concern is that creating literacies-oriented curricula is too time consuming and that there are not adequate resources (e.g., time, funding, access to professional development) to support this work.

Although teachers recognize that literacies-oriented curricula can impact language learning by "expanding learners' knowledge of the world and advancing their cognitive and academic skills" (Menke 2018, 129), teacher reticence and lack of buy-in can significantly impede curricular change. How, then, can we support teachers in crafting and implementing curricula that support students' foreign language literacies development? One strategy for ensuring teacher buy-in is to follow the backward design model of curriculum design and to involve teachers in all three of its stages. It is only through this kind of "sustained collaboration among all members of the teaching corps" (Modern Language Association Ad Hoc Committee on Foreign Languages 2007, 6) that true curricular transformation will take place and take hold. Involving teachers in this work through the collaborative drafting of learning objectives, which can take place in the methods course, during student teaching, or on the job among a team of instructors, is one way to achieve sustained collaboration. For example, Paesani (2017) documented a curriculum redesign process in a lower-level postsecondary French program that involved collaborative work with a team of twelve graduate and part-time instructors and a language program director. To create learning objectives for the program, which was anchored in communicative and literacies approaches, the team first analyzed learning objectives from existing programs that had adopted the overarching goal of foreign language literacies development. Next, they drafted, critiqued, and refined programmatic learning objectives through a series of workshops and online discussions. During the next two stages of backward design, the team created an assessment plan that aligned with these learning objectives and then retooled instructional materials with an eye toward both learning objectives and assessment. This process ensured programmatic coherence by keeping the program's goal of foreign language literacies development in focus at all times and created a culture of collaboration and collegiality among program participants.

Collaboratively constructing language curricula also contributes to enhanced communication among teachers and other program participants, another key component for establishing buy-in. Additional strategies to increase communication include sharing course syllabi to identify trends or gaps across courses or sections, particularly in relation to learning objectives and how they are realized through assessment and instruction. End-of-term teaching reflections can also increase communication and collaboration: in reflecting on how it feels to teach a course grounded in literacies-oriented objectives, teachers can identify areas of discomfort, evaluate student learning, and consider curricular improvements (Allen and Paesani 2010).

Another strategy for increasing teacher buy-in of literacies-oriented curricula is to move away from just-in-time professional development focused on problem-solving and immediate needs toward a long-term professional development program grounded in literacies principles. When teachers see consistency across professional development experiences and materials, it contributes not only to buy-in but also to their understanding of literacies concepts and their ability to apply them in language programs. Topics that might be treated in a long-term approach to professional development include curricular alignment, adapting textbook activities to realize learning objectives, critiquing course assessments, and program evaluation (Allen and Paesani 2010; Byrnes 2001; Maxim 2009; Paesani 2017). Another professional development tool to increase buy-in is the creation of materials that teachers can use to explain the curriculum to their students. Using student-friendly language to articulate why a curriculum is designed the way it is and how it is carried out through learning objectives, assessments, and instructional activities can help teachers better understand the course they are teaching and buy into its literacies orientation (Allen and Paesani 2010; C. Porter 2009).

Finally, as each of these strategies for increasing teacher buy-in suggest, curriculum construction, be it focused on foreign language literacies development or some other goal, is a process, one that is refined and revisited as the curriculum is implemented over time (Department of German 2011b). Emphasizing this fact with teachers from the outset can decrease their reticence and build their confidence. To illustrate this process, it can be helpful to show teachers how your own literacies learning objectives (or those from the research cited here) have evolved over time based on experience and more nuanced understanding of literacies concepts. Doing so will benefit both the teachers you mentor and your work as a teacher educator.

Conclusion

The purpose of this chapter was to introduce principles, strategies, and tools to help you craft literacies learning objectives and address one of the two questions framing the first stage of the backward design model: What should students know, understand, and be able to do? At the outset, we used the analogy of a roadmap to underscore the importance of beginning curricular planning with learning objectives, and this chapter also served as a kind of roadmap. To get you to the final destination of creating literacies learning objectives, we first outlined the what, why, and how of learning objectives. We then focused on integrating content, that is, literacies principles, into learning objectives. Finally, we presented various tools and strategies that served as assessments and learning experiences to help you achieve the goal of writing literacies learning objectives. Armed with this understanding, you are now ready to move on to chapter 4, in which we address the second question in stage 1 of the backward design model: What content is worthy of understanding?

Reflecting on Research and Practice

1. Analyze the learning objectives for a lesson, unit, or course in which you aim to develop students' foreign language literacies. Have you adequately addressed the what, why, and how of learning objectives presented in the first part of this chapter? Have you adequately incorporated the literacies principles addressed in the second part of this chapter? What gaps do you notice?
2. What changes do you need to make to your learning objectives based on the analysis you completed in the first question? Which of the tools and strategies presented in this chapter can you use to implement these changes?
3. Once you've revised your learning objectives to better address the what, why, and how, and to more effectively incorporate literacies principles, ask yourself the questions presented at the end of the Creating Literacies-Oriented Learning Objectives section of this chapter.

Resources

1. Bloom's Taxonomy Graphic Organizers

   Graphic organizers are a convenient tool for selecting appropriate action verbs and ensuring that your learning objectives engage students in different types of thinking. Many graphic organizers will pop up in a simple internet search for "Bloom's taxonomy graphic organizers." Two excellent examples include "Bloom's Taxonomy: Helpful Graphic Organisers" (https://bloomstaxonomy2013.weebly.com/helpful-graphic-organisers.html) and "Bloom's Taxonomy" (https://cft.vanderbilt.edu/guides-sub-pages/blooms-taxonomy/) from the Center for Teaching at Vanderbilt University.

2. Essential Questions for World Languages (https://jaymctighe.com/resources/#1521225059546-51d65de1-41c2)

   This resource, from McTighe & Associates Consulting (one of the creators of the backward design model), provides a list of essential questions appropriate for language education. To access this list, click on Essential Questions under the Downloads heading and then on Essential Questions for World Languages.

3. Georgetown University Department of German: Curriculum (https://german.georgetown.edu/undergraduate/curriculum/)

   This website provides an overview of the undergraduate German curriculum at Georgetown University, one of the first (and most well-known) postsecondary programs to adopt foreign language literacies as its overarching goal. The website has a wealth of information, including the program's rationale and organization, course syllabi, learning objectives, and an assessment plan.

Further Reading

1. "Planning for Instruction Using an Iterative Process for Backward Design" in *Enacting the Work of Language Instruction: High-Leverage Teaching Practices*, volume 2 (Glisan and Donato 2021, 33–59)

   This chapter introduces the high-leverage teaching practice of planning for instruction using the backward design process. The authors emphasize that this process is iterative. That is, through the planning process, educators may need to move between phases to adapt and adjust the curriculum for a lesson, unit, or course.

2. "Setting Goals for Learning: Stage 1 for Language Development" in *Using Understanding by Design in the Culturally and Linguistically Diverse Classroom* (Heineke and McTighe 2018, 71–110)

   This book considers the backward design model of curriculum construction in relation to multilingual and multicultural education. Chapter 4 focuses on identifying desired learning results in relation to students' language development. Although many of the examples provided are related to teaching disciplinary content through a second language, the principles presented throughout the chapter are transferable to other language learning and teaching contexts.

3. "Reconsidering Goals, Objectives, and Assessment from a Multiliteracies Perspective" in *A Multiliteracies Framework for Collegiate Foreign Language Teaching* (Paesani, Allen, and Dupuy 2016, 49–73)

   This chapter addresses goals, objectives, and assessments from the perspective of foreign language literacies development. In addition to defining goals and objectives and relating them to assessment and instruction, the chapter also provides strategies for creating goals and objectives for language education that are consistent with literacies principles.

Notes

1. Many terms are used to refer to learning objectives, including "outcomes," "performance indicators," "standards," and "benchmarks." We choose to use the term "objectives" throughout this book, regardless of whether we are referring to a lesson, unit, course, or entire language program.
2. See chapter 4 for definitions and detailed discussion of language, conventions, and cultural content.

4

Defining, Selecting, and Evaluating Target Language Texts

WHAT COMES TO MIND when you think of the content of language classes? Common answers to this question include grammar, vocabulary, culture, and communicative activities. Rarely when asked about the content of language classes—particularly those aimed at students with lower levels of proficiency—do people answer "texts." However, as a reader of this book, you know that adopting foreign language literacies as the overarching goal of language education requires placing target language texts at the center of instruction and integrating language and content at all curricular levels. The content of secondary and postsecondary language education is thus much more than grammatical forms, vocabulary lists, cultural facts, or conversational expressions. This viewpoint aligns with much current scholarship about twenty-first century language education (e.g., Byrnes 2006; Martel 2022; Paesani, Allen, and Dupuy 2016), which argues that organizing instruction around language forms and functions alone is inadequate. Instead, as you learned in chapter 1, studying language and textual content in concert provides opportunities for authentic language use, deepens linguistic and cultural understanding, and empowers and motivates learners.

Target language texts not only serve as essential content in literacies-oriented language curricula but also play an important role in the backward design model presented in chapter 2. Indeed, when identifying desired results in the first stage of this model, it is important to consider what content students should know and understand and what they should be able to do with that content (Wiggins and McTighe 2005). In stage 3 of the backward design model, we can think of this content generally at first, focusing on the themes to explore in a lesson, unit, or chapter, and then later select the target language texts to use in instruction. Alternatively, we can begin by thinking specifically about content, selecting texts that align with our learning objectives and then grounding our assessments and instructional activities in those objectives and associated content. Both approaches have advantages and disadvantages, and your choice of one over the other will depend on your teaching context and your learners. Regardless of your approach, texts should inform your decision-making as it pertains to the content of your courses. The aim of this chapter is thus to provide you with research-based tools and understandings that you can apply to select target language texts and determine their salient features in a way consistent with lesson, unit, or course learning objectives. We begin by defining target language texts and introducing the concept of genre. We then present text selection principles and a framework for identifying textual features appropriate for your learners. We conclude with a spotlight on teacher professional development and the challenge of working with target language texts in their original (versus modified) form.

Defining Target Language Texts

You may be surprised that we are devoting an entire section of this chapter to defining target language texts. Yet, as you read in chapter 1, we define texts broadly in this book to encompass much more than written documents with words, sentences, and paragraphs, and this broad definition requires some clarification. In general terms, *texts* are any concrete, observable product that communicates meaning through a set of features (Halliday and Hasan 1976; Kalantzis et al. 2016; Kern 2000). But what does this really mean? To help you develop a more nuanced understanding of what a text is, let's begin with some common research-based definitions. Each of the following statements have been used to define target language texts, but they all fall short in some way. As you read through the list, think about why each definition is inadequate, particularly in a book focused on literacies in language education. According to the research, target language texts

1. are created to fulfill some purpose in the language community in which they were produced (Little, Devitt, and Singleton 1989);
2. are composed of language samples generated by native speakers for native speakers (D. Porter and Roberts 1981);
3. reflect appropriate, natural, and quality language use (Rogers and Medley 1988);
4. are a stretch of real language, produced by a real speaker or writer for some real audience and designed to convey a real message (Morrow 1977); and
5. reflect a naturalness of form and an appropriateness of cultural and situational context that would be found in the language used by native speakers (Brosnan, Brown, and Hood 1984; Rogers and Medley 1988).

One of the most important critiques of these definitions is that they focus on the native speaker, a concept that has been much debated in language education (e.g., Canagarajah 2014; Kramsch 1997). Identifying the native speaker as the sole creator of texts suggests that there is one, idealized way to use a language when, in fact, language is used differently by different individuals (e.g., first, second, or heritage language speakers), all of whom are competent communicators. A second critique of these definitions is the use of words that arbitrarily place value on the forms a language should take. For instance, what does it mean for the language used in target language texts to be "real," "appropriate," "natural," or "quality," and who makes these value judgments? Finally, in their own ways, each definition omits one or more important elements, such as a text's component parts, its contexts of use, its purpose, or its author and audience.

To address these shortcomings, we propose the following definition of *target language texts*, crafted with the research in mind and in consultation with teachers participating in CARLA summer institutes:

> Target language texts are multimodal (i.e., reflect written, audio, audiovisual, visual, or digital modes or a combination of two or more of these modes), socially and culturally situated, and created for some real-world purpose other than language learning.

This definition addresses a text's component parts, or modes; its contexts of use, or its connection to societies and cultures; and its purpose, or its role in real-world communication. Absent from this definition is specific mention of a text's author and audience. This omission is intentional to avoid assigning value to one group of language users over another. Moreover, specifying that texts are socially and culturally situated implies that text creators and consumers are a part of or must take into consideration the specific contexts in which texts exist. The word "authentic" is also conspicuously absent from this definition of target language texts, again by design. Much like the term "native speaker," authenticity and authentic texts are concepts that have been much debated (e.g., Day 2004; Gilmore 2007; Simonsen 2019). Indeed, it is very difficult to determine what is and is not authentic without marginalizing certain language users or placing arbitrary value judgments on a text and its features.

Based on this definition, many things are target language texts that you might not have previously considered. In addition to the common textual forms of literature, print media, or historical documents, texts also include instructional videos, maps, podcasts, interviews, Instagram posts, theater performances, and the like. Likewise, some things that you may consider to be target language texts fall outside of this definition, including teacher-created stories targeting specific language forms, cultural blurbs written by textbook authors, language-learning videos, and the like. Examples of texts that align with our definition illustrate the concept of *multimodality*, or the overlapping nature of written, audio, visual, and digital communication channels (Kress 2010). For instance, an instructional video includes visual and audio modes, and their interaction enhances the way that meaning is conveyed. That is, the action of instructing through demonstration, gestures, and facial expressions (i.e., the visual mode) supports the linguistic description of the instructional steps (i.e., the audio mode) and vice versa. In addition, when an instructional video is posted on a site such as YouTube, it includes written language that provides a context (e.g., title, creator, date), viewer reactions, and when available, subtitles. This written mode provides another layer of meaning and can further enhance the messages conveyed in the visual and audio modes of the instructional video.

A final concept crucial to defining texts is that of *genre*. There are many research-based definitions of this concept, and what they share in common is that genres possess particular patterns that are culturally situated and that users expect, understand, apply, and adapt (e.g., Kucer 2014; Martin 2009; Swaffar and Arens

2005). For example, if you are an English speaker from the United States, you might expect that an infographic will have, at minimum, a title, one or more sections presenting information related to the title, images that illustrate specific pieces of information, and words, phrases, or numbers that correspond to and elaborate on these images. Based on your expectations for this genre, you can apply these features to create your own infographic and potentially adapt them to meet your needs or those of your intended audience. If you are a member of a different culture or discourse community, you might have different expectations regarding the patterns and features of the infographic genre. As such, when you encounter an English-language infographic from the United States, your expectations may not be met, which can potentially impede your ability to comprehend, apply, and adapt an infographic's features.

There are several reasons why it is important to think about genre when adopting a literacies orientation to language education. First, as the example in the previous paragraph illustrates, genre patterns and expectations may differ across cultures, and learners should be aware of these differences and understand why and how they are realized. Second, exposing students to a range of genres appropriate for their proficiency level allows them to understand and do different kinds of things with language, thus expanding their meaning-making repertoires. In fact, interpreting different written, audio, audiovisual, visual, and digital genres and understanding their features can improve students' creation of these same genres (e.g., Allen and Goodspeed 2018; Troyan 2016; Yasuda 2011). Third, the concept of genre is closely related to the definition of foreign language literacies presented in chapter 1. By exploring different genres learners can see the variability and dynamicity of language, ideas, and perspectives in a range of text types. Moreover, in exploring how genres are organized and how their specific features are realized, learners can more easily connect language forms to the meanings they express. Finally, by including a range of genres in a language curriculum, learners are also more likely to interpret and create text types they will encounter in different school subjects, as well as those they will encounter outside of the classroom. Thus, they can be better prepared to fully participate in current and future personal, academic, and workplace contexts. Of course, not all genres are appropriate for all levels of language learners; however, when we adopt a literacies orientation, it is important for learners to interact with a range of text types to increase their ability to interpret and create meaning.

Take a moment to peruse the language textbook or syllabus you are currently using and note the textual genres that are present. If you are teaching a lower-level course, your textbook or syllabus likely contains many descriptive and informational texts; if you're teaching an upper-level course, your textbook or syllabus likely contains many literary or historical texts. To help you incorporate a range of genres in instruction that are suitable for your students' age and language proficiency, it can be helpful to think of a genre continuum that moves from the informal and personal to the formal and public (Gee 2015). *Informal discourses* are those "characterized by informal communication between intimates on topics of common knowledge" (Byrnes et al. 2006, 93). Learners usually encounter informal discourses in the home, and these include genres such as personal narratives, cartoons, conversations, picture stories, or diary entries. *Formal discourses* are those genres central to participation in various societal contexts. Formal discourses are typically encountered at school or work and are thus more public in nature; examples include poetry, political debates, book reviews, and TED talks. A learner's ability to interpret and create these more formal genres is essential to their foreign language literacies development and the attainment of advanced language proficiency (Byrnes et al. 2006; Gee 2015). Thus, it is important to design courses, units, and lessons that help move students along this informal-formal continuum through deliberate genre sequencing (Ryshina-Pankova 2016). That said, keep in mind that this genre continuum is fluid and is only one factor to consider when selecting and sequencing target language texts. Returning to our infographic example, this is a formal, or public, genre but one that is appropriate for younger and lower-proficiency learners due to an infographic's specific textual features.

We can see the informal-formal genre continuum reflected in the sample curricular unit summarized in appendix A. This unit, intended for intermediate-level ESL learners, includes several informal or primary discourse genres: infographics, oral personal narratives, written letters, and images. The unit also exposes students to genres that are closer to the formal or secondary discourse end of the genre curriculum, such as statistical data and historical narratives; however, these texts are presented in a digestible format and include features of more informal genres, such as visual supports, simple sentences, clear organizational markers, and everyday vocabulary.

Selecting Target Language Texts

The research-based definitions of text and genre may feel somewhat abstract to you. You may also be wondering how you can apply your new conceptual knowledge to ensure that the texts you are using in your literacies-based curriculum are appropriate for your learners and align with your stated learning objectives. In this section, we address the topic of text selection and questions such as the following: Which texts are most appropriate for my learners? How do I ensure that a text aligns with my learning objectives? How do I identify and select textual features to target in instruction? Where do I start looking for texts? How much time must I devote to searching for and selecting texts?

Text-Selection Criteria

To develop the conceptual understanding necessary to effectively select texts, we begin with research-based criteria for selecting target language texts. This research (Paesani, Allen, and Dupuy 2016; Swaffar, Arens, and Byrnes 1991; Zyzik and Polio 2017) recommends selecting texts that

1. address a familiar, interesting topic;
2. are age appropriate;
3. are an appropriate length;
4. use the familiar to identify the unfamiliar;

5. include a substantive, discernable plot, message, or subject;
6. show clear sequential development with well-marked episodes and discourse markers;
7. fit the learning purpose and unit, chapter, or lesson theme; or
8. reflect genres relevant to the target language and its discourse communities.

The first three criteria are focused on learners and the appropriateness of a text for their personal, cognitive, and linguistic needs. For instance, if you teach Italian to high school sophomores, they are likely uninterested in texts about fashion trends among baby boomers. Likewise, given their age and cognitive development, dense literary or historical texts are probably too complex for these students. Regarding criteria 3, you may be thinking that shorter texts are best for younger or less proficient learners, whereas longer texts are better for older or more proficient learners, and you are partially right. Text length is genre dependent, so if you are selecting genres such as print and television advertisements, shorter is better. For other styles of texts, such as young adult fiction, films, or online magazine articles, length is an important consideration. Certainly, you won't select a three-page text for level I or first-semester learners in their second week of language study. Yet it may surprise you to know that for these kinds of texts, longer is just as good and sometimes better (Mehrpour and Riazi 2004). This is because longer texts (i.e., written texts of five hundred words or more) provide more context and, often, more repetition of vocabulary, grammatical structures, and ideas, facilitating rather than hindering comprehension (Kintsch and van Dijk 1978; Swaffar, Arens, and Byrnes 1991).

Text-selection criteria 4, 5, and 6 are specific to a text's content. Often when students work with a target language text for the first time, they encounter unfamiliar cultural content. When you select texts that introduce these unfamiliar ideas with concepts or vocabulary words that are familiar to your students, new cultural content can be more accessible to them. For instance, if learners of Korean have studied basic food vocabulary and typical meal patterns in the target culture, this knowledge can help them understand a text about restaurant trends in Seoul. Other ways to make textual content more accessible to learners is to select texts that have an easily identifiable message and clear sequential development. In other words, the more concrete a text is, the easier that text will be to understand. Consider the difference between a novel that follows a chronological story line versus one that moves back and forth between different time periods. Although this latter structure might create an entertaining reading experience for highly proficient language users, it can cause confusion and frustration for less proficient language users. To help you determine whether a text has a concrete message and chronology, look for features such as transition words, temporal adverbs, headings, turn taking, introductory or concluding statements, and the like.

Finally, criteria 7 and 8 focus on the purpose of the text you are selecting. Although it may seem obvious, it is very important for a text to align with your learning objectives as well as with the theme of the course, unit, chapter, or lesson you are teaching. Returning to the food example in the previous paragraph, if your learning objectives include students being able to describe food practices in the target culture, connect food practices to health and geographical location, and compare food practices in home and target cultures, appropriate themes in the texts you choose might include restaurant dining, diet culture, and connections between regional agriculture and food traditions. Less appropriate themes that do not align with your learning objectives and thus make a text less accessible to your students include the impact of drought on food crops, foodborne illnesses, and restaurant franchising. Another way to ensure that you are attending to a text's purpose is to choose texts that reflect genres relevant to the target language communities your class studies. For instance, a very salient genre in US culture is reality television; however, this genre may be less important or absent in other cultures. An awareness of these differences will help you select appropriate texts for the content of your courses and provide students with a window into the genres valued by target culture communities.

Text Complexity

In addition to the list of general text-selection criteria, it is also important to consider the complexity of the texts you are using. The Common Core State Standards Initiative (2021) provides a three-part definition of *text complexity*: (1) qualitative factors, including a text's "levels of meaning, structure, language conventionality and clarity, and knowledge demands"; (2) quantitative factors, including readability measures; and (3) reader- and task-based factors, including motivation, background knowledge, and purpose. Because we don't expect that you will run readability tests on the target language texts you select, and because the text selection criteria listed earlier address some common reader- and task-based factors, we focus here on qualitative factors that play a role in text complexity. Figure 4.1 presents a list of some of the most common qualitative factors that you might consider when selecting target language texts appropriate for your learners.

	LESS COMPLEX	MORE COMPLEX
TIME FRAMES	Primarily present tense	Multiple time frames
TOPIC	Familiar Everyday Private discourses	Unfamiliar Specialized Public discourses
VOCABULARY	Few unique words Keywords repeated Many cognates	Many unique words Limited repetition Fewer cognates
GRAMMAR	Identifiable subject Shorter sentences Simple structures	Subject not easily identified Longer sentences Complex structures
STRUCTURE	Limited dialogue Graphics Clear organizational moves	Heavy dialogue Graphics absent Vague organizational moves

◆ **Figure 4.1.** Text complexity factors (adapted from The Comprehensible Classroom 2018)

To use this figure, consider first the types of factors that contribute to text complexity. The factor of time frames is related to when in time the text is situated (i.e., past, present, future, or a combination) and the linguistic forms that are used to express time, including verbs and temporal adverbs. The topic factor is focused on the familiarity and accessibility of a text's content and overlaps somewhat with text selection criteria 1 and 4 (see previous section). The factors of vocabulary and grammar relate to the language forms used in a text and their familiarity to students, their repetition, their length, and their complexity. Finally, structure is about the organization of a text and whether that organization is concrete or abstract.

The second thing to consider when using figure 4.1 is that text complexity is measured on a continuum, as represented by the bidirectional arrow at the top. This means that determining whether a text is more or less complex is not a black and white issue; instead, you must learn to be comfortable with some gray areas when selecting texts for your learners. The factor of time frames can help to exemplify this continuum. The present tense is likely the first verb form (and perhaps the only verb form) your level 1 or first-semester students learn. This does not mean, however, that every text you select must only contain present tense verbs; rather, you should consider selecting texts that have predominantly present tense verb forms. If other verb forms are present in your text, you can design tasks that focus learners' attention on the text's most important features so that they do not get tripped up by unfamiliar verb forms (or other features that may be unknown to them). In sum, a target language text does not have to perfectly fit within learners' current knowledge base for it to be appropriate for use in your instructional context.

An Example: Selecting Texts Related to Immigration in the United States

To further exemplify the text selection and text complexity principles presented in this section, we return to the curricular unit summarized in appendix A. Before reading on, take a moment to revisit the learning objectives and textual content that form the basis of this unit and ask yourself the following questions:

1. Do the selected texts address a topic of interest for the targeted audience?
2. Are the texts age appropriate?
3. Are the texts' length appropriate given their genre and the students' level of language proficiency?
4. What new and familiar ideas do the texts present? Do the texts use students' background knowledge and experiences as a starting point to understand these ideas?
5. Do the texts have a substantive, discernable plot, message, or subject?
6. Do the texts show a clear sequential development with well-marked sections and discourse markers?
7. Do the texts fit the learning purpose and unit themes?
8. Are the selected genres relevant to the target language and its discourse communities?

Of course, since you don't have direct access to all of the texts in the curricular unit, some of these text selection questions may have been difficult for you to answer.

Nonetheless, you should have been able to answer "yes" or "partially" to most of these questions. First, because the target audience is intermediate-level high school ESL students who are immigrants or children of immigrants, the topic of US immigration is likely of high interest to them. Moreover, because many of the texts feature perspectives from young people like themselves and have varying lengths (e.g., infographics versus digital stories), they are both age and length appropriate. Learners can also use their background knowledge and experiences as recent arrivals to the United States to help scaffold their understanding of new information about US immigration. In addition, most of the unit's texts are infographics or oral and written personal narratives from immigrants; these genres are not only reflective of discourse communities in the United States, but they also provide an easily discernible subject and have a well-marked and predictable structure. Finally, the texts fit the learning purpose and unit theme because they all treat the topic of US immigration and are clearly tied to the stated learning objectives.

In terms of text complexity, it is important to determine what features from figure 4.1 indicate that the curricular unit texts are at a level of complexity appropriate for intermediate proficiency high school ESL learners. Infographics and personal narratives are two genres that are often realized using a mix of present and past tense forms, making the time frame an appropriate level of complexity for the target audience. As noted previously, the topic of immigration should be familiar to most of these students and the texts used to explore this topic represent mostly primary discourses (infographics, personal narratives), with some secondary discourses included (statistical data, historical narratives). Because students are interacting with several infographics and personal narratives (in the form of written letters, video testimonials, and digital stories), there is a high level of vocabulary repetition across texts and difficult concepts are supported with images. The grammar of the texts includes a mix of simple and complex sentences about familiar topics, and the texts are structured with limited or no dialogue and clear organizational moves, particularly in the virtual tour of Ellis Island, the infographics, and the written letters. Overall, then, the texts in this curricular unit have a level of complexity that is appropriate for the unit's learning objectives, themes, and intended audience.

Time-Saving Tips

The final point we wish to raise in relation to text selection is that of time. Through our experiences working with secondary and postsecondary teachers, we hear concerns about the amount of time it takes to find target language texts that fit with the themes of a unit, chapter, or lesson and that are level appropriate. We admit that the time it takes to find texts can be significant, particularly when you are just beginning your journey into literacies-oriented language education. We can assure you, however, that the value of adopting a literacies orientation outweighs the initial time investment required to find appropriate texts. We also echo Martel's (2013) compelling argument that preparing text-based lessons should be a professional imperative, one that is factored into teachers' regular duties. That said, we conclude this section of the chapter by offering a few tips for making the text-selection process less time consuming. First, we encourage you to always keep text selection in the back of your mind: you never know when you will encounter a target language text that may be of use for a current or future course, unit, or lesson. Similarly, maintaining a folder of bookmarked web pages, downloaded texts, references, and the like is a useful way to keep track of the texts you find. Once you have a critical mass of texts in this folder, you can create a spreadsheet that summarizes important information about each text and organize the texts into thematic subfolders or sheets, making it easier to pull out a text for use in a lesson you are developing. Finally, use existing text repositories to make searching for texts less time consuming. CARLA's Literacies in Language Education project maintains a list of web-based text resources in multiple languages (linked on the companion website, http://carla.umn.edu/literacies/book/), including less commonly taught languages, Indigenous languages, and classical languages (CARLA 2021d). In addition, many national associations for language teachers maintain sites that include resources for finding target language texts. One example is the curated resources page (https://frenchteachers.org/resources/curated-resources/) of the American Association of Teachers of French (2019), which has links to curricular and thematic resources that may include target language texts you can add to your folder. Another example is the list of Arabic manuscripts (https://aataweb.org/manuscripts) maintained by the American Association of Teachers of Arabic (2020). The website of your language-specific professional association can thus be an excellent starting point for selecting appropriate texts for use in your literacies-based courses, units, and lessons.

Textual Features

Throughout this chapter, we've referred to textual features such as images, headings, transition words, and verb forms. In this section we talk specifically about the types of features texts possess, how to identify them, and why doing so is important. In general terms, *textual features* are the building blocks of target language texts; in more specific terms, they are the meaning-making resources that reflect a text creator's deliberate or spontaneous "behind-the-scenes thinking" (Kern 2015, 21). A text creator chooses written, spoken, and visual features based upon a text's intended audience, message, genre, or tone. Textual features thus exist in a specific social and cultural context and are influenced by both the text producer and receiver (Janks 2005). These features are also interrelated; they do not function independently in a text but rather connect to one another to build textual meaning. Consider, for example, the different messages communicated by the word "hello" when it is accompanied by outstretched arms, a fervent wave, or arms folded across the chest. Each of these multimodal acts, which combine language and gesture, communicates a different meaning. Given the importance and range of textual features, it is important to identify them prior to designing instructional activities so that you have a clear idea of how a text makes meaning and which of its meaning-making features are related to your learning objectives. This systematic examination and analysis of textual features helps to "establish the patterns of meaning" and "offers a different window on the text; each feature represents a different slice of the (textual) data" (Janks 2005, 104).

In multiliteracies parlance, the meaning-making features of texts are called *Available Designs*, or "discernible patterns and conventions of representation" (Cope and Kalantzis 2009, 10). To make this definition less abstract, consider the words within it: discernible features are identifiable by and meaningful to a reader, listener, or viewer; patterns reflect the way that discernible features are organized and repeated; conventions are predictable patterns that are specific to a genre or text type; and representation refers to how these patterns and conventions are expressed, such as through different communicative modes. Because textual features are used differently across language users, genres, and contexts, they are variable and dynamic and thus reflect the definition of foreign language literacies we presented in chapter 1. Indeed, the meanings associated with a given language form, gesture, sound, or visual cue can be interpreted differently by different individuals based on their linguistic and cultural background. For instance, in the United States the expression "the country" implies outside of the city, with large amounts of land separating homes, whereas in Spain, this same expression can refer to homes outside of the city but situated in a small town with multiunit residences.

In language education, textual features can be categorized according to three interrelated types of content: language, conventions, and cultural content. *Language* includes grammatical forms, vocabulary, the sound system, spelling, metaphors, idiomatic phrases, pronoun referents, simple and complex sentences, and so on. The linguistic content of a text thus includes all of its language features in all of their many and varied forms. When you have worked with target language texts in the past, language may have been the most important—or even the only—feature you attended to. This is not surprising given the kinds of decoding activities (i.e., activities that ask students to identify specific words and phrases) prevalent in many secondary and postsecondary language textbooks. Yet to develop students' foreign language literacies, it is important to focus not just on language but also on the other types of meaning-making content a text possesses.

Conventions help learners interpret and create texts because they are crucial to understanding how different genres are constructed. Conventions are defined as "the agreed upon, or accepted, ways of using codes," and codes are the linguistic, audio, visual, gestural, and spatial systems used to communicate meaning in different types of texts (Anstey and Bull 2018, 60). Each of these systems has a flexible set of resources that are selected based on communicative need, cognitive demand, and sociocultural context (Kress and van Leeuwen 2006). For instance, in a TV talk show interview, participants might pull from a set of formal linguistic resources and might use socially neutral gestures to express meaning, whereas in an Instagram post, the text creator might use words, abbreviations, and hashtags common to that genre and might draw on visual and spatial resources such as filters or photo cropping.

The third type of textual feature essential to foreign language literacies development is *cultural content*. In chapter 1, we provided a literacies-based definition of ACTFL's culture standard as an understanding of the relationships between the social practices, cultural products, and perspectives of people in the target culture (Kern 2000; NSCB 2015). As we work to identify and understand the cultural content of target language texts, we can home in on the products, practices, and perspectives it represents and how they are expressed through language and other meaning-making systems. *Cultural products* are the tangible (e.g., books, films) or intangible (e.g., rituals, laws) creations of a particular culture; *cultural practices* are patterns of social interactions and behaviors (e.g., holiday traditions, meals); and *cultural perspectives* are the values, beliefs, attitudes, and philosophical perspectives of a society. Products, practices, and perspectives work in concert to represent a culture or community: products and practices reflect a culture's perspectives, and practices may involve the use of cultural products (CARLA 2021a; NSCB 2015).

To illustrate the textual features of language, conventions, and cultural content, we turn to one of the texts from the curricular unit presented in appendix A. "American Dreams" (I. Brown 2016) is a *New York Times* opinion piece composed of portrait photographs and statements about the American dream from fifteen individuals and families living in the United States. Each person's profile begins with a heading and subheading containing their name and geographical location. Their American dream statement is presented with their portrait in both handwritten and printed form, and each portrait is accompanied by a brief caption with biographical information. Although the individual profiles are short (e.g., the text analyzed in table 4.1 is under one hundred words), they possess features from each of the three content categories we've discussed. Table 4.1 presents a summary of these textual features for the profile of Skylar Kergil.[1]

In perusing this list of textual features, you may have noticed some overlap across the three categories. For instance, the American dream figures in all three categories: as something expressed through infinitival expressions (language), as a component of the text's structure (conventions), and as a culturally embedded ideal

Table 4.1. Example Textual Features Analysis

Language	Conventions	Cultural content
• Infinitival clauses (e.g., My dream is + infinitive; I want to + infinitive) • Informal expressions (e.g., a whole lot of; okay) • Gerund constructions (e.g., never stop growing, changing, or becoming) • Numbers to express age (e.g., by the age of 3; at 15) • Parataxis (e.g., I ask a whole lot of questions, my dream is to be okay without knowing all the answers) • Past and present tense narration (e.g., my transition . . . was; I ask) • Transgender vocabulary (e.g., transition; gender therapy)	• Dream statement and its motivation • Handwritten signature on statement • Page layout (portrait with handwritten dream and biography caption adjacent; typed dream underneath portrait) • Profile heading (name; geographical location)	• American dream • Feelings of belonging • Transgender youth

(cultural content). We point this out to illustrate that as you analyze the texts you're working with, it's perfectly normal for something that you've identified as one feature type to also be relevant for another feature type. What is important is to begin by identifying all of a text's features so that you know exactly how its language, conventions, and cultural content work to express meaning.

You may also be thinking that this list of features is quite long for such a short text. Although we encourage you to identify all of a text's features before you design instructional activities, you do not need to teach all of these features. Instead, you should make an informed decision about which feature or features to target in instruction based upon your learning objectives and your students' interests and learning needs. For instance, the text analyzed in table 4.1 is part of a lesson plan on the topic of the American dream (see appendix B), and this lesson is part of a larger curricular unit on immigration in the United States (see appendix A). The lesson-level objectives include having students define key features of the American dream, express their own American dream and its motivation, and employ images and photos to support the multimodal text they create. These objectives are directly related to two of the unit-level objectives: describe and analyze narrative, visual, and audiovisual texts presenting different perspectives on the immigrant experience in the United States and explain and critique definitions of the American dream and relate them to different immigrant experiences. Instructional activities should focus on only those textual features that help students realize these learning objectives, making only a handful of the textual features in table 4.1 relevant for the lesson: infinitival clauses, past and present tense narration (language); dream statement and its motivation, page layout (conventions); the American dream (cultural content). Although the remaining features in table 4.1 make important contributions to the text's meaning, they are unrelated to the stated learning objectives and thus should not play a role in designing instructional activities.

We have included a Textual Features Worksheet on the companion website (http://carla.umn.edu/literacies/book/) to help you carry out the two-step process of identifying textual features and deciding which of them to target in instruction. In addition to including space to note the language, conventions, and cultural content of a text and directions for identifying those features that are relevant to your learning objectives, the worksheet also includes reflective questions to help you understand how the text's features contribute to the meanings it expresses. Once you have selected texts using the criteria outlined in this chapter, you should use this worksheet to prepare for the last stage in the backward design process: planning learning experiences.

Spotlight on Teacher Professional Development

You may have noticed one topic that is conspicuously absent from this chapter: modifying target language texts. By modifying texts, we mean taking actions such as changing vocabulary or grammatical forms, omitting selected words or parts of a text, or simplifying sentence structures. We do not mean shortening or excerpting from a text (e.g., interpreting the first two minutes of a film or one paragraph of a magazine article). We have reserved this topic for the spotlight on teacher professional development because teachers often ask us if texts can be modified to accommodate their learners. Although we understand why teachers ask this question, to develop students' foreign language literacies, it is essential to work with texts in their original form. The purpose of this spotlight is thus to provide tools for teachers and teacher educators that make working with target language texts in their original form easier.

Why is using target language texts in their original version optimal for foreign language literacies development? Why shouldn't texts be modified to make them easier for students to interpret? There are several reasons why using the original version of a text is preferable to using a modified version. First, an important goal of literacies in language education is to equip students with the ability to interpret and create meaning through texts. Modifying texts can strip away some of that meaning and neutralize the cultural products, practices, and perspectives it aims to represent. Similarly, modifying texts can undermine the intent of the text creator, taking away from a text's intended meaning. Next, simplifying the language features of a text can render it unnatural through the omission of vocabulary, grammar, and conventions that exemplify the way language users speak and write. Finally, text modification can reduce some of the textual features that make interpretation easier for learners such as the repetition of words and ideas, the coherence and cohesion of the text, or the broader context of the messages being conveyed (Blau 1982; Honeyfield 1977; Swaffar 1985; Swaffar, Arens, and Byrnes 1991). The question of text modification was of great interest to researchers in the 1980s and 1990s when communicative language teaching was becoming more widely adopted. Some of the studies published at that time point to the benefits of working with original texts, including better comprehension, increased motivation and interest, and more strategic reading (e.g., Young 1993; Swaffar 1985). Other studies show that students' comprehension is better when reading simplified texts (e.g., Oh 2001; Yano, Long, and Ross 1994); however, this research focuses on surface-level comprehension of facts rather than on textual interpretation as we've defined it in this book.

Teacher educators can use a number of strategies to help teachers feel confident using unmodified target language texts in the classroom. The first is to help teachers become aware of their beliefs and prior experiences working with target language texts, which can influence their understanding and implementation of different pedagogical practices (Allen and Paesani, 2022; Menke 2018; Menke and Paesani 2021). Identifying these beliefs and then putting them into dialogue with research-based understandings of why and how to use unmodified target language texts can help teachers reconcile concerns or hesitations they may have. The work of identifying beliefs and prior experiences can take many forms, including reflective journals, one-on-one meetings between teachers and teacher educators, and professional learning circle discussions. Questions to ask of teachers during this work might include the following: What were your experiences with target language texts as a language learner? How have you used target language texts as a teacher? What successes did you have in these contexts? What challenges did you face? What are the benefits of using target language texts for you and your students? What are the drawbacks?

A second professional development strategy is to provide teachers with scaffolded help in selecting appropriate texts. The information presented in the Selecting Target Language Texts section of this chapter can support this work. For instance, in a teaching methods class, you might have students read the list of text selection criteria and the text complexity factors in figure 4.1 and then collectively apply them to a text everyone is familiar with. Methods students can then use this same information to evaluate a text of their choosing. To get feedback on their individual evaluation, students can work in small groups to discuss the reflective questions following figure 4.1 to verify that the text they've selected is appropriate for their learning objectives and audience.

Another helpful resource is the Textual Features Worksheet on the companion website (http://carla.umn.edu/literacies/book/). This worksheet can be used as a professional development tool to help teachers understand how the original and modified forms of a text make meaning. In addition to comparing the list of textual features (i.e., language, conventions, cultural content) each text possesses, teachers can consider the following questions: What meaning is changed or lost in the modified text? Do the losses outweigh the benefit of a potentially more comprehensible form of the text?

Finally, and perhaps most importantly, teacher educators should encourage teachers to adopt the well-known suggestion to "adapt the task, not the text." Indeed, a basic teaching principle "in a literacy-based language program is that students need controlled tasks, not controlled texts" (Kern 2000, 129). This means that, following careful text selection, any unmodified target language text can be used in instruction as long as the interpretive activities students carry out are level appropriate, well scaffolded, and focused on only those textual features essential for meeting stated learning outcomes. We turn to the topic of designing sound multiliteracies instructional activities—the third stage of the backward design planning model—in part II of this book.

Conclusion

The goal of this chapter was to lay a conceptual foundation for understanding how target language texts are defined and constructed and to provide tools to help you apply that foundation in the selection and analysis of texts for use in instruction. Target language texts play a crucial role in backward design planning as they are the principal content of literacies-oriented language courses and provide students with a window into how text creators use language, conventions, and cultural content to express ideas. In the next chapter, we move on to the second stage of the backward design model: determining acceptable evidence of learning through literacies-based assessments.

Reflecting on Research and Practice

1. Choose a target language text from your textbook or from a lesson you've created and use the list of text selection criteria and the text complexity features in figure 4.1 to determine if the text is appropriate for your instructional context and learning objectives. If it isn't, what strategies will you use to find a more appropriate text?
2. Working with the same text, identify its language, conventions, and cultural content using the Textual Features Worksheet on the companion website (http://carla.umn.edu/literacies/book/). Which features are most important to meeting your stated learning objectives? Which features are least important?
3. How did answering the previous questions deepen your understanding of the concepts discussed in this chapter? What items from the following list of resources and readings will you consult to fill in any gaps in your understanding?

Resources

1. Analyzing Texts Resources (https://carla.umn.edu/cobaltt/modules/curriculum/ta_form.html)

   This page from CARLA's CoBaLTT project provides several downloadable examples and resources to help you analyze the target language texts you wish to use in instruction.

2. Target Language Text Resources (https://carla.umn.edu/literacies/textresources.html)

   This page from CARLA's Literacies in Language Education project provides links to target language texts in ten languages as well as classical languages and Indigenous languages. It also includes links to general resources for finding target language texts across languages.

3. Textual Features Worksheet (http://carla.umn.edu/literacies/book/)

   Mentioned throughout this chapter, the Textual Features Worksheet is a tool to help you identify the features of a target language text, connect them to your learning objectives, and help you understand how textual features contribute to the text's meaning.

Further Reading

1. "Is This Novel Really Level 1? Understand the Factors that Contribute to Text Complexity" (https://comprehensibleclassroom.com/2018/05/16/is-this-text-really-level-1-which-factors-contribute-to-text-complexity/)

This post from *The Comprehensible Classroom* blog, written by two practicing Spanish teachers, discusses factors contributing to text complexity and how you can determine whether a text is (or is not) too complex for your learners.

2. "Concerns of Colleagues Regarding a Procedural Approach" in *Reading for Meaning: An Integrated Approach to Language Learning* (Swaffar, Arens, and Byrnes 1991, 137–51)

   The first part of chapter 8 of this classic book on teaching reading through language-content integration focuses on text selection and addresses common concerns teachers have related to using target language texts.

3. "Introduction" in *Authentic Materials Myths: Applying Second Language Research to Classroom Teaching* (Zyzik and Polio 2017, 1–12)

   The introduction to this book provides a succinct overview of target language texts—what they are, how they are used, and why they are important.

Note

1. Skylar Kergil's profile is featured here because it figures prominently in the American Dream lesson plan presented in appendix B.

5

Developing an Assessment Plan

ASSESSMENT. IT'S A WORD that elicits an emotional response from teachers and students alike. What emotions does it evoke for you? Does thinking about assessment fill you with dread or cause you stress? Does the opportunity to observe and showcase what your students can do in the target language excite you? No matter what the emotion, assessment plays an important role in teaching and learning. Moreover, educational and societal systems place great importance on the results of assessment, which leads all stakeholders—administrators, students, parents, and teachers—to value the skills and knowledge that are assessed over those that are not. In other words, assessments indicate what is important in a curriculum: if it's important, it's on the test. Assessment also plays a role in shaping student perceptions of learning objectives, determining their learning strategies, and ultimately developing their literacy skills (Zhou, Zhao, and Dawson 2020). Similarly, assessments influence what content teachers select and how they engage their students with it. Assessments, particularly standardized tests, can also have a washback effect on instruction, "exerting a stronger influence on classroom pedagogic agendas" than curricula and causing teachers to teach to the test (Unsworth 2014, 35). Finally, as we explained in chapter 2, and as evidenced in published research, when learning objectives, assessment, and instruction are aligned, students are more motivated and have a more positive perception of instruction (Davin et al. 2011; Glisan, Uribe, and Adair-Hauck 2007).

These findings emphasize the central role that assessment plays in our instructional planning; it links our learning objectives and our instructional activities, as reflected in the backward design model (Wiggins and McTighe 2005) presented in chapter 2. Assessment is essential to instructional planning as it transforms learning objectives into something more concrete; it is an evidence-based way of knowing whether objectives have been met. The question framing the second stage of the backward design model is thus the focus of this chapter: How will I know if students have achieved desired results? We address this question from a curricular planning perspective with the goal of elaborating principles and practices to craft an assessment plan. Although the principles we discuss can be applied to the creation of individual assessments, in this chapter we do not address the how-to of designing individual assessments; assessment design is addressed in chapter 10 as it relates to the knowledge process of applying. Instead, our focus here is on constructing a plan for knowing whether students have met programmatic, course, unit, or lesson learning objectives. We begin by defining key terms related to assessment and presenting principles to guide creation of a literacies-oriented assessment plan. We then discuss specific assessment types, their alignment with literacies assessment principles, and their contribution to an assessment plan prior to providing some practical steps for creating your own assessment plan. We briefly overview a template for creating literacies assessments and then spotlighting the relationship between teacher professional development and literacies-oriented assessment.

Defining Assessment and Its Varied Purposes

One potential reason for the emotional response evoked by assessment and its (over)emphasis in education is the conflation of assessment with evaluation and grading. When we mentioned assessment at the start of this chapter, did your mind automatically envision piles of compositions or exams to be graded? If so, you're not alone. Assessment, evaluation, and grading are often used interchangeably, but they refer to different activities. As you begin to develop an assessment plan, it is important to clarify these terms and to think about the role of each in your teaching.

Assessment refers to the general process of gathering information about a student's learning and measuring their level of knowledge or skills (Glisan and Donato 2021; Kern 2000; Shrum and Glisan 2016). Wiggins and McTighe (2005) narrowed this definition to focus on student learning, knowledge, or skills as related to desired results (i.e., learning objectives). *Evaluation* builds off of assessment through the analysis, interpretation, or judgment of the data or information gathered about a student (Kern 2000; Shrum and Glisan 2016). It is in evaluation that a value is assigned to student performance; these values might involve exceeding expectations, meeting expectations, approaching expectations, or something totally different. In all cases, however, evaluation is "grounded in the 'text' of a student's performance" (Kern 2000, 268). Finally, *grading* refers to the reporting of either assessment or evaluation results to any number of stakeholders, including students, parents, and administrators (Kern 2000; Shrum and Glisan 2016). It is here where performance is converted into a number or letter, something that is meaningful and understandable to those receiving the report. In short, assessment collects student performance data, evaluation interprets these data, and grading labels them. Although all are important to our practice, we narrow our focus in this chapter to assessment.

As a teacher, you likely have many different reasons for assessing student learning. Some of these might include identifying what students already know about a topic prior to starting a new unit, determining if students are progressing toward learning objectives to help adjust instruction, documenting student outcomes for stakeholders, or highlighting areas of strength or weakness to motivate students. These different purposes for assessment determine whether an assessment is diagnostic, formative, or summative. Both diagnostic and formative assessments seek to inform, adapt, or tailor instruction to students' specific needs. *Diagnostic assessment* occurs prior to the onset of instruction and allows a teacher to identify what students already know or what they can already do. Equipped with this information, you can tailor instruction to build on current knowledge and skills or to develop those things not yet learned. *Formative assessment* shares the same goal of informing instruction, but it occurs while instruction is ongoing, prior to its completion. According to Shrum and Glisan (2016), formative assessment is "designed to help form or shape learners' ongoing understanding or skills while the teacher and learners still have opportunities to interact for the purposes of repair and improvement within the instructional setting" (401). Formative assessment provides information to teachers and students alike about progress toward learning objectives. You can use this information to identify what skills or knowledge require further instructional interventions as well as which students need additional support. Likewise, students can use their performance on formative assessments to reinforce or adjust their approach to learning; based on their performance, they may decide to participate more in small group activities, slow down their reading of target language texts, consider their audience in presentational communication, or continue what they're already doing. Finally, *summative assessment* occurs at the end of instruction, when opportunities to meet specific learning objectives have concluded. As such, summative assessments seek to determine whether students have met learning targets.

Formative and summative assessment play an important role in instruction, and numerous scholars highlight the need for balance in these types of assessment practices (e.g., Kern 2000; Paesani, Allen, and Dupuy 2016; Shrum and Glisan 2016). The purpose of assessment has shifted from auditing teaching and learning to "watching and noticing what students are doing and then using that information to guide the students toward new skills and knowledge" (G. E. Jacobs 2013, 626). To this end, it is necessary to incorporate both formative and summative assessment into an overall assessment plan.

Features of a Literacies-Oriented Assessment Plan

Consistent with stage 2 of backward design, Glisan and Donato (2021) posed the following question to guide development of an assessment plan: "What evidence will show that students have produced the desired outcomes?" (48). When assessments target programmatic, course, unit, or lesson learning objectives, we elicit acceptable evidence of student learning. If after reading the first few chapters of this book you've decided to change your curricular goals to target the development of foreign language literacies (and we hope you have!), you'll need to revisit your assessment practices. Drawing on multiliteracies scholarship, Tan et al. (2020) argued that reenvisioning goals and instruction to align with literacies principles requires "*competence, ability, capacity*, and *intelligence* to be reframed" (98; italics in original). Although listening and reading comprehension questions, compositions, interpersonal speaking tasks, or written exams may provide us with some details regarding students' competencies, they do not elicit sufficient evidence to fully assess students' developing foreign language literacies.

As we discussed in chapter 3, when foreign language literacies is the overarching goal for student learning, we seek to develop their ability to interpret multiple forms of language across various genres and communicative modes; to communicate about, analyze, and transform discourse; to understand and use language, conventions, and cultural products, practices, and perspectives to make meaning; to identify and understand form-meaning relationships in texts; and to take a critical stance toward language. Assessment then necessarily "involves evaluating how students interpret and produce meaning, understanding how learners analyze texts and the knowledge they gain from that analysis, and encouraging learners to reflect on form-meaning relationships, communicative intent, and links between language and culture" (Paesani, Allen, and Dupuy 2016, 68). As in instruction, target language texts play a central role in assessment.

Kern (2000) outlined three principles to guide the development of literacies assessments and assessment plans:

1. Assessment is based on a broad view of language and literacy.
2. Assessment is multidimensional.
3. Assessment is integrated with teaching and learning.

These three principles can guide not only the types of assessments we include in an assessment plan but also the number of assessments and the contexts in which they are carried out.

The first principle, that assessment be based on a broad view of language and literacy, reflects the dynamic, socially situated view of language and the concept of foreign language literacies that undergird multiliteracies pedagogy. Assessment that adheres to this principle reflects real-world literacies practices, in which individuals actively interpret, create, and transform meaning through texts. To this end, assessment targets various communicative modes, providing students with the opportunity to both interpret texts created by others and produce their own texts. Moreover, multiliteracies pedagogy recognizes the importance of language, cognitive skills, and sociocultural knowledge when engaging in literacies practices, and so assessment must address all three of these dimensions. For example, if a learning objective targets how formal and informal forms of address (e.g., second-person pronouns in a Romance language) either create or minimize social distance, an assessment that addresses the linguistic, cognitive, and sociocultural dimensions of literacies must do more than just ask students to identify whether individuals use formal or informal pronouns or verb forms. Instead, students might be required to use their linguistic and sociocultural knowledge to interpret the relationship between two individuals in an interaction based on their pronoun use. When based on broad views of language and literacies, our assessments become less about the informational content of texts (i.e., declarative knowledge) and more about how students use their knowledge and skills to interpret the significance of a text or to create a text that meets its communicative intent (i.e., procedural knowledge). Burgess and Rowsell (2020) reported that the use of multimodal assessments with new adult immigrants to Canada was more meaningful to and stimulated greater agency in learners and teachers than the standardized, traditional literacy (i.e., reading and writing) assessments used previously.

Multidimensional assessment, the second principle, ensures that we explore a student's full range of literacies, not just a narrow subset. In contemporary society, students must be able to read more than just literary or descriptive texts and create more than just the stereotypical five-paragraph essay or family description. More than twenty-five years ago, the New London Group (1996) highlighted how multimodality and cultural and linguistic diversity were changing the competencies that students needed to be successful in their professional, academic, civic, and personal lives. Given the literacies principle that students use language for varied purposes and in varied contexts, in assessment (like in instruction) they should engage with texts from different genres for different purposes. If all of our assessments incorporate the same type of texts, we miss an opportunity to see the range of knowledge and skills students are developing. In addition to incorporating varied texts and tasks, we can also consider student performance across assessment conditions: What are they able to do independently as opposed to collaboratively? What are they able to do when allowed to go through a process versus when required to communicate spontaneously? In summary, the principle of multidimensionality encourages us to examine student performance from different angles, in different modalities, with assorted texts, across varied tasks, and in different contexts.

The final literacies principle of integrating assessment into the teaching and learning process reflects the common refrain "test the way you teach." This refrain emphasizes that the types of tasks with which students engage and the language, conventions, and cultural knowledge targeted in assessments should reflect what is used and developed in instruction. Indeed, the same activity structure can be repeated in assessment with new texts or content. Conversely, the same text can be used in assessment with different activity structures. For example, if during instruction students complete a text matrix in which they identify key characters, their relevant characteristics, and the textual features that communicate those characteristics, in an assessment they might be asked to do the same thing with a different text. Additionally, assessment can follow the same pattern as instruction. If students first interpret texts and their features in instruction and then create their own text, assessment can similarly link interpretation and creation. To continue with the text matrix example, students might then use information gathered to introduce a new character in a text continuation exercise. Paesani, Allen, and Dupuy (2016) described the relationship between instruction and assessment as "interwoven" (68), and Glisan and Donato (2021) described it as "seamless" (91). Indeed, when assessments are aligned and integrated, the boundaries between instruction and assessment are blurred.

Sample Assessment Plans

The curricular unit on immigration in the United States introduced in chapter 2 (see appendix A) includes an assessment plan that reflects the three principles of literacies-oriented assessments. This assessment plan is summarized in table 5.1. The six assessment types that compose the plan assess all four of the unit learning objectives multiple times. Some assessments primarily serve to inform teaching and learning, whereas others primarily function to determine whether learning objectives have been met. In this way, the plan demonstrates alignment with learning objectives, multidimensionality, and balance between formative and summative assessment.

Students also carry out diverse literacies practices across the six assessments in table 5.1. They engage in interpersonal communication with their peers and teacher (in-class participation) and with a community member (interview). They interact with a variety of target language texts, ranging from infographics and interactive museum tours to journalistic essays and audiovisual stories (homework, in-class participation, and quizzes). Finally, they produce traditional genres (interview, responses on quizzes and homework) as well as multimodal texts (American dream statement, digital story). At all times the assessments are grounded in textual content and students use their linguistic, cognitive, and sociocultural skills and knowledge to fulfill the demands of each assessment task. Throughout the unit, and particularly in assessments, students have agency to determine with whom they talk; what aspects of immigration data and stories are relevant; how images, audio, and text can work together to communicate the intended message; and more.

Because each learning objective is measured by multiple assessments, student performance data is gathered across distinct contexts and tasks. For example, one learning objective specifies that students will be able to describe and analyze texts that present different perspectives on the immigrant experience. As teachers, we

Table 5.1. Immigration in the United States: Unit Learning Objectives and Assessment Plan

Unit learning objectives (LOs)

At the end of this unit, in oral and/or written communicative modes students will be able to . . .

1. Discuss facts about immigration in the United States presented in narrative, visual, and audiovisual texts.
2. Describe and analyze narrative, visual, and audiovisual texts presenting different perspectives on the immigrant experience in the United States.
3. Explain and critique definitions of the American dream presented in narrative and visual texts and relate them to different immigrant experiences.
4. Plan and produce a multimodal narrative of their own experience as immigrants or children of immigrants in the United States.

Formative assessments	Targeted LOs	Summative assessments	Targeted LOs
Homework (all lessons)	1	Interview of a family member/ friend about their immigration story (lesson 2)	1, 2, 3
In-class participation (all lessons)	1, 2, 3, 4	American dream statement (lesson 4)	2, 3, 4
Quizzes (lesson 1, lesson 2)	1	Digital story (lesson 5)	2, 4

can observe whether students are able to do this by listening to their contributions to group conversations or examining their responses on worksheets. We can then provide students with feedback regarding their performance; we might guide them to use different strategies to analyze texts, ask questions to clarify the language forms or conventions they use to describe perspectives embedded in the texts, and scaffold instruction to help them identify different perspectives. Assessing the same objective through different tasks ensures that the plan is multidimensional.

Finally, instruction and assessment are integrated in the curricular unit assessment plan because assessments require students to use the skills and knowledge cultivated in instruction in tasks similar to those implemented in the classroom. For example, in lesson 4 students apply their knowledge of infinitival clauses (language forms); how images, captions, and text interact (genre conventions); and the American dream (cultural knowledge) to create a new entry in a *New York Times* essay on the American dream. The target language text they produce is a natural extension of an instructional sequence (see chapter 6) that guides students through comprehending individual entries in the essay, identifying the textual features that create meaning, and considering the essay's significance within the larger society. This instructional sequence and its associated summative assessment target learning objectives 2, 3, and 4.

Another example assessment plan that reflects Kern's (2000) three principles comes from a university course titled Spanish for Latino Students that developed the linguistic, affective, cognitive, and sociocultural dimensions of heritage students' literacies with the goal of expanding their communicative repertoires (Parra et al. 2018). The course engaged students with a broad range of textual genres that varied in communicative purpose and audience. Given the different course learning objectives, the assessment plan incorporated a range of assessments, including quizzes, an online reading program, textual creation and transformation tasks (essays, creative writing, formal letter, book/movie review, oral presentation), and a final art project. This assessment plan is summarized in table 5.2, which highlights the alignment between course objectives and assessments.[1]

What is striking about this assessment plan is the variety of textual genres with which students engage, which range from academic (presentation, essay) to critical (book/movie review) to creative (art, creative writing). Throughout the course, students also develop their awareness of how language use varies across speakers and contexts. The variety of texts students create allows them to consider these issues in their own textual production. All objectives are assessed by more than one assessment, providing the instructor with information from multiple tasks at different moments.

Whereas the alignment between assessment and objectives can be observed in table 5.2, integration with instruction cannot. The authors, however, provide examples of the multimodal texts with which students interact in instruction, how the theme of ethnolinguistic identity runs throughout the course, and how students engage in meaning design, suggesting that instruction and assessment are indeed integrated. Moreover, the authors emphasize that instruction is scaffolded, that productive speaking and writing tasks are grounded in texts that students previously interpreted, and that students receive feedback on their performance regularly.

Table 5.2. Spanish for Latino Students: Course Learning Objectives and Assessment Plan

Course learning objectives (LOs)

Through this course, students will be able to . . .

1. Advance their proficiency in all three communicative modes (interpersonal, interpretive, and presentational).
2. Reflect on and analyze the role of Spanish in their current and future lives.
3. Develop critical sociocultural and linguistic awareness.
4. Embrace their ethnolinguistic identities.

Formative assessments	Targeted LOs	Summative assessments	Targeted LOs
Short quizzes on content knowledge	1, 3	Art project	2, 3, 4
Online reading program (*Lectura inteligente herencia latina*)	1	Essay to accompany art project	1, 2, 3, 4
Textual creation and transformation tasks	1	Textual creation and transformation tasks	1

Source: Parra et al. (2018, 34–35, 37).

The assessment plans in tables 5.1 and 5.2 emphasize the interpretation and creation of target language texts, which contribute to reaching the overarching goal of students' foreign language literacies development. Moreover, there is a balance in the plans between those assessments that inform teaching and learning and those that determine if learning objectives have been achieved. As a result, these assessment plans can serve as models for your program, course, unit, or lesson, as we will see later in this chapter. One final observation regarding these plans is that traditional assessments such as exams, written compositions, or even oral interviews occupy a minimal (if any) role. Instead, performance-based assessments, in which learners "use their repertoire of knowledge and skills to create a product or a response, either individually or collaboratively" (Shrum and Glisan 2016, 404), have a more central role.

A Literacies Perspective on Traditional Assessments

In this section, we look more closely at traditional and performance-based assessments used in language education and consider what information they give us regarding students' developing foreign language literacies and their alignment with the three principles of literacies-oriented assessment.

Alignment of Traditional Assessments with Literacies Principles

In the previous section *performance-based assessments*, such as art projects, multimodal dream statements, and interviews, were privileged in the two assessment plans. Performance-based assessments require learners to employ various resources—linguistic, cognitive, and sociocultural—simultaneously to make meaning; in this sense, they resemble tasks from outside the language classroom. They are what Education Queensland (2004) calls "rich tasks," in which "students display their understandings, knowledges, and skills through performance on transdisciplinary activities that have an obvious connection to the wide world" (quoted in I. Brown, Lockyer, and Caputi 2010, 193–4). Performance-based assessments offer students an opportunity to show what they can do and capture creative language use. Moreover, if instruction encourages students to use a wide range of meaning-making resources to interpret and create texts, assessments should do the same to ensure that we assess what is taught and in the way it is taught. Because of these features, performance-based assessments serve as a lens through which to observe students' developing foreign language literacies; they provide more information about student language use than traditional assessments such as written exams, compositions, or oral presentations.

Traditional assessments do give us information about what language students know and are able to do, but when considered in relation to the three principles of literacies-oriented assessment, each falls short in some way. For example, written exams allow us to observe whether students can produce sentences with a targeted linguistic form and comprehend details from a written or audio text. Although written exams often include a real-life context, the focus on accuracy doesn't acknowledge the dynamic, socially situated nature of language and literacies. Because they do not specify who is communicating about what, for what purposes, and under what circumstances, written exams can reduce language to a static, immutable entity. The predominant focus on accuracy means that various literacies skills and dimensions are not integrated and that we only have access to one aspect of language development. Finally, written exams typically do not reflect the activities students engage in during instruction. Even in communicative language teaching, in which students regularly engage in interpersonal activities and in which the emphasis is on self-expression, written exams can feel like a departure from instruction.

Compositions give us information about how students organize their ideas in writing, and oral presentations allow us to examine a student's fluency and pronunciation in a more formal, rehearsed setting. They have some features of performance-based assessments, yet if they are devoid of context and focus only on accuracy, they too fail to align with the assessment principles laid out earlier in this chapter. Like exams, these assessments too often lack a context or purpose for communication; audience, communicative purpose, and genre considerations are not at the forefront of assessment design. Failure to consider these features results in students repeatedly crafting generic, academic essays or presentations, in which the teacher is the audience. Moreover, in rubrics for compositions and presentations, linguistic accuracy is generally prioritized over other meaning-making elements. Consequently, although aligned with the content or topic of instruction, they reflect a narrow, static view of language and literacies and are unidimensional.

You'll notice that throughout this section we qualify our statements by using adverbs such as "typically," "often," or "generally." We do this to recognize that each exam, composition, and presentation looks different; some embody more of the features we just mentioned and others, fewer. How do your exams, compositions, and presentations uphold the three principles of multiliteracies assessment? What adjustments do you need to make to bring them into greater alignment with these principles? In table 5.3 we offer a few suggestions for adapting traditional assessments to reflect a broader view of language and literacies, to incorporate multiple dimensions of literacies, and to better reflect literacies-oriented instruction. These suggested adaptations transform traditional assessments into performance-based assessments.

Alternatives to Traditional Assessments

Whereas traditional assessments focus on the product of learning, alternative assessments emphasize both the process and product of learning (Hall 2001). Given our goal of gathering data about how learners create meaning across tasks, contexts, and time, understanding a student's process is key. In this section we briefly overview four assessment types that focus on student performance and their developing literacies: digital storytelling, portfolios, Integrated Performance Assessments, and journals.

Digital Storytelling

Digital storytelling is a multimodal composition through which students tell a fictional or true story using video or a series of still images. Godwin-Jones (2012) emphasized that these are often short stories, a maximum of three to five minutes long, and that

Table 5.3. Suggested Adaptations to Traditional Exams, Compositions, and Presentations

Traditional assessment	Suggested adaptation
As part of a written exam, students complete a chart in which they identify details from an audio segment about weekend activities in a city (prices, time, activity). They then state which activity they'd like to do and why.	Students decide whether the speaker recommends each weekend activity based on how they use textual elements to convey details (e.g., positive adjectives, intonation, word order). Students then identify the target audience of the audio segment based on textual content and features.
Students research an artist from the target culture. They then write a five-paragraph composition about the artist that overviews their biography, artistic style, and major pieces of art.	Students research an artist and create a text to include on a museum's website. The text should include information about the artist, an image of a specific piece of art that they want to highlight, and commentary on the highlighted piece of art.
Students research and orally present information about an environmental concern for three to five minutes.	During instruction students learn about environmental challenges facing a specific target language community. They propose a solution to this challenge and present it to a community organization that will fund one of the initiatives. In their presentation, students describe the challenge, identify their solution, and highlight how their solution aligns with the community's values.

they allow for personal, even emotional connections. As multimodal texts, digital stories can incorporate linguistic, visual, and auditory elements and can tap into a variety of textual composition skills, most notably point of view, a dramatic question, emotional content, personal voice, soundtrack, conciseness, and pacing (Robin 2006), offering students the opportunity to expand beyond print- or language-based literacies. There are numerous published examples of digital story projects; here we highlight two that were developed specifically using literacies principles.

These projects were carried out in very different contexts, one in an intermediate (third semester) university Japanese language course (Kumagai et al. 2016) and the other in a four-week summer program for multilingual middle school ESL students (Angay-Crowder, Choi, and Yi 2013). Despite their different audiences, both projects sought to assess learning objectives related to narrative structure, genre conventions of digital stories, audience awareness, and reflection on the learning process. Perhaps what is most striking about these two projects, however, is how they exemplify the seamless integration of assessment into instruction. During instruction, students were exposed to digital stories created by others; as students interpreted the meaning of sample stories, they identified how specific textual design elements (e.g., images, words, music, rhythm, narrative structure) contributed to the meaning conveyed by the story. They then worked to articulate conventions of the digital story genre before applying these conventions to their own digital story. Because instruction demystified the way that digital stories create meaning, students were assessed on the knowledge and skills they developed and practiced during instruction.

Both sets of authors emphasized that through the digital story projects, students became critical consumers of multimodal texts and developed meta-awareness of their design choices. For instance, Kumagai et al. (2016) detailed how through engaging in digital storytelling one student deepened her awareness of "multimodal orchestration" (154), or how narration, pictures, and music interact to construct meaning. They concluded that the project encouraged "students to be intentional and purposeful in designing a text" (154), which thus allowed them to observe how students link form and meaning, language and culture, and the acts of interpretation and creation. Similarly, Angay-Crowder, Choi, and Yi (2013) noted that the digital storytelling project reframed what counts as literacy learning and teaching for teachers and students alike.

Portfolios

Portfolios involve the systematic collection of student work over time; students participate in selecting the content of their portfolio while reflecting on their learning process. Among the content, or evidence of learning, that students might select to include in their portfolio are writing samples, reading journals, recorded conversations, and textual analyses, as well as reflective statements on the creation of the portfolio. Portfolios are an ideal alternative to traditional assessments given that they "provide a portrait of what students know and what they can do, offer a multidimensional perspective of student progress over time, encourage student self-reflection and participation, and link instruction and assessment" (Delett,

Barnhardt, and Kevorkian 2001, 559). In this regard, not only do portfolios embody the principles of literacies-oriented assessment but they also provide insight into students' meaning-making and learning processes. To be meaningfully and effectively implemented, portfolios require reenvisioning teacher and student roles in teaching, learning, and assessment processes (Kern 2000). Consequently, we encourage you to think about the process of implementing portfolios as gradual, one that will require patience, commitment, reflection, and revision.

Several scholars have offered guidance on how to implement portfolios in the language classroom (e.g., Delett, Barnhardt, and Kevorkian 2001; Ferris and Hedgcock 1998; Kern 2000), and one common caveat is that teachers must articulate the purpose of the portfolio: Who is the audience? What do learners need to show evidence of? Articulating the purpose guides learners in selecting the content of their portfolio and facilitates teacher evaluation of the portfolio; a clear purpose helps us to know whether we are looking for evidence of growth, mastery, reflection, or something else entirely.

Schmerbeck and Lucht (2017) described a portfolio project grounded in literacies principles used to assess student mastery of learning objectives in a unit on German immigration in the United States in an intermediate-level postsecondary course. Through an eight-step process that included drafts, peer review, collaborative creation of rubrics, and reflection, students created a portfolio that showed their ability to interpret target language texts, collaborate and problem solve with peers, redesign textual content and features for new purposes, and reflect on their learning. The purpose of the portfolio was to assess students' comprehension of cultural content and their ability to engage in different literacies activities. The authors argued that the portfolio project afforded students a "more critical insight into concepts like the American Dream and the immigrant experience" (39), suggesting that it served as both a learning tool and an assessment tool.

Integrated Performance Assessment

Integrated Performance Assessment (IPA; Adair-Hauck, Glisan, and Troyan 2013) is a familiar performance-based assessment for many language teachers in the United States. IPAs engage learners in three different tasks across three communicative modes—interpretive, interpersonal, and presentational—around a common topic or theme. During each phase of the assessment, learners receive feedback about their performance with the goal of informing the next phase. Through IPAs teachers can assess what students are able to do with language and how their linguistic proficiency is developing. For example, as part of a unit on healthy eating, beginning, elementary-aged students of Spanish might complete an IPA around breakfast in the United States and Chile (CARLA n.d.c). First, they listen to Chilean children describe their breakfast and respond to questions (interpretive mode), then they create a presentation about their own breakfast habits (presentational mode), and finally they compare Chilean and US breakfasts with a classmate (interpersonal mode). Although the order of communicative modes and the topics of IPAs are highly flexible, there are standardized rubrics for each mode to assess students' developing proficiency and a standardized template for the interpretive mode. The questions that compose the interpretive template assess keyword recognition, main idea and supporting detail identification, genre recognition, strategy use, interpretation, identification of the author's purpose, cultural comparisons, and personal reactions.

IPAs embody some of the principles of literacies-based assessment in that they offer information on students' abilities in different communicative modes and blur the lines of instruction and assessment (Davin et al. 2011; Menke and Lake 2017; Zapata 2016). Moreover, students are engaged in meaning making when they interpret and create texts in the various phases of the assessment. Nonetheless, in their current form, proficiency-oriented IPA rubrics limit our ability to assess all aspects of foreign language literacies development. Within the interpretive mode, on the one hand, learners are asked to read between the lines to identify the author's perspective and cultural perspectives, grounding and justifying their inferences in various textual features, which provides insight into how learners interpret meaning. In the interpersonal and presentational modes, on the other hand, conventions and cultural knowledge are not incorporated into the rubric, nor are they necessarily present in the task. In addition, the language control criterion focuses on grammatical accuracy, vocabulary appropriateness, and fluency; the relationships between textual features and the meanings they communicate are not explicitly incorporated into either the task or the rubric. Bringing these aspects into focus during the feedback loop, however, would provide insight into the meanings individual learners are associating with specific language forms, conventions, and cultural products, practices, and perspectives. For instance, you might ask learners to reflect on their design choices and how those allowed them to fulfill their communicative intent. These moments of critical reflection grant you as a teacher access to learners' developing meaning-making systems, information you can then use to inform instruction.

Journals

Unlike digital storytelling projects, portfolios, and IPAs, which primarily assess what students can do with language, journals offer insights into learners' changing understandings, perspectives, identities, and knowledge base. A variety of journal types exist, and Kern (2000) makes a distinction between personal journals and intellectual journals. Given our focus on gathering data about student learning, knowledge, and skills in this chapter, we focus on intellectual journals, in which students reflect on course content, texts, or learning. Linguistic accuracy is not the goal of journaling; rather, self-reflection, idea exploration, and critical questioning are in focus. Although journals offer a space for critical reflection on textual content or perspectives, they also allow for reflection on and questioning of the features of a target language text. Journals are thus both a site for student learning and a means of gathering information about students, exemplifying seamless integration of instruction and assessment. Two examples of journaling from published scholarship demonstrate the potential of journals as a type of formative assessment to inform both your instructional practice and students' literacies practices.

As part of a Taiwanese university course titled "Gender and Reading" for advanced learners of English, Chi (2012) incorporated regular narrative journal entries into the instructional design. One student, Sue, came to better understand her own reading and inquiry process through the act of journaling. Through her journal entries she uncovered her own subconscious beliefs about what it means to be female or male and questioned how she positioned herself as a female university student in Taiwan. Simultaneously, Chi, as the teacher of the class, used the journal entries as a form of formative assessment, observing the linguistic and cultural resources that Sue (and all students) brought to the act of interpreting and analyzing course texts. Knowing how students were reading course texts allowed Chi to introduce new ways of reading into instruction and to observe how learners' reading processes and resources developed and evolved over time. In a similar way, Kennedy, Oviatt, and De Costa (2019) documented how daily journaling opened a dialogic space between an ESL teacher and her upper-elementary immigrant students, in which learners questioned and formulated ideas about their own identity, American identity, nationalism, monolingualism and multilingualism, race, and culture. Using the understandings she gained from her students' journal entries, the teacher was able to shift her classroom practices so that they reflected "a participatory model of learning that honors the cultural wealths and deep knowledges of all learners" (68). These two qualitative analyses exemplify how journaling activities "lend themselves to weaving the different types of knowledge processes and to powerful learning" (López-Sánchez 2016, 71).

Steps to Develop Your Assessment Plan

Now that you have a better feel for the nature of literacies-oriented assessments, we turn our attention to designing your own assessment plan, which you can think of as a blueprint for gauging learner attainment of learning objectives. An assessment plan specifies all the instruments we use to gather data about student development and fulfillment of learning objectives. We've emphasized throughout this chapter that a variety of measures are needed because "no single assessment instrument or single moment of assessment alone is sufficient to provide students and teachers with all the information needed to identify what to do next. The rich and balanced pool of evidence that is collected to match each specific assessment purpose will guide students in their language learning and teachers in the coaching of that journey" (Sandrock 2010, 2). We've also emphasized that assessment should reflect a broad view of language and literacies, moving beyond linguistic accuracy to understand what meanings learners attach to different language forms and conventions and how they use those understandings to interpret and create target language texts. Finally, we've underscored the need to align assessment with instruction to provide a coherent, motivating experience for students. These guiding principles form the backdrop for the steps in creating a literacies-oriented assessment plan: (1) identify learning objectives, (2) analyze existing assessment plan, (3) incorporate new assessments and/or adjust existing assessments, (4) analyze the new/revised assessment plan, and (5) assign weights for grading purposes.

The first step in crafting any assessment plan is knowing the desired results, or what the goals are for students at the end of an instructional unit (or course). Chapter 3 lays out the characteristics of good learning objectives and guides you through developing literacies learning objectives for a course, unit, or lesson. Once you've articulated learning objectives, the second step is to determine whether your current assessments provide data relevant to your learning objectives. In our work with curriculum developers, we've seen that often one learning objective is targeted heavily in assessment while others are minimally assessed (if at all). We have thus found it useful to use an assessment matrix to evaluate what objectives each assessment targets and, conversely, what assessments target each objective. A sample assessment matrix for the curricular unit on immigration in the United States (see chapter 2) is presented in table 5.4.

Table 5.4. Sample Unit-Level Assessment Matrix

Learning objective	Assessment 1: Homework	Assessment 2: In-class work and participation	Assessment 3: Quizzes	Assessment 4: Interview	Assessment 5: American dream statement	Assessment 6: Digital story
1. Discuss facts about immigration in the United States presented in narrative, visual, and audiovisual texts.	x	x	x	x		
2. Describe and analyze narrative, visual, and audiovisual texts presenting different perspectives on the immigrant experience in the United States.		x		x	x	x
3. Explain and critique definitions of the American dream presented in narrative, visual, and audiovisual texts and relate them to different immigrant experiences.		x		x	x	
4. Plan and produce a multimodal narrative of their own experience as immigrants or children of immigrants in the United States.		x			x	x

An assessment matrix like the one in table 5.4 serves as data for your critical reflection; equipped with this data, you can determine which objectives are being assessed, how often they are being assessed, and by which assessments. As you critically analyze your current assessment plan, you might ask yourself the following questions:

- Do assessments target all language forms, conventions, and cultural content identified in your learning objectives? If not, what is not assessed?
- Do assessments engage learners in all the communicative modes targeted in your learning objectives? If not, what is not assessed?
- Do assessments engage learners in using language to interpret and create target language texts?
- Do the genres and content of texts align with those targeted in learning objectives?
- Do assessments provide different contexts (e.g., independent and collaborative, process and spontaneous) for learner language use?
- Do you and students have an opportunity to monitor progress toward meeting learning objectives—either through instructional activities or formative assessments—prior to a summative assessment?

After analyzing your current assessment plan, you may find it necessary to make adjustments, either incorporating additional assessment measures or revising or eliminating existing assessments to fill any gaps you uncovered. For instance, your previous assessments may not provide adequate information about your literacies-oriented learning objectives, may all be summative in nature, or may only address presentational communication. Whatever the gaps you have identified, it is important to take action to better align objectives and assessments. The following questions, adapted from Glisan and Donato (2021), can support you as you consider what new assessments to incorporate or how to adjust your plan to align with your objectives and literacies assessment principles:

- What is the best proof that learners have met the learning objectives?
- How do the assessments fit within the larger context of the unit or course?
- What will learners do to provide you with evidence of their current knowledge and skills?
- How will you and your learners know if they are making progress toward meeting the learning objectives?
- How will learners know if they have achieved the learning objectives?

After revising your assessment plan, we suggest repeating step two—analyze your new or revised assessment measures—to ensure that no objectives are overlooked and that the plan embraces broad definitions of language and literacies, is multidimensional, and integrates seamlessly with instruction. The last reflection question in this analysis (Do you and students have an opportunity to monitor progress toward meeting learning objectives—either through instructional activities or formative assessments—prior to a summative assessment?) asks you to consider the role of formative assessments and how you and your students will know if certain topics should be revisited to facilitate meeting learning objectives. Formative assessments are pivotal to informing the teaching and learning process, and numerous scholars argue for the need for a balanced approach to assessment (e.g., Kern 2000; Paesani, Allen, and Dupuy 2016; Shrum and Glisan 2016).

The fifth and final step is to consider how the various assessments will be weighted for grading or reporting purposes. When we initially presented the assessment plan for the immigration in the United States unit in chapter 2 (see also appendix A), we included the relative contribution of each assessment type to the unit grade: quizzes comprise 5 percent of the grade; homework, 10 percent; in-class participation, 20 percent; interview, 20 percent; American dream statement, 20 percent; and digital story, 25 percent. The three formative assessments—homework, in-class participation, and quizzes—comprise a smaller portion of the unit grade than the summative assessments, 35 percent and 65 percent respectively. In addition, assessments that target fewer learning objectives have less weight in the overall grading scheme than those that assess more learning objectives. The grading scheme thus gives greater emphasis to summative assessments, which require application of knowledge and skills and greater student effort, and to those assessments that target multiple learning objectives. In sum, the nature of the assessment (formative versus summative), student effort level, and number of learning objectives addressed can serve as criteria for assigning weights to the assessment in your plan.

The five steps outlined here can lead to the creation of a blueprint for assessing students' learning and their developing foreign language literacies. These steps can be applied to instructional units, courses, or programs. Once you've crafted a plan for assessing student attainment of learning objectives, you can develop individual assessments and plan literacies-oriented instructional activities, the third stage of the backward design model (see part II of this book).

Spotlight on Teacher Professional Development

As this chapter has demonstrated, assessment is a multidimensional topic, one that becomes more complex when teachers adopt new approaches such as the multiliteracies framework. Several studies have examined the assessment practices of language teachers and how those practices reinforce or contradict the concept of foreign language literacies defined in chapter 1. Although descriptive accounts of successful assessment projects exist, several studies detail challenges teachers face in implementing and assessing literacies in language education. More specifically, studies have highlighted a number of variables that undermine efforts to realize literacies-based instruction, including disagreement about what constitutes valued knowledge (e.g., Wyatt-Smith and Kimber 2009; Yi and Choi 2015), underdefined or vague learning objectives (Wyatt-Smith and Kimber 2009), misalignment between instruction and assessment (Burgess and Roswell 2020; Menke and Paesani 2021; Tan, Bopry, and Guo 2010; Yi and Choi 2015), insufficient assessment knowledge (Choi and Yi 2016; Pirbhai-Illich, Turner, and Austin 2009), and time constraints (Yi and Choi 2015). As language education evolves to embrace new goals such as foreign language literacies development, teachers may face discomfort as they reconsider what they value in learning, how they get there, and how they assess student progress. Indeed, it can take time to concretize what evidence of literacies learning objectives looks like and to reconcile previous practices with new concepts and approaches.

Yi and Choi (2015) suggested that teachers be allowed to explore their beliefs about language, literacies, and multimodality before they integrate these concepts into instruction and assessment. This is a particularly important step for preservice teachers, who may struggle more to identify what they value in language teaching and why. Journaling is one way to explore these sometimes subconscious beliefs and values, and this can be worked into an undergraduate or graduate teaching methods course. As teacher-learners read and experience literacies-oriented objectives and assessments, they can react to them and reflect on their own experiences. Methods instructors can then ask probing questions that encourage teacher-learners to articulate the values and perspectives behind their reactions. For in-service teachers, this reflection can take place in team meetings, professional development workshops, or teacher-supervisor conversations. Elucidating our beliefs allows us to know what motivates our instructional decisions and to consider where our beliefs align with or differ from research-based practices.

The high value attributed to traditional, print-based literacy is prevalent throughout our society, and educational systems have been slow to adopt assessments that embrace a broader view of language and literacies. Expanded literacies goals are often not reflected in the "rigid and instrumental forms of assessment" (Burgess and Roswell 2020, 173) that are employed to measure student achievement in systematic ways. This mismatch sends conflicting messages about what is valued and can cause teachers anxiety and stress. For example, a participant in a study we recently published (Menke and Paesani 2021) felt constrained by her language program's proficiency goals; knowing that her students need to demonstrate a specific level on a series of proficiency assessments limited her willingness to fully implement the program's literacies approach. Instead of seeing proficiency- and literacies-based approaches as complementary, for this participant, they were in conflict. Opportunities for teachers to identify alignment among learning objectives, assessment, and pedagogy are essential for adopting new practices and approaches. Mapping activities such as that in table 5.4 support teachers as they endeavor to make this alignment.

One barrier to adopting literacies assessment practices is that they are simply unfamiliar to many teachers. Few have experienced such assessments as learners or seen such assessments in their professional development. Moreover, few examples of literacies assessment plans and formative and summative tools exist (see, however, Kern 2000; Paesani 2017; Schmerbeck and Lucht 2017). Multimodal, performance-based assessments must be incorporated not only into our language classrooms but also into teacher professional development, including methods coursework. In so doing, we provide examples of desired assessments and communicate that they are valid and meaningful. In our graduate teaching methods course, for example, we have transformed what was previously a final research paper on a topic of interest related to language teaching into a multimodal assessment. Although the assessment format varies from year to year, graduate teaching assistants must share their research findings (gathered via observations, interviews, student feedback, and scholarly articles) in a multimodal way, either as a digital story, a recorded multimedia presentation, or a conference-style poster presentation. By incorporating alternative assessments into teacher preparation, we model the practices we want teachers to implement and promote multimodal assessment as valid and valued.

Conclusion

Assessment is the lynchpin of backward design; through it learning objectives become concrete, and from it, instruction takes shape. Throughout this chapter we've explored the three key features of multiliteracies assessment: embodiment of a broad view of language and literacies, multidimensionality, and alignment with instruction. Developing a comprehensive assessment plan, grounded in these principles and balanced across formative and summative assessments, will allow you to modify instructional practices to align with literacies learning objectives and will communicate to students what is valued in the language-learning process. In part II of this book, we look more closely at these instructional practices to help you enact literacies learning objectives and align teaching and assessment.

Reflecting on Research and Practice

1. How would an assessment plan grounded in literacies principles enhance your instruction? What steps do you need to take to develop a plan for your curriculum?
2. How does literacies-oriented assessment compare with your current assessment practices? What tools and resources do you need to be able to design literacies-based assessments? How can you get what you need?
3. How do nontraditional, performance-based, or multimodal assessments align with your beliefs about valued literacies practices? What, if any, groundwork do you need to do with students, colleagues, administrators, or parents to incorporate such assessments into your curriculum?

Resources

1. Design Effective Assessments (https://teaching.berkeley.edu/resources/course-design-guide/design-effective-assessments)

   This webpage from Center for Teaching and Learning at the University of California, Berkeley, includes definitions of formative and summative assessment, sample formative assessment templates, links to alternative assessment ideas, and information on rubrics and e-portfolios.

2. Learning by Design: Assessment (https://newlearningonline.com/learning-by-design/assessment)

Part of the Works & Days website by Mary Kalantzis and Bill Cope, two of the creators of multiliteracies pedagogy, this page offers guidance and reflections on literacies-oriented assessment. It additionally includes links to assessment criteria based on the knowledge process framework, peer review forms, and teacher rating sheets.

3. Resources for Assessment-Related Topics (https://carla.umn.edu/assessment/vac/resources/index.html)

   This webpage includes a list of assessment-related resources curated by CARLA. All resources are relevant to language teaching and learning. Some resources define terms whereas others provide information on specific assessments or alternative assessment methods, such as portfolios, projects, and self-assessment. A note of caution: not all of the assessments linked from this page align with multiliteracies pedagogy.

Further Reading

1. "Designing Assessments: A Multiliteracies Approach" (G. E. Jacobs 2013)

   This brief article from the *Journal of Adolescent and Adult Literacy* summarizes essential features of multiliteracies assessment, together with key skills to be assessed. The author offers reflective questions that teachers can ask themselves as they envision new assessment practices.

2. "Redesigning an Introductory Language Curriculum: A Backward Design Approach" (Paesani 2017)

   This article from *L2 Journal* describes how a university French program used the backward design approach to redesign its courses, including the assessment plan. The author describes how program participants collaboratively developed an assessment plan and how they used assessment data to inform further program revision. An assessment matrix similar to that in table 5.4 is included in the article to illustrate this assessment plan.

3. "Creating Meaning through Multimodality: Multiliteracies Assessment and Photo Projects for Online Portfolios" (Schmerbeck and Lucht 2017)

   The authors of this article from *Die Unterrichtspraxis* promote portfolios as an assessment tool given that they foster interaction and collaboration, reflection, and critical thinking. The authors outline how they implemented a photo portfolio project into an intermediate German course and include student handouts and sample grading rubrics. This article is one of only a few published examples of literacies-oriented assessments.

Note

1. The structure of the learning objectives in table 5.2 do not adhere to the guidelines established in chapter 3. The manuscript from which they were taken did not offer sufficient detail to articulate fully observable behaviors that demonstrate student learning and the context and conditions of expected performance.

Part II

Teaching Languages through Multiliteracies Pedagogy

6

Introduction to Multiliteracies Pedagogy

YOU STARTED YOUR JOURNEY toward designing and implementing literacies curricula in part I of this book by working through the first two stages of backward design: identifying desired results and determining acceptable evidence. As a result, you now know where you are headed with your students, what content they will interact with, and how to gauge their progress toward learning objectives. Part II of this book addresses the third stage of backward design: planning learning experiences. Learning experiences are the activities in which students engage to be able to achieve desired results. Another way of thinking about this is that part I explores the what of literacies in language education (learning, objectives, target language texts, assessment), and part II explores the how (learning experiences and activities). Multiliteracies pedagogy, the approach that puts into practice the overarching goal of foreign language literacies development, provides a framework for enacting this third stage of the backward design model and is the focus of part II of the book.

Multiliteracies pedagogy is grounded in four activity types, or knowledge processes, that engage students with target language texts: experiencing, conceptualizing, analyzing, and applying. In this overview, we revisit the definitions of the knowledge processes offered in chapter 1 and explore how they contribute to the development of students' foreign language literacies. We then present a multiday lesson plan (see appendix B) on the American dream from the Immigration in the United States unit outlined in chapter 2 and appendix A, highlighting how the various knowledge processes interact to achieve the lesson's objectives. We additionally describe the planning template used to create this lesson plan (available on the companion website) to support your work in planning literacies-based instruction. We then consider concerns that teachers have raised related to implementing multiliteracies pedagogy, including time considerations, lesson scaffolding, interpersonal speaking proficiency, and student-centered instruction. Finally, we conclude with a few practical suggestions for planning your first text-based literacies lessons. Given the brief nature of this overview, we do not conclude this chapter with a list of reflective questions, resources, or further reading; you will, however, find each of these sections at the conclusion of chapters 7–10.

The Knowledge Processes in Action

As introduced in chapter 1, the *knowledge processes* framework (Cope and Kalantzis 2009; Kalantzis et al. 2016; New London Group 1996) comprises "a distinct way of making knowledge and of learning" (Kalantzis and Cope 2021l), and each is necessary to develop students' foreign language literacies. The knowledge processes framework places the learner and their thinking at the center of instructional planning. As students interpret and create texts, they experience new worlds, ideas, and ways of communicating; conceptualize how language forms, conventions, and cultural products, practices, and perspectives work to create textual meaning; analyze the importance and consequences of texts within larger social contexts; and apply their knowledge, skills, and understandings to new situations and texts. We present these knowledge processes as different pedagogical activity structures, each of which engages learners with textual content and features in different ways. Learners can use these various ways of building knowledge in other areas of study, as well as in their personal and workplace lives.

Experiencing immerses students in familiar and new ideas, textual content, and language practices. It allows students to access and share knowledge, skills, understandings, and perspectives; in doing so they can establish connections with the concepts and skills targeted in instruction. Experiencing activities thus affirm student knowledge and "provide a platform from which student learning is launched" (Kalantzis and Cope 2021j). *Conceptualizing* seeks to elucidate the textual features, including language forms, conventions, and cultural content, that are used to communicate about a topic. Not only do learners identify textual features in conceptualizing activities, but they also connect these features to the meanings they express and to other features. In other words, students discover and articulate the relationships between and among various textual features and how they work in concert to express ideas. In so doing, students develop the higher order thinking skills needed to understand complex phenomena. *Analyzing* zooms out from the design and meaning of a text to consider its significance and implications. Students might consider the role or purpose of a text in relationship to specific individuals or groups of people, social or historical events, or other texts. Alternatively, they might analyze the consequences of their own experiences, learning processes, or understandings. Analyzing activities foster problem-solving and decision-making skills and encourage principled reasoning. Finally, *applying* requires students to do something with the skills and knowledge gained through textual interpretation; they may interpret additional texts, work in different contexts, create new texts, and more. We as teachers can observe both the depth and breadth of student learning when students engage in applying activities.

In chapter 1, we presented a short lesson plan for novice ESL learners around a Grumpy Cat meme (see table 1.3). Here we include a longer lesson plan for intermediate ESL learners from within the Immigration in the United States unit that we introduced in chapter 2. The fourth in a series of five lessons, this lesson incorporates two target language texts—an infographic and a *New York Times* essay—and spans five days of class. It focuses on the cultural concept of the American dream as a lens through which immigrant experiences can be explored. During this lesson students develop their ability to explain and critique definitions of the American dream and to interpret and create multimodal texts. With the exception of applying, which is targeted only once, students have numerous opportunities to participate in experiencing, conceptualizing, and analyzing activities. As you read the lesson plan in appendix B, consider the following questions: In what ways does each activity reflect the definition of the identified knowledge process? What keywords would you use to describe the knowledge process?

To interpret the two texts in the American Dream lesson, students begin by comprehending textual content (experiencing); they then examine the textual features that communicate that content (conceptualizing) and contextualize each text's meaning within the larger topic of US immigration (analyzing). Finally, students use their new knowledge and skills to create a multimodal dream statement to include in the *New York Times* project (applying). Throughout the lesson, activities weave the various knowledge processes together; students move back and forth among experiencing, conceptualizing, and analyzing throughout all seven stages of the lesson. Because the activities encourage different types of thinking, they complement one another, and the interweaving of the various activity types deepens and refines students' linguistic, genre, and cultural understandings and skills. To illustrate the relationship between the lesson and the four knowledge processes, table 6.1 (a modified version of table 1.2 from chapter 1) defines each knowledge process and lists the associated activities from the American Dream lesson.

To further your understanding of multiliteracies pedagogy, chapters 7–10 focus on one knowledge process each. These chapters expand the definition and role of each knowledge process, provide additional sample activities that illustrate the core features of each, and examine the essential role each plays in developing students' foreign language literacies.

Planning Template for Literacies Lessons

Throughout the book, we have emphasized the centrality of texts in literacies-oriented curricula, and you may have noticed that all the instructional activities in the American Dream lesson are tied to either content from the infographic or the *New York Times* essay. The American Dream lesson follows a seven-stage instructional sequence that guides and supports students as they interact with the language forms, conventions, cultural content, and meaning of target language texts. This sequence forms the basis of a lesson planning template provided on the companion website (https://carla.umn.edu/literacies/book/). The seven stages, summarized in table 6.2, furthermore ensure that students are not only comprehending texts but also interpreting and creating them.

In the first stage, preparing to interact with texts, activities focus on activating students' current knowledge and previous experiences or building needed background knowledge to understand and interpret a target language text. This stage can also involve making predictions about a text and building the necessary linguistic skills to interact with a text and communicate about its content. The second and

Table 6.1. The Knowledge Processes of Multiliteracies Pedagogy

Knowledge process and mantra	Definition	Activities from American Dream lesson
Experiencing "Explore familiar and new ideas"	Learning through immersion in texts, activities, and social situations. Expressing thoughts, reactions, opinions, and feelings and gaining global comprehension about familiar or new experiences, objects, ideas, situations, perspectives, and ways of communicating. Does not involve deep reflection or analysis.	• Brainstorming words associated with the American dream • Reacting to textual content • Comprehending textual content • Brainstorming content for the multimodal dream statement
Conceptualizing "Connect language and meaning through texts"	Learning how language forms, conventions, organization, and other features of texts work to convey meaning. Unpacking texts, practicing skills and knowledge, and explicit learning about textual features helps learners participate more fully in communication.	• Creating a concept map of concepts related to American dream • Identifying textual components, textual organization, and language forms • Connecting textual features to meaning
Analyzing "Question the complexity of culture, language, and ideas"	Learning by connecting the content of texts to social, cultural, and historical contexts. Questioning the meaning, importance, and consequences of textual content. Critically reflecting on textual content and its relationship to one's own culture, perspectives, and learning.	• Predicting textual content • Debating statements
Applying "Create texts and showcase new knowledge"	Learning by using new knowledge, skills, and understandings and by producing language in creative ways.	• Drafting a multimodal dream statement

Source: CARLA (2021a).

third stages, building global comprehension and understanding meaningful details, target literal, factual understanding of textual content. This can involve identifying the who, what, when, and where of a text as well as understanding embedded cultural content; activities may use what is familiar to scaffold understanding of new, unfamiliar content. The goal of the fourth stage, making form-meaning connections, is to understand how a text is constructed, identifying its various textual features and how they express meaning. To this end, grammar, vocabulary, genre conventions, and organizational features are in focus. Stage 5, analyzing and contextualizing meaning, seeks to situate textual meaning and learning within a larger context. In addition to critically reflecting on their learning, students might consider the implications of a text for different groups or examine global and local practices and perspectives. In

Table 6.2. Instructional Sequence for Literacies-Based Lessons

Stage number	Stage name	Function/purpose	Suggested knowledge processes
1	Preparing to interact with texts	• Access background knowledge and prior experiences • Build new background knowledge • Make predictions about a text • Provide linguistic support	Experiencing Conceptualizing Analyzing
2	Building global comprehension	• Literal, factual understanding • Move from the familiar to the unfamiliar	Experiencing Conceptualizing
3	Understanding meaningful details	• Discover details about the cultural content of a text	Experiencing Analyzing
4	Making form-meaning connections	• Identify and understand how a text is constructed and expresses meaning • Focus on grammar, vocabulary, genre conventions, organizational features • Hypothesize about language use in a text	Conceptualizing Analyzing
5	Analyzing and contextualizing textual meaning	• Evaluate and contextualize what is learned • Build critical reflection and analysis skills • Analyze global and local practices and perspectives	Analyzing
6	Applying knowledge	• Demonstrate knowledge and skills • Use language in new and creative ways • Apply new understandings	Analyzing Applying
7	Summarizing and reflecting	• Summarize what was learned • Personal reactions to learning experience • Self-assessment of learning experience • Peer feedback	Analyzing Applying

the sixth stage, applying knowledge, students use their new cultural and linguistic understandings in new and creative ways; this is their opportunity to demonstrate what they have learned. Finally, in stage 7, summarizing and reflecting, students consolidate their learning. In addition to summarizing what they learned from texts, they might also assess or react to the content of what they learned and their learning experience.

These seven stages reflect the "pre," "during," and "post" activity structure you may be familiar with from interpretive reading or listening activities in communicative language teaching: stage 1 represents the pre phase, stages 2–4 the during phase, and stages 5–7 the post phase. These stages differ from typical communicative language teaching lessons, however, because they are expanded to ensure that students engage with texts in varied ways. For instance, in addition to building global comprehension, the during phase facilitates students establishing form-meaning connections. In a similar way, the post phase pushes students to do more than react to textual content; it engages them in critical reflection, evaluation, contextualization, and application of new knowledge and skills. Each of the seven lesson plan stages in table 6.2 targets different types of thinking so that, during a lesson, students engage with texts in different ways, allowing them to more fully understand textual meaning and how it is constructed.

A blank version of this lesson planning template is available on the book's companion website (https://carla.umn.edu/literacies/book/). The template is intended to be modular in that not all stages must be present in every lesson. The stages you enact will depend upon your learning objectives and the role of a particular lesson and text within the larger instructional unit. For example, the objective of lesson 1 of the Immigration in the United States unit is for students to be able to discuss facts about immigration. Consequently stages 4 (making form-meaning connections) and 6 (applying knowledge) may not be necessary to meet this particular lesson's objective. In a similar way, not all suggested knowledge processes must be addressed within a given stage. For example, experiencing, conceptualizing, and analyzing are all suggested knowledge processes for stage 1. In the American Dream lesson, however, instructional activities target only experiencing and conceptualizing. Analyzing is brought into the lesson in subsequent stages. Learning objectives and the role of a text in the curriculum should motivate which instructional stages compose each lesson as well as what knowledge processes are targeted.

Multiliteracies pedagogy is an inherently flexible pedagogy; the knowledge processes are nonsequential and nonhierarchical, a feature we have attempted to highlight in the planning template. It is necessary, however, to ensure that all aspects of the pedagogy are enacted at some point in a lesson or unit. Scholars have repeatedly emphasized the essential role of each knowledge process in developing students' foreign language literacies (e.g., Kalantzis et al. 2016; Michelson and Dupuy 2014; Rowland et al. 2014), yet research has also documented an overabundance of experiencing activities in teacher-created instructional materials (Menke and Paesani 2019; Rowland et al. 2014). The high prevalence of experiencing may be due to its importance in scaffolding other knowledge processes. Alternatively, experiencing activities may be numerous because individual activities require less instructional time than conceptualizing, analyzing, or applying activities, which engage students in higher-order thinking. Whatever the explanation, it is important to note that insufficient attention to each knowledge process can undermine our goal of developing students' foreign language literacies. The lesson plan template supports the design and implementation of a balanced multiliteracies pedagogy by providing a space to indicate the knowledge process(es) targeted by each instructional activity. After planning a lesson, we encourage you to examine your instructional sequence and ask yourself the following questions: Do the instructional activities support students in meeting the learning objectives? Are all knowledge processes present in this lesson? If not, which knowledge processes are missing and how might they be incorporated in this lesson or elsewhere in the unit to meet learning objectives and develop students' foreign language literacies?

As you look at the American Dream lesson and think about using the planning template, you may be struck by the fact that this lesson spans five days of instruction, not just one. Rather than thinking about the class period as the organizing principle, the template centers learning objectives and texts and acknowledges that often more than one day is needed to work with a rich text to meet literacies learning objectives. In addition, the template encourages teachers to think about both in-class and out-of-class instruction as a continuous, cohesive whole. The thinking and learning that happens in class prepares students for their work out of class, which in turn, better equips them to engage with in-class instruction the following day. In the sample lesson, all out-of-class activities are a continuation of the work modeled or begun in class. If your teaching context does not include out-of-class learning opportunities, the duration of your instructional sequences may be longer. There is no one-size-fits-all duration for lessons or units; student backgrounds, learning objectives, and learning context will all affect how multiliteracies pedagogy is enacted.

Teacher Concerns in Implementing Multiliteracies Pedagogy

As we work with teachers looking to implement multiliteracies pedagogy in their teaching, they often voice concerns related to time, interpersonal speaking opportunities, instructional scaffolding, and teacher- versus student-centered activities. These issues are addressed indirectly in the remaining chapters; we additionally respond to them here to disentangle features of the pedagogy from questions of implementation.

Although some of the issues raised by teachers are specific to language teaching, the issue of time is not. Kalantzis and Cope (2021k) note that "we don't have enough time for this stuff" is a refrain repeated by Australian teachers from across disciplines and levels when initially learning about multiliteracies pedagogy (para. 2). Time is a perpetual nemesis for teachers; we never have enough time to do all that we want to do. Concerns around time as it relates to literacies in language education stem from the position of texts in instruction as well as the integration of skills. In multiliteracies pedagogy, texts are at the heart of curricula and drive instruction. This central role of texts contrasts with their often peripheral, supplementary role in communicative language teaching where "reading and writing typically function as secondary support skills, developed to practice language forms rather than to interpret cultural content" (Paesani, Allen, and Dupuy 2016, 7). If text-based literacies lessons are seen as an add on to other instructional activities, time will be a major challenge. If, however, we center texts and use textual content and features as the foundation for all language instruction, there will be sufficient time to address all instructional imperatives. The five-day duration of the American Dream lesson may feel excessive if this lesson is in addition to grammar, vocabulary, or other more traditional language lessons. If we look closely, however, during those five days, students are practicing and using language forms, deepening their understanding of a cultural perspective, and engaging in all three modes of communication. As a complete pedagogy, multiliteracies integrates the linguistic, sociocultural, and cognitive dimensions of language learning; it does not need to be an add on to other instructional priorities. Language-content integration is essential to multiliteracies pedagogy; it blends and combines instructional foci that were previously disparate. Consequently text-based instruction can replace (not just supplement) non-text-based instruction. When the goal of foreign language literacies development is fully embraced, curricula are transformed and instruction and time are reenvisioned.

A related issue is whether students have sufficient opportunities and time in a literacies-oriented classroom to develop their interpersonal speaking skills. One of the primary contributions of communicative language teaching is its emphasis on meaning, interaction, and communication, rather than on grammatical accuracy alone (e.g., G. M. Jacobs and Farrell 2003; Littlewood 2011). In communicative approaches, interpersonal speaking is both the goal of instruction and the means to meeting the goal. Consequently, classroom instruction can be dominated by "interactive, transactional oral language use" (Byrnes 2006, 244), sometimes to the near exclusion of other language modalities. A focus on foreign language literacies places equal emphasis on all communicative modes, which may reduce the number of instructional activities with the primary objective of getting students talking. However, as seen in the American Dream lesson, students regularly engage in interpersonal speaking in text-based approaches. Indeed, in the sample lesson, all but one of the in-class instructional activities involve students talking, whether as part of a whole class discussion or in small groups. What might feel different is the content of the speaking activities. In addition to personal reactions, opinions, and stories, students discuss textual content (e.g., defining features of the American dream, whether the American dream is uniform or varied, why dreams vary) and features (e.g., how images and text interact, structure of dream statements). You likely have a large repertoire of activity structures for engaging students in interpersonal communication—information gap, jigsaw, fishbowl, speed dating, think-pair-share, and so on—and these same activity structures can be implemented in multiliteracies pedagogy. What shifts is not the number of opportunities for speaking but rather how speaking integrates with other communicative modes and the broadening of students' conversations to include the content of target language texts.

Some teachers perceive the less personal, more cognitively demanding content introduced by multiliteracies pedagogy to be too challenging or inaccessible for their students, especially beginning learners. Text selection (see chapter 4) and instructional scaffolding (see chapter 10) are key to overcoming this perceived challenge. Hall (2001) outlined several techniques for successfully scaffolding tasks, among them modeling, drawing student attention to needed linguistic forms, clarifying activity expectations, and attending to student motivation. These techniques can be applied at the level of an individual activity or at the level of a lesson, using one activity as scaffolding for the next. Returning to the American Dream lesson, the latter type of scaffolding is readily apparent. For example, at the end of stage 2, the teacher guides students to identify details about Skylar's dream and complete the text matrix prior to working independently; this same pattern is repeated in the final activity of stage 4 when examining the linguistic forms used to express dream statements. Furthermore, the first five stages of the lesson serve as scaffolding for stage 6: students first develop their knowledge of infinitival clauses, text-image interactions, and cultural perspectives on the American dream, and then they use those skills to create their own multimodal text. What is less obvious in the American Dream lesson plan is the internal scaffolding of activities. For example, the brief description of the debate activity (Is the American dream the same for all?) does not specify how the teacher prepares students to state their opinion and support it with evidence. To scaffold student participation in this activity, however, the class could collectively brainstorm ways of expressing agreement and disagreement and the linguistic forms needed to introduce evidence (e.g., based on, according to, because). Essential to developing quality scaffolding is clarity around the intent of an activity, both for you as the teacher and for your students. Knowing what tasks students are assigned and what knowledge and skills are necessary to do so will allow you to provide the necessary scaffolding and articulate clear instructions and expectations for students.

The final issue raised by some teachers is that multiliteracies pedagogy requires significant teacher-fronted instruction and is consequently not sufficiently student centered. We consider this to be a question of implementation rather than a feature of the pedagogy. As a critical pedagogy, multiliteracies positions learners as active participants in the learning process, as individuals who bring their previous experiences and knowledge to the task of learning and who are responsible for their own learning. In other words, multiliteracies is a student-centered pedagogy. In student-centered instruction, teachers facilitate learning by structuring activities so that students discover their own questions, explore answers to those questions, build their repertoire of strategies and tools for learning and communicating, evaluate ideas and knowledge, and construct their own understandings (as opposed to being told what to understand). Teachers can facilitate this active engagement in the learning process in various ways, including whole-class, teacher-fronted instruction, in which the teacher models, questions, redirects, provides feedback, and more. We understand how teacher-fronted instruction can reflect a transmission model of education in which students are passive recipients of knowledge; however, this is not what multiliteracies pedagogy espouses. A number of the instructional activities in the American Dream lesson are teacher fronted, yet in each case, students actively contribute to and shape the creation of knowledge in the class. They share stories and ideas, make and verify predictions, identify and compare textual features, synthesize information, and clarify misunderstandings. At no point are they passive; instead, they coconstruct knowledge with their classmates through the teacher's careful facilitation of class discussions, in which students engage in interpersonal listening and speaking. When implementing multiliteracies pedagogy, you may notice a shift in the distribution of activity structures (whole class, partners, small group, individual), but a shift in structure does not necessitate a shift in participation or engagement on the part of the learner.

Conclusion

Multiliteracies pedagogy is a flexible, student-centered framework for planning and implementing instruction. It centers target language texts, using them as a springboard for learning and creating new knowledge; by examining the meanings created by language forms, conventions, and cultural content, learners uncover new ideas, perspectives, and ways of communicating. The framework offers us a vehicle through which we can develop students' foreign language literacies. It is exciting, but it can also be daunting given the opacity of some of the terminology and the rethinking of instructional practices it involves. As you delve into the specifics of the pedagogy in chapters 7–10, we encourage you to revisit definitions and sample activities and to reflect on how each knowledge process resembles or differs from strategies you already use. Doing this critical analysis will allow you to understand the pedagogy more fully.

We also recognize that implementing a new pedagogy can be intimidating. Instructional planning might initially take longer as you articulate new instructional objectives, wrestle with how to enact each knowledge process, and consider how to scaffold learning experiences for student success. It may also mean letting go of activities that you've done in the past and having a few new activities flop. This is mentally and emotionally challenging work. We remind you that you don't have to overhaul your entire curriculum at once; even one new lesson can have an impact on student learning. From that single lesson you might redesign a curricular unit or develop a second text-based lesson for a different unit. The more you work with multiliteracies pedagogy, plan lessons with literacies objectives, and use the unit and lesson templates provided on the companion website (https://carla.umn.edu/literacies/book/), the more familiar you will become with activities that target each knowledge process, which will accelerate your planning process. And by reflecting on what works well and what doesn't work well during implementation, you can refine your activities and enhance their effectiveness.

7

Experiencing: Building Textual Understanding

Explore familiar and new ideas

WHEN WE EXPERIENCE SOMETHING, we are active participants; we use our senses to engage in the activity or with our surroundings. We don't typically use all our cognitive resources to make sense of what we're immersed in or to reflect critically upon it and its significance, yet we can learn through these experiences. For example, Mandy learned how to dance the Macarena and the Electric Slide by dancing alongside friends and family at school dances and weddings; no one taught her step-by-step but rather she learned by participating in this social, group activity. Similarly, young children learn words and patterns of communication through experiencing and participating in numerous, varied communicative events; through their participation in activities, they are socialized into patterns of meaning and interacting in their community. In essence, experiencing is learning through immersion.

The multiliteracies knowledge process of *experiencing* may feel familiar to you. With its focus on learning through doing, experiencing resembles communicative activities that ask students to immerse themselves in the language, draw on their previous knowledge and experiences, or react based on their opinions or feelings. Gaining surface-level comprehension of target language texts, sharing reactions, and gathering information about classmates' activities are all examples of communicative activities that fall within experiencing.

In this chapter, we dig into experiencing with the goal of deepening your understanding of this knowledge process and expanding your repertoire of experiencing activities. We begin by defining experiencing and exploring its role in developing foreign language literacies. We then describe five experiencing activities, detailing how each reflects the key characteristics of this knowledge process. Finally, we conclude with a practical tool that you can use to reflect on your current instructional practices, focusing on identifying the number and variety of experiencing activities.

Defining Experiencing

In chapter 1 you learned that experiencing does not involve deep analysis of target language texts but rather comprehension of and reactions to textual content. The textual content that students experience might be familiar to them, part of their lived realities, or it might be new, outside their daily experiences. Opportunities to experience the known and the new are valuable to learners as they encourage students to connect knowledge and communicative practices from outside the classroom with new ideas, new ways of communicating, or new situations. *Experiencing the known* activities, in which students discuss their worlds using familiar patterns of communication, open a space to bring cultural backgrounds, identities, and interests into the classroom. For example, in a unit on professions, students might draw on knowledge gained through observing and interacting with individuals in their community to associate qualifications and responsibilities with various professions. They can compare and contrast what they know and have experienced with what their classmates know and have experienced. Such activities not only validate the learning students gain in the world but also provide them the opportunity to bring to the forefront knowledge, assumptions, or beliefs that might otherwise be implicit or below the level of consciousness. Additionally, these activities provide you, the teacher, with insights into the motivations, knowledge, and lifeworlds of your students. *Experiencing the new* activities, in contrast, expose students to ideas, information, or situations outside or beyond their reality. Continuing with the jobs theme, exploring job ads for a target language community allows students to see valued skills, required application materials, salary information, and the like. As they comprehend the information communicated in texts, students experience new ideas, new language, and new perspectives. They do this by using and building upon the strategies, language, and knowledge that they already possess; they use familiar patterns of communication to explore new, unfamiliar worlds. Pedagogically weaving between what is known or familiar and what is new or unfamiliar allows students to refine and expand their communicative repertoires and knowledge base (Kalantzis et al. 2016).

Although students may work independently, an important component of experiencing activities is collaboration among students to describe, explore, react, and compare their varied knowledge bases or perspectives. Alternatively, they might share the experience of immersing themselves in a new world, working together to make sense of it, to respond to it, and to connect it to their previous understandings. By grounding linguistic and cognitive processes in interaction, experiencing activities recognize and respect that learning and human cognition are always socially situated. Experiencing can thus include the likely familiar activity of listening to an advertisement for a job search website and working individually to answer comprehension questions, as well as various alternative, collaborative activities such as conducting a class poll around what services on the job search website students are most likely to use.

Many teachers use experiencing activities as a warm-up or scaffold for conceptualizing and analyzing activities, which are more cognitively demanding knowledge processes. For instance, teachers can help learners identify the linguistic forms (e.g., vocabulary, grammatical structures, communicative patterns and strategies) needed to discuss or reflect on a topic prior to doing more interpretive work. Continuing with the jobs example, the teacher can introduce vocabulary related to professions as well as structures for expressing qualifications or work schedules as students compare familiar jobs within their own communities. In addition, teachers can connect these concrete, lived experiences with unit or course concepts (e.g., jobs are culturally situated, jobs that are afforded great respect and prestige may vary from one community to the next).

Experiencing and Foreign Language Literacies

Although providing scaffolding for other instructional activities is important, experiencing activities perform a significant role in developing learners' foreign language literacies on their own. When students use familiar vocabulary, grammatical structures, or conversational patterns to share their experiences or comprehend texts, they develop fluency and automaticity in the target language (Kern 2000). Foreign language literacies foregrounds the creation and interpretation of meaning across contexts; to be able to do this efficiently and effectively, learners need extensive practice in using target language forms to make meaning. Interaction figures prominently in theories and hypotheses of second language learning (e.g., interaction hypothesis [Long 1981, 1996], output hypothesis [Swain 1985], sociocultural theory [e.g., Lantolf 2000; Vygotsky 1978]). When interacting with others for different purposes and across varied topics, learners access linguistic forms to express their message, receive feedback on the efficacy of their choices, and collaborate to clarify meaning. Multiple meta-analyses have concluded that "interaction plays a strong facilitative role in the learning of lexical and grammatical target items" (Mackey and Goo 2007, 438), a finding that is not limited to oral interactions but that holds true for interaction in computer-mediated environments as well (Gurzynski-Weiss and Baralt 2014, 2015; Ziegler 2016).

Experiencing activities additionally play an important role in creating a learning community. Experiencing the known activities, in which students bring their experiences, practices, and knowledge into the classroom, acknowledge the identities, interests, and cultural backgrounds of learners. The whole learner is recognized and valued, and learners have the opportunity to connect their outside-the-classroom self with their school self. In other words, they can connect their various communities and knowledge bases. Foregrounding the knowledge and experiences of students removes the teacher as the sole authority figure and positions all students as valuable contributors to the classroom community of practice. Learners are active participants and drive their learning rather than being passive receivers of information from others. In addition, experiencing activities allow students to make their own discoveries about the target culture and language as well as their own. By participating in collaborative, meaning-based activities, learners can reflect on why they engage in certain practices and make observations about the target language and culture. They're not receiving knowledge from others but rather constructing this knowledge themselves. Although at first glance, this process of constructing knowledge may only seem appropriate when experiencing the new, many of our everyday practices and beliefs form part of our existing knowledge that lies below the level of consciousness. Bringing unconscious and implicit practices and knowledge into the classroom allows us to examine them and make them explicit (e.g., What jobs are valued in my community? What jobs are valued in other communities?) (Kalantzis et al. 2016).

Experiencing plays a key role in developing foreign language literacies, yet instruction that overemphasizes experiencing to the near exclusion of other activity types runs the risk of not fully developing learners' meaning-making repertoires. If instruction focuses exclusively on comprehending target language texts without examining the way texts are constructed or without considering their meaning within a broader sociocultural context, learners do not have an opportunity to connect language, meaning, and culture. And if learners only interact with familiar genres such as everyday conversations, they're denied the opportunity to observe how language is used in diverse contexts and between varied groups of people, again losing the opportunity to develop necessary cognitive, linguistic, and cultural competencies. It is interesting to note that these potential pitfalls are often cited as limitations of CLT (e.g., Byrnes 2006; Kern 2000; Kramsch 2006; Levine et al. 2008).

You likely already have a toolbox of activities that you use to engage students in communicative activities; this toolbox can be useful as you seek to design experiencing activities. As you incorporate and center target language texts more in your curriculum, you may find it necessary to adapt tried-and-true activities or even incorporate new ones to ensure that your teaching fully embraces literacies principles. In this next section, we share a few sample experiencing activities. In addition to allowing students to share their experiences or ideas and comprehend texts, these activities provide scaffolding for other knowledge processes and prepare learners to take an active, critical stance toward language and texts, interpret multiple forms of language use in various contexts, and analyze, interpret, and transform discourse.

Sample Experiencing Activities

Comprehension questions, brainstorming, personal reactions, and information gap activities are experiencing activities that you likely already employ. With the goal of expanding your instructional toolbox and deepening your understanding of the knowledge process of experiencing, we present five sample experiencing activities, highlighting how they bring students' lived experiences into the classroom, immerse them in new language and ideas, and build off of previous knowledge and skills to scaffold engagement in other learning activities.

Story Maps

Interpreting and creating narratives or historical recounts requires sequencing events to create the chronology of a story. This task can prove challenging for language learners who may overlook temporal adverbs, be unfamiliar with the cultural activities or locations referenced, or rely on lexical rather than morphological cues for time. These challenges are exacerbated by texts that move between time frames, such as those that have flashbacks or foreshadowing. To support learners' comprehension of a text, they can map key events, locating them in time or space. In a second-year university German course, Redmann (2005b) asked students to trace the route characters in a youth novel took as they traveled by bike through a region of Germany. Not only did students locate the various towns mentioned on a map, but they also recorded information about the town that was included in the book. This experiencing the new activity provided students with insight into the distance between towns and differences between towns in different areas; it additionally supported their understanding of the storyline and their later transformation of the text into other genres (postcards, diary entries).

Story mapping is a flexible activity type that can be applied to texts of different genres and modalities. For instance, students might map out events on a timeline or a narrative plot structure diagram (orientation/exposition, complicating problem, rising action, climax, falling action, resolution/denouement), or they might diagram family relationships between individuals named in a text. Carrying out these activities allows students to refine their understandings of textual content, most notably the relationships between events, places, or people.

Story mapping can also be used to prepare students to interact with texts by visualizing their own experiences. For example, students might map out their day—where they are at what times and how they travel from one location to another in their town or city. They can compare their movement (or lack of movement) through their town or city with that of classmates to see how similar they are and whether any generalizations can be made. Participation in such an experiencing the known activity can prepare students to listen to a target language speaker recount their daily activities. Through it, they build their fluency with the language forms necessary to express time, location, and daily activities and they bring cultural practices, products, and perspectives to the level of consciousness. Illustration or visualization supports learners as they seek to identify and comprehend textual details or their daily practices. To this end, you might also consider how illustration and visualization can be used with other content, whether familiar or new (e.g., drawing an individual or location described in a written or audio text).

Digital Social Annotated Reading

Reading is often considered an independent, solitary activity, one based on print texts. Book clubs or literature circles bring reading into the social realm when readers share their reactions, questions, and understandings. Digital texts, together with new technologies, have further expanded the possibilities for social, collaborative reading. In particular, *digital social annotated reading* (DSAR) allows students to "construct, revise, and fine-tune their understandings and interpretations of a text synchronously or asynchronously" (Michelson and Dupuy 2018, para. 9). A body of emerging work points to the benefits of DSAR: it encourages students to share personal reactions, reread, shift their role within a group, and communicate about a text. In DSAR environments, individuals can mark up and annotate a digital text and share these annotations with others.

DSAR has been used across languages and levels. For example, Blyth (2014) and Thoms, Sung, and Poole (2017) reported on DSAR in beginning-level university

French and Chinese courses, respectively. In both instances, students were asked to read texts outside of class and use a digital annotation tool, eComma, to comment on and ask questions about the texts. The French teacher reported that through their annotations, students reacted to new cultural practices and coconstructed meanings. Students in both classes made connections to their own personal experiences, clarified the meaning of words and phrases, and responded to one another's reactions. Each of these activities aligns with the knowledge process of experiencing, as students collaboratively immerse themselves in, understand, and respond to target language texts.

DSAR can fulfill a similar function as reading journals, but the former is more social and grounded in the text itself. As with reading journals, teachers can see students' areas of confusion and understanding. Unlike reading journals, classmates' annotations can serve to scaffold or mediate the learning of peers in addition to fostering social connections. Based on published reports of DSAR, we recommend putting students into small groups (3–5 learners) to allow space for all to connect with, respond to, and immerse themselves in the target language text.

Grouping or Categorizing Activities

Grouping or categorizing activities are a great way to have students interact with ideas or vocabulary before, during, or after interacting with a text. When grouping familiar words and ideas, students experience the known and identify unconscious or implicit categories they already possess. If, however, students are asked to group items, words, or images based on information in a target language text, they experience the new.

For example, Hsiaomei (n.d.) included a variety of categorizing activities in her lesson around *The Very Hungry Caterpillar* for elementary immersion learners of Chinese. As they collaboratively read the story, students classify the foods mentioned according to those that make the caterpillar feel good and those that make its stomach upset (experiencing the new); words that describe the caterpillar's physical appearance and physical feelings (experiencing the new); and foods eaten in China, foods eaten in the United States, and foods eaten in both China and the United States (experiencing the known and the new). Through these activities learners build their familiarity with target vocabulary, understanding of the story, and cultural practices and perspectives. In addition, the teacher gains insight into what students already know about Chinese food practices. These activities serve as scaffolding for other instructional activities in which students critically consider why food practices and products vary across cultures (analyzing) and in which they transform the story, creating their own text about a different insect (e.g., flea, moth, ladybug) in China, the unusual foods it eats, and how it transforms (applying).

Similar classification activities were employed by Barnes-Karol and Broner (2010) in an intermediate-level university Spanish class, in which students were asked to group foods depicted in photographs of what individual families from around the world eat in a week (e.g., frozen foods, boxed foods, produce). In this experiencing the new activity, students immerse themselves in the visual text and notice what is present. At this point, students are not delving into what cultural values or perspectives underlie the differences but rather are making observations, connecting what they already know (ways of grouping food) with something new (information conveyed in the visual text).

Instructional Conversations

Instructional conversations are classroom conversations, designed and managed by the teacher, with the pedagogical purpose of "greater language proficiency and complex thinking about academic topics" (Todhunter 2007, 607). Unlike some teacher-student interactions in which teachers ask questions with correct or known answers (e.g., What is the weather today? What do bees do with the pollen that they collect?), instructional conversations are modeled on every day, noninstructional conversations. Teachers ask open-ended questions that encourage students to form, express, and exchange ideas, and then through responsive feedback, they assist students in further elaborating or clarifying their understandings and language. To a casual observer, instructional conversations may sound like a naturally evolving conversation, but they require intention (identifying the pedagogical purpose), planning, and skill (responsive questions and feedback, scaffolded language, strategic turn taking) in order to realize their goals.

L. Brown, Iwasaki, and Lee (2016) provided an example of an instructional conversation in an intermediate, university Korean language class. The teacher began a lesson by gathering perspectives on the word *oykwukin* (foreigner), including whether it has a positive or a negative connotation. The teacher then presented statistical information about the increase of foreigners in South Korea, asking students to react and respond to these statistics. Finally, students were asked to order images of foreigners to South Korea from those that Koreans would treat with the most kindness and respect to those that they would treat with the least kindness and respect, sharing their reasoning with the class. Through this instructional conversation, students experienced the known as they expressed their own thoughts on the word "foreigner" and how others might be received based on what they already know about South Korea. The conversation structure was familiar, and they had opportunities to produce extended language (multiple sentences), connect with the topic, and observe conversational moves modeled by the teacher (e.g., turn taking, uptake, follow-up questions). Students also experienced the new as they learned vocabulary specific to groups of foreigners (e.g., *oykwukin kunloca*, "foreign laborers," and *kyopho*, "overseas Korean") and about the rapidly changing demographics of South Korea. This new information set the scene for their viewing of a clip from a Korean drama series, *My Lovely Sam Soon,* in which they could observe how a US-raised, Korean character is positioned as foreign through visual effects, costuming, and language (e.g., honorifics, English and Korean use). The initial instructional conversation prepared students to view the video, identify how foreignness was communicated in this clip (conceptualizing), and interpret the social position of foreigners in Korean society (analyzing). In addition, it offered opportunities for elaborated language and gave the teacher insight into what features students focus on when grouping individuals. Through an analysis of student talk during instructional conversations, L. Brown, Iwasaki, and Lee (2016) observed learners creating their own meanings, (re) positioning themselves, and considering diverse perspectives and meanings of the word *oykwukin.*

Instructional conversations are a flexible activity type. Indeed, in much of the multiliteracies scholarship, they are presented as an analyzing activity given their potential to guide students' complex thinking, yet in this example, students used a familiar conversation structure to explore a new topic: foreignness in Korea. The instructional conversation focused on what they already knew about the topic and their reactions to new information. Changing the nature of the questions could, however, transform this activity into either conceptualizing (identifying how language forms position foreigners) or analyzing (critical reflection on the sociohistorical reasons for the respective positioning of foreigners in Korea).

Reader's Theater

Unlike the instructional conversation example that occurred prior to interacting with a target language text, *reader's theater* (Tanner 1993) takes place after students read a text. In this activity, students work in groups to perform a written text, using their multiple voices to create and express the meaning that they make from the text. They work collaboratively to segment the original text and perform it aloud with different voices. In this activity, students do not rewrite the text in any way; rather they use the words as produced by the author and give them voice. Reader's theater has been successfully used across languages, levels, and age groups. Students find it engaging and fun, and teachers report that it increases student fluency, comprehension, and awareness of textual features (McKay 2008).

López-Sánchez (2014) provided an example in which small groups of students identified the voices in *M-111*, a poem by Jacobo Morales. Students first highlighted who was saying different lines (husband/narrator, guests, daughter) and then read the poem aloud. In this example, identifying the voice is somewhat straightforward as the various speakers are explicitly referenced in the poem. In other instances, the task is a bit more complex as students must interpret or negotiate which words, phrases, or sentences should be attributed to whom as words or passages aren't specific to a character. This is the case in the reader's theater activity included in Paesani, Allen, and Dupuy (2016), in which lower-level French students assign segments of a written cultural vignette to voices that aren't explicitly identified in the text. In both examples, students continually and repeatedly immerse themselves in the text. As students collaborate and use their linguistic skills to express their ideas, ask questions of others, and reach consensus, they use familiar communication patterns and thus engage in experiencing the known. In contrast, they experience the new as they individually read the text, collaboratively work toward global comprehension, and view or listen to the performances of their classmates. By assigning voices in different ways, each group's performance creates new meanings and becomes a new, transformed text to be experienced. Collectively, students experience how multiple interpretations of a single text are possible.

We've highlighted here how reader's theater engages students in experiencing, yet tweaking or expanding the activity can engage students in additional knowledge processes. For example, directing student attention to specific textual features or asking them to reflect on changes in meaning that result from different assignments of voices engages them in conceptualizing and analyzing.

Spotlight on Teacher Professional Development

Throughout this chapter we've mentioned that experiencing activities might feel familiar to you given their overlap with many communicative activities. This statement reflects findings from several studies that have explored teacher learning around multiliteracies pedagogy and analyzed the instructional materials they have created. For example, two different materials analyses—one in a university English as a foreign language (EFL) program in Japan (Rowland et al. 2014) and one in a university Spanish program in the United States (Menke and Paesani 2019)—found that between 65 percent and 75 percent of all instructional activities targeted the knowledge process of experiencing. Similar findings were reported from a Chinese language class for young learners (Kim and Xing 2019). An unintended consequence of this practice is that learners are not afforded the opportunity to think critically about language and culture, develop a diverse set of meaning-making resources (e.g., language forms, cultural knowledge in their first and second languages, understanding of genres), or participate in varied literacies activities. Indeed, a study of the reading practices of Yemeni EFL students revealed that when independently reading English texts, students primarily engaged in experiential thinking, focusing on comprehension and reaction, which was reflective of their learning experiences (Bhooth, Azman, and Ismail 2015).

Menke and Paesani (2019) hypothesized that the frequent use of experiencing activities might stem from one of the following: narrowly conceived literacies learning objectives, the conceptual challenge of integrating content and form, overreliance on the same activity structures, and fear that low proficiency will hinder students' ability to engage in cognitively demanding tasks. Some of these obstacles to a balanced multiliteracies pedagogy are addressed in future chapters, but here we want to focus on lesson analysis as a tool to identify patterns in instructional practices and reflect on whether materials and practices align with curricular goals. Rowland et al. (2014) recommended analysis of instructional materials as a valuable practice for teachers and programs moving toward literacies-oriented curriculum and instruction.

CARLA's Lesson Analysis Checklist, available on the companion website (https://carla.umn.edu/literacies/book/), is a way for you to determine whether text-based lessons rely too heavily on experiencing and whether students always engage in the same activity types—and types of thinking—during instruction across the lessons of an instructional unit. We recommend starting with a text-based lesson from your textbook or of your own creation that you've already taught. In the initial phase of the analysis, you will contextualize the lesson: its learning objectives, targeted language forms, and cultural content. Then in the second phase you will classify each instructional activity in the lesson according to the elements from the teaching context addressed and the targeted multiliteracies knowledge processes. In the third and final phase, you will evaluate how well the lesson meets the identified objectives, how the knowledge processes are distributed across the lesson, and what changes are necessary to more fully develop students' foreign language literacies. As you work with this checklist and determine if an activity targets experiencing, ask yourself the following questions:

- Are students' own experiences, feelings, and reactions the basis of the activity?
- Are students using familiar ways of communicating?
- Are students focused on comprehending and responding to a text?

If the answer is yes, the activity is most likely experiencing. How many experiencing activities are included in your lesson? What is the distribution of oral, interpersonal activities in relation to activities in other modalities? Taken together, do the lesson's activities lead to different types of engagement with the text? If nearly all activities target experiencing or if students do not engage in other ways of knowing, the next three chapters of this book will be important for you. If experiencing activities rely only on comprehension questions, can you incorporate one of the experiencing activities introduced in this chapter? Similarly, we encourage you to look across lessons within a unit to determine the variety of experiencing activities included. Can some activities be modified to more fully immerse students in the text and develop their comprehension in different ways?

Conclusion

Experiencing is foundational to developing students' foreign language literacies. When actively engaged in experiential learning, students explore previous knowledge and experiences as well as new, unfamiliar ideas and worlds. They connect their lived experiences with those of others by immersing themselves in diverse texts and communicative events. Such activities can give teachers insight into who their students are while simultaneously valuing what each learner brings to the classroom and offering them opportunities to build on this knowledge. Moreover, they allow students to use their communicative skills to learn with and from others. Experiencing activities can occur at any point in an instructional sequence and deepen students' ability to communicate about and understand their own experiences and those of others. But experiencing is only one activity type contributing to students' foreign language literacies development. For language learners to be truly multiliterate, they must also engage in conceptualizing, analyzing, and applying activities, which we address in detail in the next three chapters.

Reflecting on Research and Practice

1. What are five keywords you would use to define experiencing? Why are experiencing activities important?

2. In what ways do the sample activities presented in this chapter align with or differ from experiencing activities that you typically use in your teaching? What other experiencing activities do you regularly use? How can you incorporate some of the sample activities overviewed in this chapter into your teaching?
3. How does each of the sample experiencing activities develop students' foreign language literacies?

Resources

1. CARLA's Literacies Activity Repository (https://carla.umn.edu/literacies/book/)

   This repository allows you to view sample experiencing activities from various languages and instructional levels. Activities are pulled from literacies-oriented lesson plans created by practitioners and researchers.

2. Techniques for Digital Social Reading (https://www.coerll.utexas.edu/coerll/social-reading-webinar)

   In this webinar, Joanna Luks (2018) overviews digital social reading. In addition to showing how one specific tool works, she highlights the affordances of this instructional tool, explores ways to apply it to curricula, and shares resources.

3. Sample Experiencing the Known (https://newlearningonline.com/learning-by-design/the-knowledge-processes/activities) and Experiencing the New Activities (https://newlearningonline.com/learning-by-design/the-knowledge-processes/experiencing)

   Developed by two members of the team who created the multiliteracies framework, these two web pages provide additional sample activities that target experiencing (Kalantzis and Cope 2021i, 2021j). Although they are from other subject areas and not specific to language teaching, the activities can be adapted to the language classroom.

Further Reading and Viewing

1. "Experiential and Conceptual Learning" (https://newlearningonline.com/literacies/chapter-3/experiential-and-conceptual-learning)

   In the first several minutes of this video (end at minute 3:33), Kalantzis and Cope (2016b) overview the knowledge process of experiencing. They identify its purpose and offer some caveats for creating experiential learning opportunities.

2. "Analysing Foreign Language Instructional Materials through the Lens of the Multiliteracies Framework" (Menke and Paesani 2019)

   In this research article published in *Language, Culture, and Curriculum*, Menke and Paesani detail the materials analysis process and report findings on how instructional materials incorporate the four knowledge processes of multiliteracies pedagogy. In their discussion, the authors consider implications for student learning and teacher professional development.

8

Conceptualizing: Connecting Form and Meaning

Connect language and meaning through texts

WHEN ASKED WHAT LANGUAGE learning entails, some teachers respond with memorizing word lists, declensions, or verb conjugations. Others may even describe the goal of language learning as using new words and grammar to express yourself. Such a structural view of language fails to recognize that meanings are socially constructed and that language forms are but one tool for making meaning. Linguistic elements are indeed important, yet on their own, independent of context and language users, they do not have meaning. Language learning is thus about learning how to use all the resources available in a language to interpret, create, and negotiate meaning across contexts.

Language is one of the many semiotic, or meaning-making, systems humans use to communicate with and understand one another; other ways of making meaning include gestures, images, and sounds. Learners must be able to identify the meaning-making resources that are available in the language they are learning, understand the meanings those resources communicate, and apply them to the interpretation and creation of messages. In other words, knowledge of language forms, conventions, cultural content—the textual features we discussed in chapter 4—and their associated meanings enables language learners to interact with target language texts as we've defined them throughout this book.

This chapter builds on the understanding of textual features you have developed and prepares you to design instructional activities that help students connect the forms used in texts with the meanings they express. We begin by defining key features of the knowledge process of conceptualizing and its role in foreign language literacies development. We then examine sample form-focused activities and how they embody (or not) these features. Next, we address common misunderstandings of conceptualizing by contrasting what it is with what it is not. Finally, we conclude with some of the challenges teachers encounter with the knowledge process of conceptualizing and ways that these might be addressed through professional development.

Defining Conceptualizing

Conceptualizing is about understanding the meanings conveyed by specific textual elements and how those textual elements work together to express a message. Conceptualizing activities bring language forms and conventions into focus, but as the mantra "Connect language and meaning through texts" suggests, conceptualizing is not just about the structure of language. Although language is the "most distinctive human possession" (Wardhaugh 1999, viii) and "at the core of our being human" (Reagan and Osborn 2021, 15), we saw in chapter 4 that meaning is not created through language alone but through the combination of language with audio, visual, gestural, and spatial systems: filmmakers leverage lighting, background noise, music, and camera angles to set the scene, and bloggers use headings, font size, colors, images, videos, and hyperlinks to guide readers through their texts. Thus, a learner's meaning-making toolbox must contain more than just linguistic resources. Both the resources used and the meanings they convey are socially constructed and governed; as such, they vary across and within languages and communities. Conceptualizing seeks to uncover and make explicit the agreed-upon codes and conventions of a target culture with the goal of developing students' "awareness of the relationships between textual conventions and their contexts of use" (Kern 2000, 16), a key element of foreign language literacies. To this end, conceptualizing activities might guide students to explore how verbal aspect (e.g., preterit versus imperfect) shapes the meaning of a story; how genre conventions guide a reader through a text; how color, size, or angle influences the emotion a photo evokes; or how gestures and movement enhance or alter a presenter's message.

Kalantzis et al. (2016, 79) identified the overarching goal of conceptualizing activities as getting students to "describe the underlying structures of meaning." This requires students to name the elements used to make meaning and their similarities and differences. In doing so, they develop a language for talking about textual features, also known as a metalanguage. To fully realize the goal of "describ[ing] the underlying structures of meaning," learners must identify the concrete form-meaning connections present in a text, speculate about patterns, and build conceptual models of how meaning-making resources work together. Thus, learners not only name linguistic forms and their meanings but also theorize about the larger meaning-making system and gain understanding of how meaning is constructed in specific contexts.

Given its focus on language and other meaning-making resources, many teachers equate conceptualizing with traditional, language-focused instruction. To make conceptualizing more concrete and differentiate it from other language-focused instruction, we've identified three core criteria: conceptualizing is explicit, meaning based, and learner centered. These three criteria have been applied to other instructional approaches, so we take a moment here to clarify and expand on their connection to multiliteracies pedagogy before applying them to example conceptualizing activities.

- Explicit: You might associate this word with explicit grammar instruction, such as charts, grammar drills, or vocabulary lists. Our use of the word explicit, however, refers to intentionality and focus. Students are not expected to just pick up grammar and vocabulary from the language that surrounds them; rather, in conceptualizing, they consciously attend to textual features and the meanings they communicate. Identifying and naming meaning-making elements, establishing patterns and relationships between them, and connecting them to textual meaning is planned for, not assumed or incidental.
- Meaning-based: Conceptualizing activities are always tied to the interpretation or creation of textual content. As a result, linguistic forms are not learned or practiced in isolation, and activities are not designed to only practice forms. Instead, language forms facilitate students' ability to interpret and create meaning (i.e., to communicate). It is for this reason that text-based instructional activities typically focus on meaning before form. Given that form-meaning associations are dynamic and context dependent, the meaning of language forms and conventions must be grounded in textual content and not presented as static, immutable rules.
- Learner-centered: Learners are active and involved in identifying and understanding patterns and relationships when engaged in conceptualizing. They are not just told what a form means or how a text is organized, but rather they are guided to notice textual features, question their function, establish patterns in usage, and link textual features and meaning. Bull and Anstey (2019) emphasize the importance of students using this kind of inquiry process as it develops their metacognitive skills and increases their ability to interpret and produce texts. This approach to conceptualizing shares similarities with inductive teaching approaches, which have also been shown to improve learners' acquisition of language forms (e.g., Dotson 2010; Grim 2008; Haight, Herron, and Cole 2007; Herron and Tomasello 1992).

In the American Dream lesson plan presented in appendix B, there are several conceptualizing activities, each of which embodies the three criteria we just described. In stage 1 of the lesson, learners focus on the concept of the American dream and diagram the relationship between its various componential parts. Learners actively theorize or construct relationships based on information gained from the infographic text, making this activity explicit, meaning based, and learner centered. In stage 4, learners direct their attention to specific language forms (infinitival clauses, past tense narration) and genre conventions (motivation statements, headings, photo captions, photographs), and how these features contribute to textual meaning. These forms were preselected for instruction through an analysis of the textual features (see the Textual Features Worksheet referenced in chapter 4) and aligned with learning objectives. The conceptualizing activities explicitly target these features by having learners identify the forms and their meanings. The activities are also meaning based because learners explore how the language forms and genre conventions contribute to the text's meaning. Finally, learners are the ones making observations, hypothesizing, and identifying form-meaning connections, making the activity learner centered.

In another example, Ready (n.d.) engages intermediate, postsecondary learners of Spanish in identifying descriptive words (adjectives) and expressions (metaphors) in a poem by Pablo Neruda. Through guided inquiry and critical focus questions, students identify the descriptive language forms and then consider how the specific words and expressions employed paint a negative perception of a specific food company. Likewise, Paesani, Allen, and Dupuy (2016) describe a lesson in which beginning learners of French differentiate dialogue and description in a short story, examine what information is conveyed via each text type, and then identify the linguistic forms and conventions used to signal dialogue. In both examples, students actively identify textual features, the meanings they convey, and patterns across them, making the activities explicit, meaning based, and learner centered.

The Role of Conceptualizing

In language classes, textual content typically refers to the information a text conveys: presentational mode rubrics assess the details and messages a student expresses in a text, interpretive mode assessments hold students accountable for comprehending the ideas communicated in a text, and interpersonal mode communication involves both the expression and interpretation of meaning. When seeking to develop foreign language literacies, however, focusing solely on textual ideas, details, or messages is insufficient; we must also examine how this content is expressed. The focus of instruction around target language texts must therefore include what the text means, what forms are used to create meaning, and the meanings each form communicates. Insufficient attention to form-meaning connections may impede a learner's ability to meet the varied communicative demands placed upon them by society (Bhooth, Azman, and Ismail 2015) as well as inhibit development of more advanced language functions (Menke and Paesani 2019). Indeed, the failure of many university language majors to achieve advanced-level proficiency is often attributed to the separation of language and content in curricula and insufficient attention to language development in upper-division, content-focused courses (e.g., Donato and Brooks 2004; MLA 2007; Zyzik and Polio 2008).

Several studies have reported on the importance of conceptualizing in developing students' communicative repertoire. Michelson and Dupuy (2014) found that students in a fourth-semester university French course who participated in a semester-long multiliteracies global simulation developed awareness of how language use varies across speakers and contexts. In this simulation, students enacted Parisians who lived in the same apartment building, and as they interacted with other characters in the simulation, they varied the register (i.e., level of language from formal to informal) in which they communicated according to both the interlocutor and the context of the communication (e.g., a public Facebook post or a private phone conversation). The researchers observed that students who enacted younger residents used informal vocabulary and emoticons, whereas students portraying older, more professional residents employed more formal language features. In a second study, Allen and Goodspeed (2018) engaged students in conceptualizing as part of a unit on social issues in France. During the conceptualizing phase of instruction, students examined the rhetorical, stylistic, and organizational conventions of a persuasive letter written by a French president, focusing on the use of personal pronouns, repetition, and a call for action. Students later wrote their own persuasive letter to a politician in which individual students employed on average eight of the fourteen textual features present in the model text. The authors concluded that engaging students in the analysis of textual features equipped learners not only to create their own texts but also to personalize them through their choice of features. Finally, Maxim (2006) reported on the effectiveness of a literacies-oriented approach to reading a novel in a first-semester German class. The beginning-level learners initially struggled to understand who the agent (or subject) was in sentences that did not follow the prototypical subject-verb-object word order of English. After a series of conceptualizing activities in which they developed awareness of nominative and accusative case markings, however, students were more successful in comprehending the novel. As these three studies demonstrate, conceptualizing increased student awareness and knowledge of target language forms and conventions; students then used this knowledge to interpret and create target language texts. They also developed an awareness of the dynamic, contextually dependent nature of language; their linguistic productions reflected language that varies according to interlocutor and purpose as opposed to being a fixed set of rules.

Conceptualizing or Not?

Not all language- or genre-focused activities are conceptualizing activities. In table 8.1 we present a series of activities and invite you to consider whether each engages students in conceptualizing. You can use the three criteria presented in the previous section—explicit, meaning based, learner centered—to help you determine why each activity is or is not a good example of conceptualizing.

Each of the activities described in table 8.1 is based upon a target language text, be it a song, a video, or a written text, yet not all of them engage students in conceptualizing. Only five of the activities—cohesion relationships, substitutions, revising and editing, demystifying pronunciation, and mapping—target form-meaning connections and involve conceptualizing. The other two activities—fill in the blank and sing-along—do not entail conceptualizing.

The first activity, fill in the blank, focuses on a specific linguistic form within the context of a text, but it does not explore the meaning communicated by the subjunctive. As it is written, this activity is not meaning based, as student attention is exclusively focused on producing the correct conjugation and making sound-spelling correspondences; their attention is not focused on how using the subjunctive affects the song's meaning. Exploring the changes in meaning that result when using the indicative instead of the subjunctive in the same text would transform this particular activity into a conceptualizing activity. Moreover, doing so would help students see

Table 8.1. Conceptualizing or Not?

Activity	Description
1. Fill in the blank	Students are given a handout of song lyrics with all instances of subjunctive verb forms removed. As students listen to the song, they fill in the blanks with the verb form they hear.
2. Cohesion relationships	Prior to reading a short text (but after previous work with transitions and connectors), students receive strips of paper, each with a sentence from the text. Students put the strips in order, creating a complete text. They then discuss how transitions and connectors served as clues for the text's organization.
3. Substitutions	After reading a short story, students turn their attention to the use of verbal aspect throughout the narrative. They exchange all imperfect forms for perfect (preterit) forms and then discuss how the change impacts the overall storyline.
4. Revising and editing	Based on feedback from peers and/or their teacher, students revise and edit their own movie reviews. They make decisions regarding their text's organization, the forms used to express their opinion, and the use of explicit or null subjects based on feedback and their intended message and audience.
5. Sing-along	To practice pronunciation and pay attention to the sounds in a song, students sing a song as a class.
6. Demystifying pronunciation	Students listen to a stanza of a song and identify all examples of pronounced and unpronounced mute-e. They then try to explain the pronunciation and spelling conventions used by the songwriter based on the use of mute-e. Finally, they explore how these patterns interact with the song's message and tone.
7. Mapping	After reading a description, students create a concept map that illustrates the relationships between items in the description, words used to describe them, and what they as readers infer from the descriptions.

Sources: Kern (2000) and Paesani, Allen, and Dupuy (2016).

the meaning communicated by subjunctive forms as opposed to just memorizing a list of phrases that cue its use.

In the second activity, *cohesion relationships*, students focus on devices, specifically transitions and connectors, that make paragraphs or texts cohere. Having to put the sentences in order without having previously read the text forces learners to rely on these devices; they see how these words contribute to the overall meaning of the text. The final step of the activity, discussion of how the transitions and connectors served as clues, then develops students' metalinguistic knowledge as they abstract from the text to explore the function of cohesive devices more generally. Throughout this activity, students are cognitively engaged in constructing a text and patterns that guide the use of transitions and connectors.

Substitutions (activity 3) draws student attention to the meaning communicated by past tense verbal aspect within a specific text. Students observe how using the preterit versus the imperfect changes the meaning that is created. Rather than memorizing a list of rules to be followed (e.g., repeated or ongoing actions use imperfect), they scrutinize what the use of the imperfect means within this text (e.g., went on for a long time, with no specific start or end). They do this by contrasting the imperfect with a different form in the same context, noting how that change affects the overall meaning of the text. Through this examination students can begin to understand language use as a series of choices between forms that communicate different meanings rather than as an arbitrary set of rules. In this activity, students consciously attend to verbal aspect and the meanings it creates. They are also active in making observations, hypothesizing meaning contrasts, and creating their own meaning-based rules to govern imperfect-preterit use. Choosing between imperfect and preterit is no longer a question of right or wrong but rather of what meaning language users want to communicate.

Revising and editing (activity 4) is a common presentational communication activity; when revising and editing are focused on making edits to more effectively and precisely communicate meaning, this is a conceptualizing activity. One difference between the revising and editing activity presented here and those commonly used in language classrooms is the agency of the learners and the focus on textual meaning. As presented in table 8.1, students have agency to make decisions about forms based upon the meanings they communicate. This differs from other revision activities in which students are focused on producing the one correct form, without thinking about why. To successfully carry out this activity, students must consider the choices they've made in light of their reviewer's comments and decide how to clarify their intended meaning.

Activities 5 and 6, sing-along and demystifying pronunciation, both focus on pronunciation, yet demystifying pronunciation engages students in conceptualizing whereas a sing-along does not. When students sing along, they are focused on articulating sounds in the same way as the singer; they do not consider how the singer's pronunciation patterns create cohesion within the text, contribute to the song's tone, or indicate the singer's identity. In contrast, in activity 6 students look for patterns across the singer's articulations and how those patterns contribute to the musicality and message of the song. Consequently, the focus on pronunciation is grounded in textual meaning, making this a meaning-based conceptualizing activity.

Mapping as described in activity 7 is very different from the mapping activities used to exemplify experiencing in chapter 7. In the latter, students experience a text by mapping out relationships based on textual content (geographic locations, family relationships, timelines); in the former, students conceptualize the text by focusing on the textual features that communicate its content. In the mapping activity in table 8.1, students look at not just what elements are included in a description but also the forms used to describe each element (adjectives in this case). Additionally, students articulate what readers infer about those elements based upon the descriptions. In other words, through mapping students uncover how the linguistic forms work together to communicate the author's perspective of and stance toward the place being described. Grounded in the meaning of the text, focused on the connection between form (adjectives) and meaning (overall sense of the place), and based on relationships observed by students, this activity is meaning based, explicit, and student centered.

The activities in table 8.1 that are not conceptualizing differ importantly from activities we just described because, although they are explicitly focused on linguistic forms found in texts, they do not connect the forms to textual meaning in any way. Moreover, in the two nonconceptualizing activities, students do not construct patterns or make generalizations, but rather they work to apply rules that have been given to them. Along these lines, Saudelli and Rowsell (2013) caution that conceptualizing can be misunderstood as drill and practice. And although nonconceptualizing, language-focused activities may play a role in developing automaticity with forms, they do not promote the development of foreign language literacies.

Reconceptualizing Form-Focused Instruction

Throughout this chapter, we have focused on what conceptualizing is, defining it as an explicit, meaning-based, student-centered activity that analyzes the what, how, and why of textual features. To further differentiate conceptualizing from other approaches to the instruction of language forms, we share a table that summarizes both what conceptualizing is as well as what it is not. Table 8.2 was originally created by classroom teachers as they sought to deepen their understanding of conceptualizing. The descriptors they identified highlight that conceptualizing is always grounded in textual meaning and that it involves the joint construction of patterns. Presenting a list of vocabulary or paradigms to be memorized and asking students to complete mechanical drills do not engage the necessary cognitive processes to establish form-meaning connections, and thus they are not good descriptors for conceptualizing. The descriptors in table 8.2 also underscore the dynamic nature of language in that conceptualizing is not thinking of rules and vocabulary as set in stone; instead, language varies across users and sociocultural contexts.

As we've argued throughout this book, language and conventions are dynamic meaning-making resources: language exists to meet our communicative needs,

Table 8.2. Conceptualizing Is (Not)

Conceptualizing is . . .	Conceptualizing is not . . .
• connecting form with meaning • text-based and contextualized • learner-centered • inquiry-based (e.g., speculating, testing, generalizing) • planned attention to textual features that will help individuals to interpret and create meaning • grammar, vocabulary, and more (e.g., genre, organization, other semiotic systems)	• memorizing grammar rules or vocabulary • thinking of rules and vocabulary as set in stone or independent of context • isolated grammar instruction • mechanical drills that don't require understanding of meaning to be completed • a lecture or telling students about grammar concepts, rules, or lists of vocabulary • identifying "the right" form • focused solely on grammar and vocabulary • surface-level comprehension of textual facts

and conventions reflect the patterns that characterize different textual genres. Individuals leverage linguistic, conventional, and other meaning-making resources (e.g., grammar, vocabulary, font sizes, visual images, sounds, spatial relationships, gestures) to express themselves. Second language learners must discover not just what these meaning-making resources are but also the meanings they convey. To do this, they need to be exposed to and create numerous and varied target language texts. Unpacking how these texts construct meaning through the knowledge process of conceptualizing develops language learners' explicit knowledge of the tools that will help them communicate appropriately, effectively, and accurately (Cope and Kalantzis 2009; Kern 2000).

Spotlight on Teacher Professional Development

Conceptualizing might be the most difficult of the activity types for teachers to plan for and implement. We highlighted in chapter 1 the finding that teacher-created instructional materials target some knowledge processes more than others. Of the four knowledge processes, conceptualizing was the least emphasized in two different studies: it comprised fewer than 10 percent of all instructional activities in analyses of postsecondary English and Spanish multiliteracies materials (Menke and Paesani 2019; Rowland et al. 2014). Minimal to no attention to language forms is similarly reported in some studies of content-based language instruction (e.g., Bigelow 2010; Cammarata and Tedick 2012). Two questions naturally follow from this conclusion: Why is this the case? And how do we support teachers in their efforts to incorporate conceptualizing in instruction?

Several explanations for the lack of form-meaning or form-content integration have been offered in the literature. First, incorporating interesting and meaningful content allows teachers to develop students' critical thinking and other cognitive capacities, expose learners to other perspectives and ideas, connect with students' lives outside of the language classroom, and engage learners at the appropriate cognitive levels (Kim and Xing 2019; Menke 2018; Menke and Paesani 2021). The positive outcomes teachers associate with this meaningful content may lead them to prioritize "understanding the world" (Menke 2018, 124) and to "overlook the language exploitation aspects of instruction" (Stoller and Grabe 1997, 93), similar to what happens in content-based classrooms.

A second explanation offered by scholars is the conceptual challenge literacies concepts present to teachers (e.g., Allen 2011; Dupuy and Allen 2012; Paesani 2013; Menke and Paesani 2021). Literacies concepts can sometimes be opaque, and they often differ from the lived experiences and beliefs of most language teachers because they have been socialized into separating the "language acquisition imperatives" (Maxim 2014, 93) of form and meaning. Despite the many calls for language-content integration, "a lack of theoretical foundation and practical guidance as to how to conceptualize that integration and implement it . . . has impeded its realization" (Ryshina-Pankova 2013, 227). Consequently, few teachers have had the opportunity to experience language-content integrated instruction as a language learner or observe it as a teacher, which means that they don't have concrete, lived experiences to draw on to support their developing understanding of concepts or design of instruction. Additionally, previous learning experiences that have focused on limited, formal aspects of language may handicap teachers when they consider what forms and conventions to incorporate into instruction.

Finally, for some teachers explicitly attending to language forms or textual conventions is inconsistent with their beliefs about language teaching. Some theories of language acquisition and approaches to language teaching sustain the idea that learners will acquire language forms through meaningful exposure to target language input and that instruction of language forms does not alter or affect this process (e.g., the monitor model [Krashen 1981], generative second language acquisition [e.g., Hawkins 2001; White 2003], input processing [VanPatten 1993]). Additionally, some forms of communicative language teaching embrace minimizing or excluding form-focused instruction from the classroom. Teachers whose beliefs align with these theories of language acquisition and instructional approaches may consider activities that explicitly target language forms and conventions "anathema" or "anachronistic" (Rowland et al. 2014, 147) and may struggle to reconcile their beliefs with the intentional focus on form required in conceptualizing activities.

Based on this brief review, we identify two primary needs of teachers moving to multiliteracies pedagogy: (1) reflection on their personal beliefs and learning histories and (2) increased "knowledge about language" (Andrews 2007). Increasing awareness of one's experiences and beliefs about the goals of language learning and the teaching of language forms opens a space for teachers to consider what they value, what their practices are, and why. These beliefs, experiences, and practices can then be linked to pedagogical concepts as a means of identifying points of dissonance and alignment. Practically speaking, this reflection work can be woven throughout professional development experiences. For example, as part of their coursework, preservice teachers might initially write a language learning autobiography and complete a language learning beliefs survey. Once in the field, they might review a lesson plan that they've designed to see how it reflects their previous experiences, their beliefs, or other pedagogical concepts to which they have been introduced. If preservice candidates share these documents with their methods instructors, field supervisors, or cooperating teachers, it opens a space for conversation with experts who can facilitate connections with and deeper understanding of pedagogical concepts such as foreign language literacies, language forms and conventions, and conceptualizing. For those who are already teaching, peer observations provide an opportunity for reflection on practice and dialogue around the reasoning behind one's instructional practices. A colleague or mentor conducting the observation might inquire about the teacher's motivations for specific instructional activities: How does this activity resemble activities that you engaged with as a learner? How does this activity align with or differ from your beliefs about language learning? What pedagogical concepts align with this practice and how?

Morton (2016) identified "content and language knowledge for teaching" as an essential component for all language teachers (150–51); it embodies the form-meaning mappings that we have discussed throughout this chapter. Numerous scholars have emphasized the gradual nature of developing teachers' understanding of the interdependence of language and content. Cammarata and Tedick (2012) described it, for example, as an "awakening" that happens (257), and Morton (2016) commented that this interdependence is not "understood theoretically and then applied but emerges in and through contact with the complex social world of content-based classrooms" (152–3). To initiate such an awakening or emergence, professional development should engage teachers in textual analysis. Teachers can collaboratively analyze multimodal texts with the goal of discovering all the different features that create the text's message. The Textual Features Worksheet presented in chapter 4 and available on the companion website (https://carla.umn.edu/literacies/book/) can scaffold this work, which seeks to answer the question of how an author achieves their communicative goal. To carry out this kind of textual analysis, teachers should become "language explorers" (Tarone 2009, 19), embracing a spirit of inquiry that acknowledges the dynamic nature of language. Academic programs can foster this disposition and skill set in pre- and in-service teachers by offering abundant examples of language use in varied contexts that illustrate typical or standard uses of language forms and creative language play. Doing so can awaken teachers' sensibilities to how language creates meaning.

With respect to how to integrate language and content in instruction, models are useful for both preservice and in-service teachers. In a needs analysis, postsecondary instructors of Spanish indicated that model lesson plans and activities were the most needed professional development resource to develop their understanding of and ability to implement multiliteracies pedagogy (Paesani and Menke 2019). By observing how others have brought textual features and their meanings to the forefront, the abstract concept of conceptualizing becomes more concrete. Furthermore, instructional teams might collaboratively plan or develop conceptualizing activities, an experience that postsecondary instructors evaluated as extremely impactful (Paesani and Menke 2019). The PACE model (Presentation, Attention, Coconstruction, and Extension) of teaching language forms supports teachers in designing explicit, meaning-based, learner-centered, form-focused instruction and can thus facilitate this work (Donato and Adair-Hauck 1994). Glisan and Donato (2017) explained that the sequence includes selecting examples of the target textual feature from the text, determining how to draw learner attention to the feature, identifying the desired generalization (What is the form-meaning connection?), scripting questions to guide students to the generalization, and preparing responses to student questions and misunderstandings.

Equipped with an understanding of form-meaning connections, awareness of their own natural tendencies, and research findings that point to the underrepresentation of conceptualizing in teacher-created materials, teachers can make a commitment to incorporate conceptualizing activities regularly into instruction. Instructional teammates or mentors can then check in with teachers on their progress toward their goal.

Conclusion

In this chapter, we have encouraged you to rethink your approach to the teaching of language forms through the knowledge process of conceptualizing. Because language teachers consider conceptualizing to be the most challenging knowledge process to understand and implement, we have deconstructed its essential features and offered concrete examples to use in text-based literacies lesson plans. As you continue the in-depth exploration of the knowledge processes of multiliteracies pedagogy in the remaining chapters, keep in mind the importance of form-meaning connections to students' foreign language literacies development and how it can prepare them to more effectively interpret target language texts and apply their knowledge to the creation of new texts.

Reflecting on Research and Practice

1. Has your thinking around the role of grammar and vocabulary in language education changed over the course of reading this chapter? If so, how? How can you communicate the role of grammar and vocabulary to students?
2. Are the form-focused activities you typically use in instruction explicit, meaning based, and learner centered? If not, how might you modify them to make them align with the core features of conceptualizing?
3. How has your understanding of conceptualizing evolved since you were first introduced to the concept in chapter 1? How has it evolved based on your reading of this chapter?

Resources

1. CARLA's Literacies Activity Repository (https://carla.umn.edu/literacies/book/)

   This repository provides examples of activities from all four knowledge processes, including conceptualizing. Activities are pulled from literacies-oriented lesson plans created by practitioners and researchers.

2. Sample Conceptualizing Activities (https://newlearningonline.com/learning-by-design/the-knowledge-processes/conceptualising; https://newlearningonline.com/learning-by-design/the-knowledge-processes/conceptualising-by-theorising)

   Kalantzis and Cope (2021g, 2021h) list numerous examples of activities that target conceptualizing from other academic disciplines, not necessarily language teaching. The activity templates can be adapted to draw out specific textual features and their meanings.

3. "How Does a Caterpillar Become a Butterfly?" Lesson Plan (https://drive.google.com/file/d/0Byg7PyauMJRSbmxGampCOG1STok/edit)

In this lesson created by Hsiaomei (n.d.), young Chinese immersion learners develop understanding of temporal adverbs and cultural food products through their engagement in instructional activities based on *The Very Hungry Caterpillar*, a book by Eric Carle. The lesson is part of the Foreign Languages and the Literary in the Everyday (FLLITE) database.

4. "What's in a Name?" Lesson Plan (https://docs.google.com/document/d/1Dit7mWCRmGoRvUHM32WXk3euMdRfD6c7Xsl6cNbUJwE/edit)

   This lesson, created by Luks (2013b), is part of the FLLITE database. In it, beginning, university learners of French explore the use of nouns as adjectives and rhyming to interpret and create metaphorical language in poems.

Further Reading and Viewing

1. "Experiential and Conceptual Learning" (https://newlearningonline.com/literacies/chapter-3/experiential-and-conceptual-learning)

   In the second half of this video (start at minute 3:33), Kalantzis and Cope (2016b) discuss the knowledge process of conceptualizing. They provide examples of naming different components of communication as well as the patterns and relationships that guide their use.

2. "Integrating Textual Thinking into the Introductory College-Level Foreign Language Classroom" (Maxim 2006)

   This article published in the *Modern Language Journal* describes an instructional sequence that guides beginning, university learners of German through the reading of a short romance novel in German. As part of the sequence, learners engage in conceptualizing activities around descriptive language and nominative and accusative cases.

3. "Reconceptualizing Grammar and Vocabulary as Meaning-Making Resources" in *A Multiliteracies Framework for Collegiate Foreign Language Teaching* (Paesani, Allen, and Dupuy 2016, 86–105)

   In this chapter, Paesani, Allen, and Dupuy review key concepts and research related to the teaching of language forms prior to presenting a template for teaching language forms within the multiliteracies framework. The template is complemented with a sample instructional sequence for a lower-level French class.

9

Analyzing: Exploring Cultural Practices and Perspectives

Question the complexity of culture, language, and ideas

ANALYZING ACTIVITIES—AS THE PRECEDING mantra emphasizes—involve having learners question what is learned from the target language texts they read, listen to, and view. In fact, developing students' foreign language literacies, or their ability to build meaning from texts and interpret their cultural and linguistic content, relies crucially on analyzing. Yet many teachers report that analyzing activities are the most complex for them to carry out, particularly when students have lower language proficiency, and research shows that these activities are often absent from or deemphasized in multiliteracies lessons (Menke and Paesani 2019; Rowland et al. 2014). The aim of this chapter is to demystify analyzing activities and to guide you through how to engage language learners in higher-order activities that lead to critical analysis of texts. We begin by expanding the definition of analyzing presented thus far and developing a rationale for implementing analyzing activities at all levels of language instruction. Next, we provide examples of analyzing activities and break down common barriers to their successful implementation. We then conclude with a spotlight on teacher professional development in relation to analyzing.

Defining Analyzing Activities

In earlier chapters of this book, we defined *analyzing* activities as those providing a big-picture view of textual meaning that includes connecting what is learned to social, historical, cultural, or political contexts and purposes. Not only do students step back from a text to question its meaning, importance, and consequences, but they also consider the role and purpose of textual ideas and relate them to their own culture, perspectives, and learning (Cope and Kalantzis 2009, 2015; New London

Group 1996). In doing so, learners are able to answer the question of why: why do cultural products, practices, and perspectives exist, and why are they important; why did the author create this text in this way, and how do they want us to feel about it; and so on. Analyzing activities are thus quite different from the experiencing activities you learned about in chapter 7, which are more immersive in nature and are more personal to the learner and their experiences, feelings, and opinions. They also differ significantly from the conceptualizing activities you learned about in chapter 8, which require students to zoom in on specific textual features to understand how they make meaning. Analyzing activities are also likely quite different from the types of text-based activities found in the textbooks and other materials you use in language instruction, particularly those grounded in communicative language teaching, which prioritize surface-level comprehension of facts, decoding, and practice of language forms.

As the definition presented here makes clear, analyzing involves higher-order thinking and cognitive abilities. Indeed, this multiliteracies activity type can be correlated with two cognitive processes in Bloom's Taxonomy of Educational Objectives: analyzing and evaluating (Anderson and Krathwohl 2001; Bloom 1956; Kalantzis et al. 2016). In Bloom's taxonomy, analyzing involves the ability to distinguish and draw connections among ideas, whereas evaluating involves the ability to justify or critically examine a stand or decision. Engaging in these two cognitive processes allows learners to tease apart the cultural products, practices, and perspectives represented in target language texts; to construct informed opinions about the impact of these products, practices, and perspectives on target and home cultures; and to contextualize them in relation to different contexts and purposes. Through the multiliteracies activity type of analyzing, then, learners analyze and evaluate ideas and texts beyond the literal level; they read between the lines by examining different viewpoints, they critically reflect on these viewpoints, and, potentially, they transform new understandings into action (Kalantzis and Cope 2021a). As such, analyzing activities are also an essential component of the multiliteracies framework as a *critical pedagogy* that integrates teaching and learning, on the one hand, with social justice and critical consciousness, on the other hand.

At this point, the concept of analyzing may still feel abstract to you, and in our experience, it's helpful for teachers to think about keywords related to this activity type. After reading the previous two paragraphs, what words do you think best characterize analyzing activities? Some keywords that the teachers we have worked with use to define analyzing are reasoning, inferencing, drawing connections, and evaluating perspectives. Other keywords proposed by multiliteracies scholars include comparing, critiquing, arguing, concluding, judging, synthesizing, and justifying (Kalantzis and Cope 2021a). It may also be helpful to consider these keywords in relation to a classroom example. For instance, in the four corners activity in the sample lesson presented in appendix B, the teacher presents the following statement: "The American dream is the same for all." Students must choose the corner of the classroom that reflects their level of agreement with the statement: strongly agree, agree, disagree, or strongly disagree. Once in their corners, students provide evidence to support their selection and identify factors that might influence how an individual defines the American dream. Going back to our list of keywords, this four corners activity involves reasoning, evaluating perspectives, judging, and justifying. We will continue to provide examples of analyzing activities throughout this chapter, but first it is important to understand why analyzing activities are essential for students' foreign language literacies development.

Why Ask Why?

Analyzing activities often focus on answering the question why, but why ask why? That is, how does exploring the deeper meaning of texts, their purposes and consequences, and their relationship to the world help develop students' communicative abilities and their literacies in another language? As chapter 1 explained, foreign language literacies involve a range of knowledge and abilities, including interpretation, inferencing, problem-solving, and reflection, all of which are connected to the definition of analyzing we presented in the previous section. Indeed, analyzing represents one of "the things you do to know" (Kalantzis et al. 2016, 67), or the things we do in the real world to understand and take action. For example, the ability to analyze allows us to be critical consumers of information; in combination with conceptualizing, analyzing activities train us to recognize whether information is credible or fake. Likewise, analyzing improves our ability to negotiate, be assertive, and assess the impact of our own behavior on others (Kalantzis and Cope 2021a). Finally, analyzing is an essential component of informed decision-making and ethical reasoning, skills that are not only important for working with target language texts but also transferable to many academic, workplace, and personal settings.

In addition to developing essential literacies knowledge and skills, prioritizing analyzing in curriculum and instruction fills an important gap in many commercially available language learning materials. Many of these materials encourage learners to focus on themselves—their personal reactions, experiences, and beliefs—in relation to textual content without also considering the impact of that content on others or the text's purpose in the target culture. Ennser-Kananen (2016) points out that cultural content is often "light, curious, and often pleasantly amusing" (55). Moreover, questions of identity, access, power, and beliefs are rarely present in textbooks (Glynn and Wassell 2022). Instead, these materials are largely focused on linguistic development; that is, on how reading, listening to, or viewing texts can help reinforce and practice the grammar and vocabulary learned throughout an instructional unit and how working with texts can contribute to reading and listening proficiency. Literacies-oriented materials have these goals as well, but with the addition of analyzing activities, they also encourage students to question why ideas are presented the way they are and why they are representative of target language cultures. Analyzing activities, therefore, provide a means for enriching students' linguistic, cultural, and intellectual development simultaneously.

These ideas are reinforced by research showing that analyzing activities help students connect language and culture, engage more deeply with texts, and explore multiple points of view. Reporting on a global simulation project grounded in multiliteracies pedagogy and implemented in an intermediate-level postsecondary French course, Michelson and Dupuy (2014) found that analyzing activities are essential for helping learners move beyond the what and how of a text—perspectives often addressed in experiencing and conceptualizing activities—to also consider the who of a text. That is, analyzing helped students situate target language texts in terms of an author's perspective and a text's intended audience and thus allowed them to see how culture is played out in the linguistic, organizational, and stylistic choices an author makes. Focusing on the development of critical literacy, Chun (2009) described the application of multiliteracies pedagogy in a high school ESL class. Students read a graphic novel treating topics of racism and power relations that were relevant to their lives as second language speakers of English residing in the United States. The analyzing activities (e.g., critical questions, multiple interpretations, personal reflection) implemented by the teacher deepened students' engagement by drawing on their own resources and experiences, fostered critical reflection about the graphic novel, and empowered students as cocreators of knowledge. Finally, Mills (2006) investigated a culturally and linguistically diverse English-medium sixth grade classroom in Australia and found that when teachers enacted analyzing activities, students were able to critique the underlying social, cultural, political, and ideological assumptions in texts, to evaluate the intentions behind textual meaning, and to consider different textual interpretations and points of view. Analyzing activities helped these students move beyond the more traditional strategy of finding the correct interpretation of texts; instead, they understood and evaluated how texts make meaning, why, and for whom. Taken together, these studies not only illustrate the benefits of analyzing activities for language learning but also suggest that analyzing can and should take place in all language courses, regardless of students' age or proficiency level.

Designing and Implementing Analyzing Activities

With an understanding of what analyzing activities are, why they are important, and how they contribute to students' foreign language literacies development, we turn now to considerations for designing and implementing effective analyzing activities. To begin, take a moment to reflect on what you've learned to this point and create a list of characteristics that good analyzing activities embody: What knowledge or skills must these activities develop in your students? How should they engage your students with target language texts? In collaboration with participants in CARLA summer institutes, we have identified five characteristics of good analyzing activities:

1. They make connections between the text and the external world and across cultures and perspectives.
2. They get at the why of the text: the author's perspective, the cultural content within the text, the genre, and so on.
3. They encourage justification and reasoning by grounding ideas and perspectives in textual evidence.
4. They don't always have a right or wrong answer.
5. They include clear instructions and are well scaffolded within a lesson.

Were any of these on the list you generated? What additional characteristics might you add to this list? We encourage you to use this list, as well as the mantra that started this chapter, to help you craft effective analyzing activities as you design your own text-based lessons.

You can find many examples of analyzing activities in CARLA's Literacies Activity Repository (https://carla.umn.edu/literacies/book/) and in the sample lesson plan provided in appendix B. We'll talk about four examples here to help you see the five characteristics of good analyzing activities in action. The first example is a *3-2-1 activity*, a task that asks learners to summarize and analyze the knowledge they have gained from target language texts and to identify areas of misunderstanding (Zygouris-Coe, Wiggins, and Smith 2004). A 3-2-1 activity can serve as a useful formative assessment for both students and teachers, allowing students to assess their own learning and teachers to identify topics that need further attention. The 3, 2, and 1 components may take many forms. One common format is to summarize learning in three words or sentences, analyze learning in two words or sentences, and identify questions or areas of confusion in one word or sentence. For instance, after reading a text on food practices in countries of the Arabic-speaking world, learners might summarize the text in three sentences, make two comparisons to food practices in their own country or region, and identify one food practice they didn't understand fully. Alternatively, students might list three dishes they learned about, two regional features that might affect food practices (e.g., climate, industry, geography, history), and one personal connection with the text. The specific content of a 3-2-1 activity is therefore flexible based on a lesson's content and learning objectives and on your students' language proficiency. In addition, the implementation of 3-2-1 activities is also flexible: they can be carried out as individual or small group activities, include written or recorded responses, take place in or out of class, or incorporate technology such as an online discussion board or breakout rooms. Returning to the characteristics of good analyzing activities listed earlier, we see that 3-2-1 activities encourage learners to make connections between the text and the external world and across cultures and perspectives, encourage justification and reasoning by grounding ideas and perspectives in textual evidence, and include open-ended questions that do not have a right or wrong answer. In addition, 3-2-1 activities touch upon many of the keywords we introduced earlier in this chapter, including drawing connections, comparing, concluding, and synthesizing.

A second example of an analyzing activity is peer feedback, which is used to improve the content of the presentational products students create. A common form of peer feedback is peer editing of written work, but for it to fall within the multiliteracies activity type of analyzing, peer feedback must be focused on the content of students' written work and the relationships between language forms and their purpose and meaning, rather than on the accuracy of language forms (Kern 2000; Paesani, Allen, and Dupuy 2016). For example, a content-focused peer feedback activity for a descriptive essay might include the following steps: (1) students underline the introductory and concluding statements of the essay as well as the topic sentence of each paragraph and then make one suggestion for improvement, (2) they identify details the author has provided about the topic and make one suggestion for making the details clearer or more vivid, and (3) they ask one question or make one positive statement about the perspective the author is communicating in the essay. The traditional way to implement peer feedback activities is through in-class pair or small group work with the help of a printed handout; in an online environment, these activities can take place synchronously in breakout rooms or asynchronously via a collaborative document. Two of the characteristics of good analyzing activities that are relevant for peer feedback are getting at the why of the text to understand an author's perspective, the cultural content within the text, or its genre and encouraging justification and reasoning by grounding ideas in textual evidence. Content-focused peer feedback activities are also consistent with the analyzing keywords of drawing connections, critiquing, judging, and justifying.

The third example activity that encourages analyzing is *critical focus questions*. The purpose of this activity type is to raise students' awareness of the significance of the language and ideas in a text and their effect on a reader, listener, or viewer (Kern 2000). Critical focus questions can take many forms, but they must target the why and how of a text, rather than the who, what, where, and when. In other words, critical focus questions should not ask about textual facts but rather about why those facts are important within larger cultural, social, historical, or political contexts and how language contributes to that importance. To help you discern good critical focus questions from bad ones, consider the following examples:

- Which cultural perspective presented in the text did you like the best?
- Is this a good example of a cultural practice from this country?
- Who is your favorite character in the text?

These kinds of questions are not uncommon in the reading, listening, and viewing activities found in many commercially available teaching materials; however, they are not critical focus questions because they do not raise students' awareness of the significance of the language and ideas presented in a text. Instead, they simply ask students to identify facts about the text or to relate the text to their personal opinions and preferences. More appropriate examples of critical focus questions include the following:

- How do these words in the text reflect cultural perspectives?
- How does the representation of the cultural practices presented in the text differ from your own culture?
- Why do you think the author presented this character in this way?

These critical focus questions are more appropriate than the original examples because they require students to focus on the why and how of the text, and thus they reflect the second item on our list of characteristics of good analyzing activities. These questions also encourage students to make connections between the text and the external world and to justify their answers by grounding ideas in textual evidence. Finally, critical focus questions reflect the analyzing keywords of reasoning, inferencing, evaluating perspectives, and justifying.

Finally, in the lesson plan on the American dream (see appendix B), students carry out several predicting activities, including one in which they imagine the audience, authors, content, and positionality of American dream statements from a *New York Times* article. This predicting activity encourages students to get at the why of the text before they even read it, and this information is revisited at later points in the lesson to scaffold students' detailed interpretation of the American dream statements. This activity is also open-ended, leaving room for students to make educated guesses about the text's purpose and intent without risk of providing a wrong answer. Predicting thus meets two of the characteristics of good analyzing activities provided earlier and furthermore aligns with the keywords of reasoning, inferencing, evaluating perspectives, and judging.

Overcoming Potential Roadblocks

After reading the previous section, you may be feeling that analyzing activities are too challenging for your students, particularly those in younger grades or those with lower-level language proficiency. Although analyzing activities encourage higher-order thinking and may be abstract for some learners, the research summarized earlier in this chapter shows that analyzing activities have many benefits for language learners of all ages and at all levels of instruction. Two common roadblocks teachers identify in relation to designing and implementing analyzing activities are that they are (1) too cognitively demanding and (2) too complex to take place in the target language. Overcoming these roadblocks involves redesigning activities to meet the needs of all learners, even those who struggle to use the target language to think critically.

The analyzing activities from the previous section can all be redesigned to overcome these roadblocks. For instance, in discussing 3-2-1 activities we underscored their flexibility: these activities can take many forms and can be simplified to meet the needs of different learners. The easiest way to adapt a 3-2-1 activity is to have students respond with individual words rather than with complete sentences. Another alternative is for students to represent their analysis of a text through images or drawings. In table 9.1 we show three different versions of the 3-2-1 activity on food practices in the Arabic-speaking world that incorporate these alternatives and meet the needs of learners of different ages and proficiency levels.

The peer feedback activity presented in the previous section encouraged learners to improve the content of a descriptive essay by following a three-step process. A simple way to adapt this activity for lower-proficiency learners is to have them carry out the peer feedback activity in their first language (or the dominant language of the class, such as English in US learning contexts). This suggestion may make you bristle, particularly if you strive to implement the high-leverage teaching practice of facilitating target language use by employing the language for 90 percent or more of classroom instruction (ACTFL n.d.; Glisan and Donato 2017). However, this high-leverage teaching practice also encourages teachers to be specific and deliberate about their choice not to use the target language. Given the benefits of peer feedback on students' presentational writing, such as influencing discourse-related aspects of writing, developing writing strategies, gaining inspiration from peers, and reducing writing anxiety (e.g., Hyland and Hyland 2006; Lundstrom and Baker 2009; Yu and

Table 9.1. 3-2-1 Activity with Modifications

Activity stage	More proficient learners	Less proficient learners	Young learners
3	Summarize the text in three sentences	List the three most important words from the text for understanding its main message	Find or draw three images that illustrate what you understand from the text
2	Compare food practices in your own country/region in two sentences	List two food practices mentioned in the text that are different from your own	Complete a Venn diagram with words or images to illustrate areas of overlap and difference in food practices in the target and home cultures
1	Identify a misunderstood food practice in one sentence	Ask one question about food practices in your home or target culture	List one new word or draw one idea you learned from the text

Lee 2016), the choice to use students' first language during this activity type is justified. Alternatively, to encourage target language use during peer feedback among lower-proficiency or younger learners, modifications can be made. For example, in the first peer editing step outlined earlier, instead of generating original suggestions for improving descriptive writing, the teacher can provide a list of options from which the peer reviewer selects. Likewise, in step 2 students can underline or highlight descriptive words that are repeated in the text and then provide one new word. Finally, in step 3 peer reviewers can select one positive comment about the written work from a teacher-provided list.

At first glance, critical focus questions may seem like the most challenging activity type to adapt for younger or less-proficient learners because they raise students' awareness of the significance of language and ideas in a text by focusing on the questions of why and how. Certainly, critical focus questions require higher-order thinking that can be difficult for learners to carry out in their first language, let alone in the target language. One strategy for facilitating target language use in critical focus questions is to provide adequate linguistic support. For instance, students can use sentence starters to structure their responses, or the teacher and students can discuss relevant grammar forms and brainstorm vocabulary lists prior to carrying out the activity. In the American Dream lesson presented in appendix B, linguistic support for the critical focus questions in stage 5 is provided in two ways. First, students build vocabulary knowledge as they read the infographic, tying images used to represent aspects of the American dream to the words that describe them. Second, this vocabulary is revisited in the handout students complete prior to answering critical focus questions to scaffold their analysis of the dream statements. To make critical focus questions more appropriate for younger learners, the complexity of the questions can be reduced or the questions can be broken down into smaller parts. For instance, instead of asking how the representation of the cultural practices presented in the text differ from their own culture, students might instead list the cultural practices from the text, then list similar practices from their own culture, and lastly identify one difference between the two.

Finally, the predicting activity from the American Dream lesson can be simplified so that learners do not have to produce language on their own to answer complex questions. For instance, younger learners can be provided with two or three possible answers to each predicting question. With the help of their classmates or teacher, they pick the one that makes the most sense to them. In so doing, students are not required to produce complex language and ideas on their own. Although analyzing activities can take on different forms and require students to produce varying amounts of language, they are engaging in the same cognitive processes regardless of proficiency level or age.

Spotlight on Teacher Professional Development

As we have explained throughout this book, teachers' understanding and application of literacies concepts—including the knowledge process of analyzing—are influenced by their previous experiences and beliefs as language teachers and learners. For instance, in the previous section we mentioned that some teachers feel that analyzing activities are too complex for their learners. This concern is often based on previous experiences with teaching approaches and materials that focus more on students' personal impressions of the messages in a target language text and less on their interpretation of those messages. This anecdotal evidence provides only limited insight into how teachers learn about and implement analyzing activities; in this section we focus on what the research says about analyzing activities from a teacher learning perspective, including implications for professional development.

One of the six key findings from the teacher development research reviewed in chapter 1 is that teacher-created instructional materials emphasize some knowledge processes over others and that analyzing is the knowledge process that appears least frequently in these materials. An analysis of text-based English language materials from a Japanese university revealed that only 5 percent of activities focused on analyzing, suggesting that there was little "concern with the structures and functions of texts or the motivations and intentions of text producers" in their design (Rowland et al. 2014, 147). Likewise, an analysis of interpretive communication materials from a lower-level postsecondary Spanish program in the United States found that analyzing comprised only 10.4 percent of activities, whereas experiencing activities represented 65 percent of the analyzed corpus (Menke and Paesani 2019). Finally, a study of two teachers of Chinese for linguistically diverse young learners found that few of the teachers' literacies practices focused on analyzing (Kim and Xing 2019). In discussing this finding, the researchers argued that "merely being exposed to innovative instructional strategies and pedagogies does not necessarily lead to the acquisition of innovative instructional strategies and pedagogies. The process of 'designing' in multiliteracies needs to be a transformative process" (13). The findings from these three studies are troubling, particularly given the benefits of analyzing outlined earlier in this chapter. As our summary of a study on a global simulation in an intermediate-level postsecondary French course demonstrated, analyzing activities are essential for understanding an author's perspective or a text's intended audience and connecting the cultural messages expressed in a text to its linguistic, organizational, and stylistic features (Michelson and Dupuy 2014). Likewise, a study of student writing in another intermediate-level postsecondary French course underscored the benefits of both analyzing and conceptualizing activities for expanding students' writing repertoires and raising students' awareness of the complexity of communication through writing (Allen and Goodspeed 2018).

There is clearly a mismatch between teacher uptake of analyzing activities and the benefits of analyzing for student learning. How do we reconcile this mismatch? How can we use these research findings to inform teacher professional development? The first step in helping teachers overcome their reticence in relation to analyzing activities is to encourage them to think critically about their language teaching and learning histories. Itself an analyzing activity that encourages teachers to question the complexity of their ideas about teaching, this work can take many forms: questioning beliefs about language proficiency and student ability, examining biases based in experiences with communicative language teaching or other instructional approaches, or evaluating past experiences in which analyzing activities had a positive or negative impact on their students or themselves. Critical reflection of this kind shouldn't be a one-time event; rather, it should take place at multiple points during teachers' formation. In a K–12 teacher preparation program, for instance, teachers can develop a language teaching and learning autobiography in their initial methods course and then expand and evaluate it at the end of their first year of coursework, at the start of their student teaching, and so on. In a postsecondary language department, teachers can develop this autobiography during their preservice orientation workshop, revise it during or after their required methods class, and use it as a point of reference during postobservation conversations. In all of these scenarios, the beliefs and experiences teachers identify as influencing their teaching should be put into dialogue with pedagogical concepts such as analyzing to make explicit theory-practice connections.

To further encourage theory-practice connections that improve teacher understanding and implementation of analyzing activities, it is important to think critically about learning objectives at the lesson, unit, or course level and how they align with the knowledge process of analyzing. By asking themselves how implementing analyzing activities helps them reach their objectives, teachers can begin to see whether and how their learning objectives emphasize the various aspects of foreign language literacies defined in chapter 1 and how to align those emphases with different knowledge processes and classroom practices. When learning objectives are narrowly conceived in relation to the concept of foreign language literacies, it can offer both an explanation for why analyzing activities are absent from or deemphasized in instructional materials and an opportunity to broaden learning objectives and instructional practices (Menke and Paesani 2019).

Professional development related to instructional practices is also important for helping teachers understand and implement the knowledge process of analyzing. The

Lesson Analysis Checklist from CARLA's Literacies in Language Education project (CARLA 2021c; https://carla.umn.edu/literacies/book/) is a professional development tool that provides a structure for evaluating existing text-based instructional materials using literacies principles and adapting those materials to better reflect the four knowledge processes, including analyzing. Rehearsal, a professional development strategy borrowed from the literature on high-leverage teaching practices (Glisan and Donato 2017, 2021), provides teachers with scaffolded support in a safe environment prior to trying out analyzing activities with their students. Rehearsal takes place within the context of a methods course and involves a three-step process of deconstructing the instructional practice to identify the steps involved in its implementation; rehearsing the practice in front of classmates to implement steps identified in the deconstruction phase; and assessing the practice to receive feedback on its implementation. Given the challenge teachers face in designing and implementing the knowledge process of analyzing, both lesson analysis and rehearsal can be powerful tools for reinforcing the importance of activities that reflect the mantra of questioning the complexity of culture, language, and ideas.

Conclusion

In this chapter we deconstructed the knowledge process of analyzing and provided several tools (e.g., keywords, characteristics of good analyzing activities) to help you deepen your understanding of this important activity type. We furthermore provided several examples of analyzing activities and presented alternatives to these activities to help you meet the needs of lower-proficiency and younger language learners. In chapter 10, we move on to the last of the four knowledge processes—applying—and explore ways that students can demonstrate what they have learned from texts through the experiencing, conceptualizing, and analyzing activities they have carried out.

Reflecting on Research and Practice

1. How has your understanding of analyzing evolved since you were first introduced to the concept in chapter 1? How has it evolved based on your reading of this chapter?
2. What aspects of the knowledge process of analyzing are still unclear? What professional development activities or resources presented in this chapter can help solidify your understanding?
3. What analyzing activities from this chapter or from CARLA's Literacies Activity Repository will you implement in your teaching moving forward? What modifications do you need to make to those activities to fit your learners' needs?
4. What is the relationship between analyzing and the remaining knowledge processes of experiencing, conceptualizing, and applying? How can you scaffold lessons using these other knowledge processes to effectively prepare students to engage in analyzing?

Resources

1. CARLA's Literacies Activity Repository (https://carla.umn.edu/literacies/book/)

   This repository provides examples of activities from all four knowledge processes, including analyzing. Activities are pulled from literacies lesson plans created by practitioners and researchers.

2. Sample Analyzing Activities (https://newlearningonline.com/learning-by-design/the-knowledge-processes/analysing; https://newlearningonline.com/learning-by-design/the-knowledge-processes/analysing-critically)

   These web pages, designed by Kalantzis and Cope (2021b, 2021c), provide additional examples of analyzing activities. Although not designed specifically for language learners, these activities can be adapted using the principles and strategies presented in this chapter.

3. Text-based lessons that exemplify analyzing:

   - Alles offen: Öffentliche Verkehrsmittel und Weltoffenheit: German, secondary/postsecondary (https://drive.google.com/file/d/0Byg7PyauMJRSMGMxUHh3c0gxTFk/view)
   - Interpreting *La Belle et la bête*: French, secondary (https://www.learner.org/series/teaching-foreign-languages-k-12-a-library-of-classroom-practices/french-interpreting-la-belle-et-la-bete/)
   - Un portrait chinois: French, postsecondary (https://docs.google.com/document/d/1z-Dd7kKMnrLbYaB0C75k42Nk_8yyi-gA004Nnw1RQgk/edit)

Further Reading and Viewing

1. "Critical Literacies and Graphic Novels for English-Language Learners: Teaching Maus" (Chun 2009)

   This article published in the *Journal of Adolescent & Adult Literacy* focuses on graphic novels as a text type that can help students understand and explain how language works both for and against different groups of people, thus fostering students' critical understanding of texts and the perspectives they portray.

2. "Analytical and Applied Learning" (https://newlearningonline.com/literacies/chapter-3/analytical-and-applied-learning)

   In the first half of this recorded lecture (end at minute 3:05), Kalantzis and Cope (2016a) discuss the knowledge process of analyzing and its two subprocesses: analyzing functionally and analyzing critically.

3. "An Interactive Reading Journal for All Levels of the Foreign Language Curriculum" (Redmann 2005a)

Published in *Foreign Language Annals*, this article presents a flexible tool for helping students critically interpret target language texts: an interactive reading journal. Examples of how the tool can be implemented for intermediate and advanced levels of instruction are provided.

10

Applying: Assessing Student Learning

Create texts and showcase new knowledge

AS THE SAYING GOES, "Knowledge is power." Or is it? At the core of a literacies approach to language education is enabling learners to interpret, transform, and create target language texts. Engaging in these activities prepares learners to participate fully in a range of personal, academic, and workplace contexts. It is thus more apt to say that "applying knowledge is power." The knowledge process of applying allows language learners to use the knowledge, skills, and understandings they gain while working with texts in oral and written production activities. Applying activities can occur at any point but, given their nature, are often found at the end of a lesson plan or instructional unit because they provide a way for teachers to assess student learning. Indeed, applying activities are familiar to most language teachers and can take many forms such as compositions, oral presentations, or IPAs (Adair-Hauck et al. 2006). Despite their familiarity to many teachers, however, the multiliteracies knowledge process of applying differs from these common production activities because at its essence is the creation of something new through the deliberate integration of the language features, textual conventions, and cultural content students work with during experiencing, conceptualizing, and analyzing activities. The aim of this chapter is to explain and exemplify the characteristics of applying activities and to consider their role in instructional and assessment practices. As with the previous chapters in this book, we conclude by considering applying in relation to teacher professional development.

Defining Applying

As you learned in chapter 1, and as the mantra at the beginning of this chapter suggests, through the knowledge process of *applying* students demonstrate and transform what they have learned—be it language forms, genre features, cultural products, practices, and perspectives, or a combination of these things—by using language in new and original ways (Cope and Kalantzis 2009, 2015; New London Group 1996). Applying activities thus allow students and teachers to enact one of the critical components of our definition of foreign language literacies: the creation of target language texts. We understand texts broadly, as we have throughout this book, to include not only written texts such as essays but also audio texts such as podcasts, conversational texts such as interviews, and multimodal texts such as infographics. Applying activities also integrate language and content by drawing on students' growing repertoire of meaning-making resources and by emphasizing multiple communicative modes and technological tools. Finally, the knowledge process of applying goes beyond the simple practice or regurgitation of language forms and instead encourages learners to meaningfully retool, remix, and personalize what they have learned from texts.

Depending on their focus, applying activities provide evidence of students' depth of textual understanding, their breadth of textual understanding, or both. When demonstrating their *depth of understanding*, learners apply in ways that are consistent with the ideas, genres, language forms, and skills they have encountered throughout a unit or lesson. When demonstrating their *breadth of understanding*, learners apply in innovative or nontraditional ways across multiple modes (e.g., written, visual, audio, gestural), thereby preparing them to engage with diverse peoples and contexts outside of the classroom context (Kalantzis and Cope 2021d, 2021e). The applying activity in the American Dream lesson plan presented in appendix B illustrates both aspects of applying: retooling the genre features of the dream statements students have interpreted demonstrates their depth of understanding, whereas presenting their own dream statement in a multimodal (text and image) format demonstrates students' breadth of understanding.

Focusing on students' depth and breadth of understanding in applying activities affords opportunities for formative and summative assessment of learning throughout a lesson or instructional unit. As we stated in chapter 5, *formative assessments* serve to monitor student learning during a lesson or unit; feedback from formative assessments helps students identify areas of struggle or gaps in learning and helps teachers address problems in real time. *Summative assessments* serve to evaluate student learning against a standard or benchmark (e.g., a rubric) at the close of a lesson or unit. Both forms of assessment can help teachers evaluate students' depth and breadth of understanding, although typically formative assessments are more focused on depth whereas summative assessments are more focused on breadth. For example, students might create a storyboard of a short story they have read, providing a visual representation of their depth of understanding. As a formative assessment, this activity allows students and their teacher to identify gaps or errors in understanding before moving on to deeper textual interpretation activities. At the close of the same short story lesson, learners might demonstrate their breadth of understanding by retelling the story in a different genre (e.g., movie, graphic novel, poem) or from the perspective of a different character. This summative assessment differs from the formative storyboard example because it requires students to apply what they learned about the language forms, genre conventions, and cultural content of the story in new and creative ways.

Differentiating Communicative Production and Applying Activities

What kinds of communicative production activities are present in your textbook or curriculum? What do these activities ask your learners to do? Are these activities meaningfully connected to the target language texts students have interacted with? In our experience, communicative production activities in secondary and postsecondary textbooks are quite different from the American dream statement, storyboard, and story retelling examples. The purpose of textbook activities such as writing a postcard, describing someone or something, or comparing information in a text to one's personal experiences is usually to encourage meaningful practice and replication of the grammar and vocabulary students have learned throughout the chapter. When these activities occur at the close of a reading, viewing, or listening lesson, they may ask students to communicate their opinions and personal experiences without explicitly connecting them to the textual content they've interpreted. Indeed, such communicative production activities typically lack grounding in the language, conventions, genre features, and cultural products, practices, and perspectives embedded in target language texts. Likewise, many textbook writing activities relate to the themes and grammatical forms presented in a chapter or unit but lack connection to a particular text studied in the chapter. Yet if students are to appropriately and creatively apply all the meaning-making resources they have learned throughout a lesson or unit, it is crucial that applying activities connect to the texts they have interpreted.

It may feel uncomfortable for you to rethink the way you design and implement communicative production activities to be more in line with literacies principles. To mitigate this discomfort, we provide some evidence of the impact of applying activities on student learning. Overall, encouraging the knowledge process of applying can improve students' communicative abilities in a language, their awareness of language forms and textual conventions, and their understanding of how those textual features express meaning in a text. Thus, through applying "learners . . . create and reshape meaning through explicit manipulation of forms" and "test hypotheses about the new language" (Kern 2000, 172). Several studies of postsecondary language learners support this overall claim. For example, research into the literacies-based undergraduate German curriculum at Georgetown University has shown that when students attend to the language and genre features of target language texts during interpretation activities and then transform these features during applying activities, the quality of their oral and written productions improves. Evidence of this improvement includes increases in the number of turns students take during conversational exchanges, enhanced coherence in their narrative writing, and the use of more complex grammatical structures over time (e.g., Byrnes, Maxim, and Norris 2010; Warren and Winkler 2016). In another study, Kumagai et al. (2016) described a digital storytelling project in a second-year intermediate Japanese class designed using multiliteracies pedagogy. The researchers analyzed one student's digital story and found that applying activities increased her awareness of how various multimodal textual features (e.g., narrative structure, images, music) work together to convey meaning and her ability to justify meaning-making choices. Finally, Zapata (2018) described a curriculum for heritage speakers of Spanish grounded in multiliteracies pedagogy. To investigate the impact of curricular materials on students' learning, the researcher analyzed several data sources, including students' written and multimodal narratives on the topic of immigration. Findings showed that students increased their metalinguistic awareness and could apply what they had learned through the study of narrative texts in innovative ways. Taken together, this research demonstrates not only students' language development but also their ability to "engage with, inquire into, and express themselves in multiple ways, increasing the likelihood that they will connect with and be understood by others" (Kalantzis and Cope 2021e).

The examples provided up to this point demonstrate the characteristics, importance, and effectiveness of applying activities, but their design and implementation may still be unclear to you. We thus now turn our attention to the practice of applying, focusing on characteristics of effective applying activities, concrete examples, scaffolding, and rubrics.

Designing and Implementing Applying Activities

To help you move from communicative production to the design and implementation of applying activities, we begin this section by looking more closely at common textbook activities. To summarize the definition of applying presented up to this point, consider the following list of keywords: creation, transformation, textual connection, multimodality, depth, and breadth. Using these keywords as a point of reference, reflect on why the following production activities, common in many communicative textbooks, are not good examples of applying:

1. Students perform the dialogue presented in their textbook by reading its different parts aloud.
2. Students read a travel brochure and then write a postcard to their family about a trip they have taken in the past.
3. Students watch a movie from the target language culture and then write one paragraph about why they did or did not like it.
4. Students listen to a podcast and then write questions using five of the verbs presented in the recording and interview their partner.

When students perform a dialogue, they are simply repeating what has been presented to them in their textbook; they are not using the language forms embedded in the dialogue to create something new or to demonstrate their knowledge. In fact, all a teacher can assess from such a performance is students' accurate pronunciation of the target language. Writing a postcard is more like the knowledge process of applying than performing a dialogue. In this writing activity, students showcase the depth of their grammatical and lexical knowledge; however, they do not demonstrate their cultural understanding of the travel brochure genre. Moreover, there is no explicit link to the text they have read and its meaning-making features. The third example, in which students write a paragraph about preferences, demonstrates even more clearly a lack of textual grounding. Although students might describe aspects of the movie they watched in their paragraph, there is no requirement to do so. Rather, students react personally to the video without explicitly connecting to its linguistic, organizational, or cultural features. As such, the teacher is unable to assess the depth or breadth of students' knowledge. Finally, when students write questions using verbs from a text, they are focused on grammar only; nothing about this production activity connects to the meaning conveyed in the podcast. Instead, students are practicing language forms rather than transforming what they've learned from a text in creative ways.

How might these common textbook production activities be transformed to better reflect the multiliteracies knowledge process of applying and its associated keywords? Table 10.1 presents alternatives to the four activities just critiqued as well as the applying keywords they reflect.

Table 10.1. Multiliteracies Alternatives to Common Textbook Production Activities

Original activity	Multiliteracies alternative	Relevant applying keywords
1. Students perform the dialogue presented in their textbook by reading its different parts aloud.	Students complete a *reader's theater* (Kern 2000; Tanner 1993) activity in which they do a dramatic reading of the dialogue that demonstrates their understanding. To enhance their interpretation, students add interjections, gestures, props, and so forth that they think are necessary for effectively conveying meaning.	Creation Textual connection Depth
2. Students read a travel brochure and then write a postcard to their family about a trip they have taken in the past.	After interpreting the travel brochure, students transform the genre by creating a promotional video for the travel destination.	Creation Transformation Textual Connection Multimodality Depth Breadth
3. Students watch a movie from the target culture and then write one paragraph about why they did or did not like it.	After watching and discussing the movie, students write a movie review for the target culture's version of IMDb, focusing on the story's chronology and how the filmmaker expressed that chronology in the script and through filmic conventions.	Creation Textual connection Depth
4. Students listen to a podcast and then write questions using five of the verbs presented in the recording and interview their partner.	After listening to and gaining a detailed understanding of the podcast, students then question the text. They ask questions focused on what additional information they want to know about the topic of the podcast and then use the ideas from their questions to write a comment for posting on the podcast's website.	Transformation Textual connection Multimodality Breadth

With this understanding of how communicative production activities can be modified to better reflect the knowledge process of applying, we turn now to different types of applying activities you can add to your teaching toolkit. You are likely comfortable with presentational writing as a form of applying. A few examples of presentational writing common in literacies-based instructional materials include genre reformulation, a personal action plan, and story retelling. You already read about two examples of *genre reformulation* earlier in this chapter: the reformulation of a short story into a movie, graphic novel, or poem and the transformation of a travel brochure into a promotional video. A *personal action plan* is a second type of presentational writing activity that helps learners turn an idea gleaned from a text into action by identifying a goal, the steps and resources needed to carry it out, and possible barriers to achieving the goal. Finally, a *story retelling* encourages students to rewrite a text from a different point of view, such as that of a different character, narrator, time period, or culture, using language forms and conventions learned through textual interpretation activities.

It might surprise you to know that story retelling can also be implemented as a presentational speaking activity in the form of a video recording or an in-class presentation, both of which can be carried out individually or in small groups. Other presentational speaking activities that reflect the knowledge process of applying are a news broadcast and a reading reaction. A news broadcast allows learners to research and present in depth a topic treated in a text they have interpreted. Students take on different roles in the news broadcast (e.g., anchor, interviewer, interviewee, commentator) to provide various perspectives on the topic. The news broadcast can be presented live in class or as a video recording. Reading reactions are often implemented as writing activities but can be transformed into presentational speaking when students audio or video record their response to a text. Although commonly implemented as experiencing activities (see chapter 7), reading reactions can also be applying. For instance, in addition to describing their understanding of and personal reaction to a text, learners can relate their knowledge and experience to a unit's (or lesson's) essential questions and learning objectives. Alternatively, they can be asked to relate their learning to previous course units or to other texts they have read, listened to, or viewed.

Interpersonal communication also plays a role in the knowledge process of applying. For example, interpersonal writing activities might include collaborative drafting, texting, and dialogue journals. *Collaborative drafting* activities involve the whole class or small groups of students working together to create a document, such as a letter to the principal about an issue at their school. The issue addressed should be one that students explored in the lesson's target language texts, such as school lunch programs or gender equity in sports. Texting or instant messaging are activities students carry out regularly in their everyday lives through their phones and social media. We can capitalize on this reality in the language classroom by having students first interpret a target language text about the abbreviations, emojis, and other conventions commonly used in texting from the target culture. Then students apply this knowledge by texting one another about the potential impact of these conventions on speakers' ability to communicate effectively. Like reading reactions, you may be familiar with *dialogue journals* as a form of written interpersonal communication between teacher and student. Dialogue journals are usually informal in nature, allowing students to react to, contemplate, and personalize their understanding of a text. To ensure that dialogue journals fit within the parameters of applying (rather than the knowledge process of experiencing), prompts should encourage students to further interpret issues taken up in target language texts and to draw on the meaning-making resources learned from texts to do so. Dialogue journals thus provide opportunities for open, teacher-student written dialogue and can serve as a low-stakes, formative assessment of the depth of students' learning.

Applying can also take the form of interpersonal speaking in activities such as fishbowl, role play, and debating. A *fishbowl* activity provides opportunities for multiple perspectives on a topic addressed in a text-based lesson and can serve as a formative assessment of students' depth of knowledge related to the vocabulary and cultural themes in a text. A common format for a fishbowl activity is to arrange classroom chairs in a circle with two "hot seats" in the middle. Two students take the hot seats and answer questions from their classmates about a multidimensional topic from a text (e.g., mask wearing during the COVID-19 pandemic, language standardization). After several minutes, two different students take the hot seats, and the activity continues. Role play provides students with another opportunity to explore a text's cultural content from multiple perspectives and to express those perspectives by taking on a specific role. For instance, if the class has been learning about mask wearing during the COVID-19 pandemic, they might carry out a role play in which one student is a public health expert, one is anti-mask, and another is pro-mask. For the role play to truly be an interpersonal speaking activity, students should not read a prepared script but instead refer to notes as they perform their role for the class. Finally, in a debate, students take a side on an issue explored in a unit and apply their knowledge of language features used to effectively take turns, express an opinion, and disagree. This summative assessment pushes students to both deepen and broaden their understanding of the issue and, in some cases, take a side that they do not personally agree with. Because debating also requires students to relate the issue to broader social and cultural contexts, this activity has characteristics of two knowledge processes: applying and analyzing.

Taken together, the examples in this section serve to both expand your teaching toolkit and demonstrate that applying is much more than presentational writing. Table 10.2 summarizes these examples and their relationship to the presentational and interpersonal modes of communication.

Scaffolding Applying Activities

Knowing what types of applying activities to implement with your students is the first step in integrating this knowledge process into your multiliteracies teaching practices. Another important consideration is how to scaffold instructional activities to ensure that students apply what they've learned during a lesson or unit. As we've stated throughout this book, the primary aim of a literacies approach to language education is the interpretation and creation of target language texts. But how do we

Table 10.2. Examples of Applying across Communicative Modes

Communicative mode	Modality	Examples
Presentational	Writing	Genre reformulation Movie review Personal action plan Story retelling
	Speaking	News broadcast Promotional video Reader's theater Reading reaction Story retelling
Interpersonal	Writing	Collaborative drafting Dialogue journals Texting/instant messaging
	Speaking	Debate Fishbowl Role play

move students from one to the other? Instructional scaffolding (Wood, Bruner, and Ross 1976) is crucial to answering this question. *Scaffolding* involves guided assistance by a peer or more capable other by "focusing learners' attention on the task, directing their attention to essential and relevant features, modeling expected behaviors, and keeping learners motivated throughout" (Hall 2001, 33). There are three important scaffolding considerations in relation to the knowledge process of applying: (1) textual interpretation activities that lead students to applying, (2) the structure of the applying activity itself, and (3) the relationship of the applying activity to your learning objectives and assessment plan.

The knowledge processes framework is a flexible pedagogy that allows teachers to choose and order activities based on their learning objectives and their students' needs. That said, applying activities most frequently occur at the end of a lesson or unit, so how do we scaffold the other knowledge processes within a lesson to successfully lead students to applying? Why are experiencing, conceptualizing, and analyzing important in preparing students to apply? Relating the knowledge processes to Bloom's Taxonomy of Educational Objectives shows that all four place different cognitive demands on students: experiencing activities require students to remember through recognizing and recalling information and to understand through inferring and summarizing information; conceptualizing activities require students to understand through classifying, exemplifying, comparing, and explaining language and conventions; analyzing activities require students to analyze cultural content through differentiating, organizing, and attributing and to evaluate that content through checking and critiquing; and applying activities require students to apply cultural and linguistic knowledge through executing and implementing and to create texts through generating, planning, and producing language and ideas (Anderson and Krathwohl 2001; Bloom 1956; Kalantzis et al. 2016).[1] Experiencing, conceptualizing, and analyzing can thus lay the groundwork for the more cognitively complex process of applying, providing scaffolding for students as they work to meet a lesson's learning objectives. For example, the applying activity in the American Dream lesson plan is to create a multimodal American dream statement. Prior to this summative assessment, students engage in experiencing activities to activate background knowledge related to the American dream before reading; they complete experiencing, conceptualizing, and analyzing activities to gain global and detailed understanding of facts and perspectives on the American dream; they carry out conceptualizing activities to understand and explain the genre features and grammatical forms in dream statements that they will later apply; and they do analyzing activities to evaluate and contextualize their learning and prepare for applying. Not only does the lesson provide scaffolding through the deliberate sequencing of the four knowledge processes, but it also illustrates how the individual activities of a lesson relate to one another in terms of the language forms, conventions, and cultural content students are learning. All of these forms of content are relevant for textual interpretation and creation.

Once you have ensured that the lesson is well scaffolded, it's time to turn to the structure of the applying activity itself. As is the case for the lesson as a whole, the steps of an applying activity should be scaffolded such that they relate to one another and provide a clear process for carrying out the activity. For instance, if students are completing a story retelling activity, simply providing a prompt (e.g., Retell the story from the perspective of your favorite character) is not adequate. Instead, it is important to identify the steps that lead to the creation of the final written or oral product. A suggested structure (Allen and Goodspeed 2018; Paesani, Allen, and Dupuy 2016) for doing this work is as follows:

1. Pool knowledge of relevant language forms, conventions, and cultural content studied throughout the lesson or unit.
2. Understand the genre of the final product, including is context, purpose, audience, and organization.
3. Plan for writing or speaking by researching new ideas, brainstorming content and organization, and drawing connections to information learned in the lesson or unit.
4. Draft and revise the final product.
5. Present or publish the product and reflect on the process.

Of course, not all of these steps are necessary for each applying activity you create. That said, this structure provides clear scaffolding for students and connects the product and process of the applying activity to the interpretive work students have done up to this point. For instance, in the American Dream lesson, students have already pooled knowledge (step 1) and analyzed the genre (step 2) in previous parts of the lesson. In the applying activity, students plan for writing or speaking by brainstorming their future dreams and aspirations (step 3) and draft the final product following the specific prompt in the lesson (step 4). Finally, students present their statement to classmates and reflect on their role in society (step 5). This five-stage structure for applying activities is summarized in table 10.3 and incorporated into a template for summative assessments on the companion website (https://carla.umn.edu/literacies/book/). We encourage you to use this template as a flexible tool for scaffolding summative applying activities for your learners.

A final consideration regarding scaffolding is ensuring that individual applying activities relate to your learning objectives and assessment plan. Doing so reflects the backward design model of curriculum construction presented in chapter 2 and ensures that all parts of a lesson, unit, or course are aligned. In chapter 5 we discussed principles of literacies-based assessment, including the importance of providing multiple opportunities for students to demonstrate their knowledge through different types of assessment activities. Following this recommendation ensures that you are assessing all of the learning objectives in a given lesson, unit, or course and that all learners have the opportunity to shine based on their different skills and abilities. In addition, through the use of formative and summative applying activities,

Table 10.3. Sample Instructional Sequence for Scaffolding Applying Activities

Stage number	Stage name	Function/purpose	Suggested knowledge processes
1	Pooling knowledge of relevant unit content	• Access background knowledge and prior experiences • Build new background knowledge	Experiencing Conceptualizing Analyzing
2	Understanding the product's genre	• Understand the context, purpose, and audience of the product • Review relevant text(s) for organization, genre conventions, and form-meaning connections	Experiencing Conceptualizing Analyzing
3	Planning for writing/speaking	• Research new ideas • Brainstorm content and organization • Draw connections between knowledge developed in the unit and its application in the final product	Experiencing Conceptualizing Applying
4	Drafting and revising	• Draft final product based on planning activities • Provide or review feedback from peers, teacher, or both • Revise final product based on feedback	Conceptualizing Analyzing Applying
5	Presenting and reflecting	• Publish or present product • Reflect on product and learning related to language, culture, and communication	Experiencing Applying Analyzing

students gain feedback on whether and to what degree they are meeting stated learning objectives, and teachers gain insights into the depth and breadth of students' understanding. In the American Dream lesson, for instance, the summative applying activity assesses students' depth of knowledge in relation to two learning objectives: the ability to express one's American dream and its motivation and the ability to employ images to support written or spoken texts.

Rubrics also play a role in scaffolding applying activities because they tell students how they will be evaluated, what is important in an assignment before they complete it, and which learning objectives are being assessed. Indeed, rubrics provide a means for concretely showing how learning objectives and assessments are aligned with each other and how a specific applying activity puts that alignment into practice. When constructing rubrics that reflect literacies principles and capture the purpose and focus of applying activities, it's important to consider (1) how students are demonstrating the depth and breadth of their knowledge and (2) what form this knowledge takes. To answer the question of how, rubrics should focus on the language forms, conventions, and cultural products, practices, and perspectives that form the basis of the text-based lesson, unit, or course and that are relevant to the specific applying activity. To answer the question of what form, rubrics should focus on the process of completing the applying activity and the successful creation of a product that reflects the genre of the activity. The rubric in appendix C reflects these ideas: the first three categories of the rubric—Content Knowledge, Language Control, and Task Appropriateness—evaluate how students are demonstrating their knowledge; the last category—Task Completion—as well as parts of the third category evaluate the form that this knowledge takes. For students to successfully apply their knowledge of language forms, conventions, and cultural products, practices, and perspectives, rubrics should also reflect the unit, lesson, or course learning objectives and support students as they create their own target language texts. We thus encourage you to adapt the rubric in appendix C to meet your specific needs, keeping in mind the literacies principles you've learned throughout this book as well as the learning objectives and linguistic, cultural, and textual content your assessment is targeting. A downloadable version of this rubric is available on the companion website (https://carla.umn.edu/literacies/book/) to facilitate this adaptive work.

Spotlight on Teacher Professional Development

To conclude our discussion of the knowledge process of applying, we once again turn to the research on teacher learning around multiliteracies pedagogy and its implications for professional development. One of the research findings we highlighted in chapter 1 is that teachers find it challenging to implement literacies concepts in the classroom (Allen 2011; Dupuy and Allen 2012; Menke 2018; Paesani 2013). For example, this challenge is evident in novice and experienced graduate teaching assistants taking methods coursework grounded in literacies concepts: both groups claimed to be using the knowledge processes—including applying—in their teaching; however, their actual classroom practices were not aligned with the literacies concepts underlying these knowledge processes (Allen and Dupuy 2013; Dupuy and Allen 2012).

Contributors to this misalignment may include the constraints imposed by the textbook being used and the relationship between instructional practices and assessments. For instance, in one study, novice graduate teaching assistants "grappl[ed] with the contradiction between the approach of the textbook and principles of literacy-based teaching" (Allen 2011, 100). Not only did participants find their textbook less useful for implementing multiliteracies pedagogy than they had hoped, but they also found it lacked authenticity and engagement. Participants also reported "a lack of alignment between literacy-based instruction and assessments designed at times by colleagues who did not hold the same concept of literacy-based teaching" (Allen 2011, 100). In other words, there was sometimes a mismatch between participants' understandings and applications of literacies concepts and those of other instructors in their program. The study participants, however, saw this challenge as an opportunity to confront their colleagues' more traditional conceptualizations of language education and to model literacies-oriented instructional and assessment practices.

Additional research findings suggest that formal learning experiences (e.g., reading and discussing research), although valuable for solidifying conceptual understanding, are insufficient. Instead, a combination of formal and experiential learning is needed to provide teachers with opportunities to apply literacies concepts to classroom practice. That is, a praxis orientation (i.e., the reciprocal relationship between research and practice) is ideal for facilitating teacher learning. For instance, Allen's (2011) study participants found activities like sharing literacies lessons with peers and designing a literacies-oriented course syllabus were most useful for moving from comprehension to application of literacies concepts. Likewise, for Dupuy and Allen's (2012) participants, examining concrete examples of and creating their own lessons contributed to praxis-based understandings of literacies concepts and pedagogical tools.

What do these research findings mean for teacher professional development? How can you use them to improve teachers' understanding and implementation of applying activities? One strategy for honing teachers' understanding of the knowledge process of applying is to analyze and then implement the five-step structure for creating applying activities presented earlier (pool knowledge, understand the genre, plan for writing, draft and revise, present and reflect). Within the context of a methods course, for instance, teachers and teacher educators can discuss how various literacies concepts (e.g., foreign language literacies, meaning design, interpretation, creation, form-meaning connections, textual features) are reflected in the five steps. Next, they can critique their own instructional practices by identifying which of the steps they typically carry out when creating applying activities and which they do not. Once they've analyzed the five steps, teachers can use this structure to create their own applying activities, provide feedback on their colleagues' activities, and revise based on feedback received. Not only does this process of analysis and implementation support a praxis-oriented approach to teacher professional development, but it also helps teachers deepen their understanding of the knowledge process of applying by becoming more aware of their existing knowledge and practices.

A second strategy for honing teachers' understanding and implementation of applying activities is to analyze and adapt communicative production activities in the textbooks they use. As with the first strategy, working from familiar materials taps into teachers' existing knowledge and practices. It also illustrates that when adopting multiliteracies pedagogy, one needn't start from scratch. We introduced the idea of working from existing textbook materials in chapter 9 with the Lesson Analysis Checklist (https://carla.umn.edu/literacies/book/) from CARLA's Literacies in Language Education project. Here, we home in on applying activities using a checklist grounded in the principles presented in this chapter. The checklist is presented in table 10.4 as well as on the companion website (https://carla.umn.edu/literacies/book/).

To use the checklist, teachers first identify the orientation of activities in their textbook based on whether they are more reflective of communicative production or applying. When this analysis is complete, teachers can then identify gaps in a textbook activity and brainstorm ways to adapt it in line with the knowledge process of applying. The tool in table 10.4 can be used in various contexts in which teachers are learning about multiliteracies pedagogy: a methods course in which teachers are introduced to the approach, a professional learning circle among colleagues, meetings between a team of teachers and their supervisor, and so on. Through the two professional development strategies presented in this section, teacher educators can overcome some of the challenges identified in the research summarized earlier, and teachers can more effectively craft applying activities that allow students to create texts and showcase new knowledge.

Table 10.4. Working with the Textbook: Communicative Production versus Applying Activities

Part I: Use the checklist below to determine if your textbook activity is more reflective of communicative production or applying.

Characteristics of communicative production	Characteristics of applying
Unclear or weak connection to unit text(s)	Clear or strong connection to unit text(s)
Practice or replication of unit grammar and vocabulary	Transformation or retooling of textual language, conventions, and cultural content
Focus on personal reactions or opinions	Focus on breadth and depth of textual understanding
Language-content separation	Language-content integration

Part II: If your activity is more reflective of communicative production, what steps must you take to adapt it to be more reflective of applying?

Conclusion

In this chapter, we concluded our examination of the four knowledge processes of multiliteracies pedagogy by focusing on applying. Although applying activities are likely familiar to you, this chapter revealed that applying is quite different from the kinds of communicative production activities found in many textbooks. Among these differences is the focus on students demonstrating both the depth and breadth of their textual understanding across communicative modes. The examples and strategies presented in this chapter illustrate how to achieve this focus and encourage you to expand your current understandings and practices en route to effectively developing your students' foreign language literacies. In the epilogue we consider applying and the other knowledge processes of multiliteracies pedagogy within the broader field of language education and discuss questions and strategies for moving the field toward literacies-oriented curriculum, assessment, and instruction.

Reflecting on Research and Practice

1. How has your understanding of applying evolved since you were first introduced to the concept in chapter 1? How has it evolved based on your reading of this chapter?
2. What aspects of the knowledge process of applying are still unclear? What professional development activities or resources presented in this chapter can help solidify your understanding?
3. What applying activities from this chapter or from CARLA's Literacies Activity Repository will you implement in your teaching moving forward? What modifications do you need to make to those activities to fit the specific needs of your learners?
4. Review the three scaffolding considerations presented in this chapter. Which do you already carry out in your lesson and activity planning? How can you improve the way that you scaffold applying activities?
5. What applying activities from this chapter or CARLA's Literacies Activity Repository can you adopt or adapt as formative and summative assessments of your students' depth and breadth of understanding? How will you ensure that these activities align with stated learning objectives? How will these activities fit within your overall unit or course assessment plan?

Resources

1. CARLA's Literacies Activity Repository (https://carla.umn.edu/literacies/book/)

   This repository provides examples of activities from all four knowledge processes, including applying. Activities are pulled from literacies-oriented lesson plans created by practitioners and researchers.

2. Sample Applying Activities (https://newlearningonline.com/learning-by-design/the-knowledge-processes/applying; https://newlearningonline.com/learning-by-design/the-knowledge-processes/applying-creatively)

   Kalantzis and Cope (2021d, 2021e) detail sample applying activities on these two web pages. Although not designed specifically for language learners, these activities can be adapted using the principles and strategies presented in this chapter.

3. "Interpreting Literature: View & Analyze the Video" (https://www.learner.org/series/teaching-foreign-languages-k-12-a-library-of-classroom-practices/spanish-interpreting-literature/view-analyze-video/)

   This video shows a high school Spanish lesson that incorporates two applying activities grounded in the texts students have worked with: an oral report and alternate story endings. The video provides an excellent model of how to scaffold a lesson that moves from interpretation to creation.

Further Reading and Viewing

1. "Putting Multiliteracies into Practice: Digital Storytelling for Multilingual Adolescents in a Summer Program" (Angay-Crowder, Choi, and Yi 2013)

   This article from *TESL Canada Journal* describes a digital storytelling project for middle school students that integrates the four knowledge processes of multiliteracies pedagogy. The project involves both presentational writing and speaking and provides an example of a multimodal applying activity.

2. "Analytical and Applied Learning" (https://newlearningonline.com/literacies/chapter-3/analytical-and-applied-learning)

   In this video, Kalantzis and Cope (2016a) explain the knowledge process of applying (start at minute 3:05 and watch until 5:31). In it, they discuss the two applying subprocesses: applying appropriately, which focuses on students' depth of knowledge, and applying creatively, which focuses on students' breadth of knowledge.

3. "Teaching Writing as Designing Meaning through Texts" in *A Multiliteracies Framework for Collegiate Foreign Language Teaching* (Paesani, Allen, and Dupuy 2016, 168–99)

   This chapter homes in on presentational writing as a form of applying. The chapter provides an overview of writing research in language education, example lessons and activities, and a lesson plan template that can be used to craft multistage writing activities and assessments grounded in target language texts.

Note

1. See chapter 3 for a discussion of Bloom's taxonomy in relation to literacies learning objectives and the four knowledge processes.

Epilogue
Advancing Literacies in Language Education

AS YOU REACH THE final pages of this book, you may be considering the next steps for advancing literacies in your language classes, asking yourself questions such as the following: What have I already learned? What do I still need to learn? And how can a literacies orientation frame my work as a language teacher or language teacher educator? We are asking ourselves similar questions as we consider ways to advance literacies in the field of language education beyond this book: What have we already accomplished? What work still needs to be done? And how can we facilitate widespread adoption of literacies principles in language programs? The purpose of this epilogue is to begin to answer these questions by briefly reviewing what we know about literacies in language education and providing practical suggestions for moving the field toward curricula, instructional practices, and assessments that reflect literacies principles.

This work began over twenty five years ago after the publication of the New London Group's (1996) manifesto, "A Pedagogy of Multiliteracies: Designing Social Futures," which aimed to change both the goals and processes of literacies education. Rather than conveying information to be memorized and reproduced, the New London Group argued that literacies education must acknowledge our increasingly globalized and diverse societies and the greater variety of text types that exist, due in large part to changing technologies. Doing so allows learners to "see themselves as active participants in social change, as . . . active designers—makers—of social futures" and ensures "that all students benefit from learning in ways that allow them to fully participate in public, community, and economic life" (60). Over time, this educational philosophy took hold not only in first language literacies education but also in diverse disciplines such as the arts (e.g., Crafton, Silvers, and Brennan 2009), mathematics (e.g., Joutsenlahti and Kulju 2017), science (e.g., Hilton, Nichols, and Gitsaki 2010), special education (e.g., Lawson et al. 2012), teacher education (e.g., Cloonan 2010), and importantly for this book, language teaching and learning.

Two important phenomena sparked the move toward literacies in language education. The first was the publication of Kern's seminal book, *Literacy and Language*

Teaching (2000), which repackaged principles from the New London Group's manifesto and applied them to language curriculum, assessment, and instruction. Importantly, Kern presented the definition of foreign language literacies that has informed not only this book but also much of the scholarship in this area. Kern furthermore argued that adopting a literacies orientation can serve to unify language programs, including the sometimes-disparate educational aims of developing students' communicative and textual analysis abilities. The second important phenomenon was the overhaul and widespread documentation of the undergraduate German curriculum at Georgetown University (Department of German 2011b), one of the first, and most well-known, US postsecondary programs to adopt foreign language literacies as its overarching goal. This multiyear curriculum revision project is oft cited in the literacies literature and has served as a model for other language programs (e.g., Maxim et al. 2013; Paesani 2017).

This book provides another resource for constructing programs that develop students' foreign language literacies. Throughout, we have explored how you can transition your curricula, assessments, and instructional practices (chapter 2) to reflect this overarching goal by establishing literacies learning objectives (chapter 3), selecting rich textual content (chapter 4), overhauling your assessment plan (chapter 5), and planning for and implementing literacies learning experiences (chapters 6–10). This kind of curricular and pedagogical change, however, is slow, and we recognize that reading this book is just one step in reenvisioning and retooling your work as language educators in line with literacies principles. To help you move forward, this epilogue summarizes what we know about literacies in language education and identifies future needs in relation to three main topics: teachers, students, and pedagogy.

Advancing Teacher Knowledge and Resources

As the Spotlight on Teacher Professional Development section in each of this book's chapters has indicated, teachers react positively to literacies-oriented curriculum and instruction and recognize its impact on learning, feelings of accomplishment, interest in language study, higher-order thinking abilities, and connections to other disciplines (Kim and Xing 2019; Menke 2018; Menke and Paesani 2021). Nonetheless, you have also read that learning about and enacting literacies pedagogy can be challenging, in part because teachers' "entrenched practices [prove] difficult to alter" (Swaffar 2014, 13). In addition to reconciling previous beliefs, values, and experiences with new literacies concepts, teachers find literacies terminology to be complex and sometimes difficult to apply in the classroom. The teacher-friendly language and practical tools presented in this book are one step toward making this approach accessible. Yet there is also an important need for sustained teacher professional development beyond this book around literacies pedagogy (e.g., Allen 2011; Allen and Dupuy 2013; Paesani and Allen 2020). In addition to adopting foreign language literacies as a guiding principle in pre- and in-service methods courses, it is also important to provide what Johnson and Golombek (2020) call structured mediational spaces, where teachers can practice the work of language instruction with feedback and support from peers and teacher educators. Examples of such structured and mediated professional development include a yearlong workshop series addressing one or more literacies concepts (Nauman 2011) and professional learning circles in which participants discuss and experiment with literacies instructional practices (Menke 2018). Lacorte (2018) suggested that these activities should model the four knowledge processes of experiencing, conceptualizing, analyzing, and applying to provide pre- and in-service teachers with the opportunity to experience literacies pedagogy themselves. After completing such activities, teachers can then reflect critically on their experience and relate it to their own teaching and students.

Another strategy for overcoming the challenges teachers face in relation to literacies principles and practices is to provide them with praxis-oriented resources. Identified as a primary need among postsecondary language instructors (Paesani and Menke 2019), such resources help teachers make the connection between theoretical concepts and research-based evidence, on the one hand, and beliefs, experiences, and classroom instruction, on the other. There is a growing body of published, praxis-oriented resources in teaching methods books (e.g., Paesani, Allen, and Dupuy 2016) and scholarly articles and book chapters (e.g., Kumagai, López-Sánchez, and Wu 2016; Michelson 2018; Redmann 2005b). However, these resources are not always freely available and, with a few exceptions, are focused on postsecondary language learning contexts in more commonly taught languages. The companion website to this book (https://carla.umn.edu/literacies/book/), CARLA's Literacies in Language Education project (https://carla.umn.edu/literacies/), and the FLLITE project (https://fllite.org/) are three examples of free, praxis-based resources that are applicable across levels and languages. One resource in the Literacies in Language Education project is the activity repository we have referred to throughout this book. This repository exemplifies the knowledge processes with multiple practical examples to help teachers implement multiliteracies pedagogy. To increase the benefit of this resource, it would also be helpful to include videos of teachers enacting each knowledge process as well as teacher commentary on how this enactment expands their understanding of literacies principles. Also needed are additional examples of literacies assessments. Although this book provides tips for building a literacies assessment plan (chapter 5), a template and sample rubric for creating literacies assessments (see appendix C and the Template for Summative Assessments on the companion website), and several examples of both formative and summative assessments (chapter 2, chapter 5, chapter 10, appendixes A and B), more examples are needed. Indeed, there is a dearth of resources illustrating how to design, scaffold, and implement assessments that reflect literacies principles and that are aligned with the four knowledge processes. Publishing praxis-based materials as open educational resources (OERs) is one way to increase access to all of these needed professional development supports. Moreover, OERs increase teacher agency in that existing resources can be adapted (and reshared) to fit teachers' contextual needs (WikiEducator 2010). Teachers can also create and share their own resources, thereby contributing to the literacies knowledge and resource base.

Advancing Student Learning

Although much of this book has focused on teachers and teaching (e.g., building a literacies knowledge base, effectively enacting literacies principles in the classroom), adopting a literacies orientation to language education is meaningless if it is not beneficial to learners. Luckily, a robust body of research illustrates that this approach benefits learners in multiple ways. Overall, this research shows that students have positive perceptions toward literacies-oriented curriculum and instruction: they see it as beneficial to their language and culture learning and enjoy interpreting and creating multimodal texts (Leier 2018; Paesani 2015, 2016; Zapata and Ribota 2021). Students also identify personal benefits to language study grounded in literacies principles, such as improving their time management skills, increasing collaboration with peers, fostering creativity, and feeling empowered (Chi 2012; Choi 2015; Turpin 2019; Zapata and Ribota 2021). Other studies have shown that, with teacher guidance, students recognize that grammar and other textual features are important meaning-making resources that help them read and write more effectively (Paesani 2015, 2016; Yáñez Prieto 2010, 2015).

As you read in many of this book's chapters, a literacies approach also positively affects students' language acquisition and proficiency development. In addition to documenting its curricular revision, members of the Georgetown University German program referenced earlier also conducted extensive research on students' learning as they experienced the curriculum. Findings showed improvements in the linguistic dimension of foreign language literacies development: students' writing improved and became more complex over time, and students exhibited advanced-level abilities as a result of instruction focused on textual interpretation and creation (e.g., Byrnes, Maxim, and Norris 2010; Liamkina 2008; Warren and Winkler 2016). Research from this and other language programs also illustrates that a literacies orientation can help students identify and use language features specific to different genres, thereby increasing their linguistic repertoire and meaning-making capabilities (e.g., Allen and Goodspeed 2018; Maxim 2006; Ryshina-Pankova 2010). Relatedly, empirical research also documents the benefits of revision and editing in relation to writing improvement and language acquisition (Turpin 2019; Zapata and Ribota 2021).

Less research exists on the sociocultural dimension of literacies-oriented curriculum, instruction, and assessment. The few studies published in this area show that students gain awareness of how language use varies across contexts and modalities such as formal versus informal encounters and written versus oral language (Michelson 2018, 2019; Michelson and Dupuy 2014; Zapata and Ribota 2021). Other studies have shown that using a literacies approach to expose students to language varieties used by real speakers can destabilize the native-speaker model; help students see themselves in the texts they read, listen to, and view; and encourage appropriation of language forms beyond the standard variety (Losada Rivas and Suaza Cardozo 2018; Rilliard 2021; Turpin 2019).

Despite these encouraging findings, more research into the sociocultural dimension of foreign language literacies development and its impact on student learning is needed to better understand not only how students benefit from this approach but also how teachers can leverage these findings to create effective pedagogical materials. Also missing from the research on student learning is an understanding of the cognitive dimension of foreign language literacies development. Although research shows that a literacies orientation can improve students' linguistic abilities, it's not yet clear how this shapes the cognitive demands placed on students or the strategies they use to navigate literacies learning activities. This line of research would help teachers understand how to scaffold lessons to meet the needs of diverse learners (e.g., younger versus older, more versus less proficient) and how to interweave strategy instruction to bolster student learning. Equally important in understanding the impact of a literacies orientation on student learning, particularly as it pertains to the goal of preparing students "to fully participate in public, community, and economic life" (New London Group 1996, 60), is looking toward other disciplines. That is, what does the research tell us about student learning in disciplines such as art, mathematics, science, or special education? How might those findings inform language education? What transferable skills result from a focus on literacies development across disciplines? Exploring such questions will ensure that we are meeting our students' needs both now and in the future.

Advancing Multiliteracies Pedagogy

If you were to do a search of this book, the word "critical" would pop up repeatedly. Throughout, we have emphasized the importance of literacies in language education for promoting critical thinking, critical engagement with texts, critical reflection, and the like. This focus is consistent with the idea that "world language education is not only about the teaching and learning of a second or additional linguistic system, but it is also about social and cultural knowledge, and, perhaps even more, about helping students to develop critical approaches to examining and understanding such knowledge" (Reagan and Osborn 2021, 215). In fact, the literacies approach we have outlined in this book is an example of a *critical pedagogy*. Critical pedagogies have become more prevalent in recent years given the increased interest in social justice in language education and elsewhere. Exactly what are critical pedagogies? Many definitions exist, and some salient characteristics include understanding "the deep meaning, root causes, social contexts, ideology, and personal consequences" of texts, events, actions, and the like (Shor 1992, 129); "transforming existing social inequalities and injustices" (McLaren 2003, 186); and "asking fundamental questions about knowledge, justice, and equity" (Wink 2000, 71). In a nutshell, critical pedagogies are about equipping students with the skills needed to interrogate the knowledge they receive and create.

In language education, critical pedagogies prioritize language development for the purposes of engaging with target language cultures and recognizing students' multilingual and multicultural identities. They additionally develop students' ability to think critically, communicate clearly, and address complex social issues. By integrating target language texts through the literacies orientation described in this book, language education is centered around rich content that can be critically examined and is reflective of multiple voices, perspectives, experiences, and ways of using language. A literacies orientation can thus free language educators from the constraints of the textbook, which is the de facto curriculum in most language classrooms and which often presents sanitized, hegemonic, and superficial information about target language speakers and cultures (Ornstein 1994). Instead, we can use the textbook as a flexible tool to be adapted and augmented based on the target language texts and textual features we bring into the curriculum and the needs and interests of our students.

As we illustrated in chapters 6–10, the knowledge processes of multiliteracies pedagogy provide a structure for critically engaging students with target language texts. This activity framework is also compatible with other critical approaches, such as teaching for social justice, which has become a central focus of language education in recent years (Glynn, Wesely, and Wassell 2018; Goodspeed et al. 2021; Randolph and Johnson 2017). Clearly, the knowledge process of analyzing is an important component of critical and social justice approaches because it allows students to situate cultural products, practices, and perspectives within a larger social context and to consider why and how different voices are included or excluded. It is perhaps less obvious that conceptualizing is another knowledge process with implications for critical and social justice approaches. Through conceptualizing activities learners can identify the meanings that specific language forms or conventions express, what perspectives they convey, and how they might contribute to or challenge linguistic and social marginalization. In so doing, students develop skills in critical thinking and analysis, a key component of Hackman's (2005) model of social justice education. Viewed in this way, conceptualizing can also address the diversity and identity standards from the Learning for Justice (2021) framework as students learn that language is more than a tool for communication but can also signal individual differences and group membership or exclusion. Taken together, the four knowledge processes, as well as the overarching concept of foreign language literacies, seek to empower all learners and prepare them to be engaged participants in their current and future academic, professional, personal, and civic lives. These goals align with those of social justice approaches, which seek to challenge, confront, and disrupt misconceptions, untruths, and stereotypes; provide all students with the resources needed to learn to their full potential; draw on students' unique talents and strengths; and promote critical thinking and agency for social change (Nieto 2010).

To advance literacies in language education and facilitate its widespread adoption, maximizing the affinities among social justice, critical pedagogies, and literacies principles is crucial. Supporting this work will involve additional research to investigate how literacies pedagogy contributes both to teacher and student learning in relation to social justice topics and to the creation of praxis-oriented resources to help teachers effectively implement literacies in language education with a social justice focus. Several professional groups exist to support teachers in this kind of work, including ACTFL's Critical and Social Justice Approaches special interest group (https://tinyurl.com/2az5bz7n) and language-specific groups such as the Diversity, Decolonization, and the French Curriculum collective (https://ddfccollective.weebly.com/) and the Diversity, Decolonization, and the German Curriculum scholarly collective and forum (https://diversityingermancurriculum.weebly.com/). Moreover,

CARLA's Social Justice in Language Education project (https://carla.umn.edu/socialjustice/) creates and disseminates praxis-based resources that marry social justice and multiliteracies pedagogies. These resources include a scholarly and practical bibliography, planning templates, curricular units in multiple languages, a repository of target language texts on social justice topics, and professional development workshops.

Conclusion

A literacies approach to language education has the potential to transform language teaching and learning and to significantly affect students' lives. This book is one contribution to realizing this potential, but more work is needed. Throughout this book we have invited you to engage in this work by experiencing new ideas, concepts, and instructional examples; conceptualizing relationships among literacies concepts, pedagogical practice, and student learning; and analyzing how your goals and practices align with literacies principles. It is now up to you to showcase the knowledge and skills you have acquired through reading this book by applying them to your own teaching context, reflecting critically on their efficacy, and retooling as needed. In so doing, you will play an essential part in advancing literacies in language education.

Appendixes

A

Literacies-Based Curricular Unit

THE MODEL UNIT IS provided in an abbreviated format here. The complete unit, which is presented using the planning template referenced throughout the book and which includes links to all target language texts, is available on the companion website (https://carla.umn.edu/literacies/book/).

Unit Title: Immigration in the United States

Learning Context

- Language: English as a second language
- Level: US high school; intermediate-level course
- Unit duration: four and a half weeks (twenty-two sixty-minute class periods)

Essential Questions

- What is the immigrant experience in the United States?
- How do immigrant experiences differ across individuals?

Unit Learning Objectives

At the end of this unit, in oral and/or written communicative modes, students will be able to . . .

1. Discuss facts about immigration in the United States presented in narrative, visual, and audiovisual texts
2. Describe and analyze narrative, visual, and audiovisual texts presenting different perspectives on the immigrant experience in the United States
3. Explain and critique definitions of the American dream presented in narrative, visual, and audiovisual texts and relate them to different immigrant experiences
4. Plan and produce a multimodal narrative of their own experience as immigrants or children of immigrants in the United States

Unit Content: Texts

Infographics (written + visual):

- "Explore Immigration Data" (by decade, by region) (Lesson 1; US Department of Homeland Security n.d.)
- "Ten Things You Probably Didn't Know About Immigrants" (Lesson 1; National Academy of Sciences 2021)
- "What Immigration Means to the United States" (Lesson 1; American Immigration Council 2017)
- "The US Immigration System" (Lesson 1; US Department of Homeland Security 2017)
- "What Americans Think of the American Dream" (Lesson 4; The Center for a New American Dream 2014)

Interactive website with maps, images, and descriptive text (written + visual):

- Interactive Tour of Ellis Island (Lesson 2; Scholastic Inc. n.d.)

Digital Stories (audiovisual):

- Profiles from the Immigrant Stories Collection (Lesson 3; Immigration History Research Center n.d.)

Journalistic Essay (written + visual):

- "American Dreams" (I. Brown 2016)

Unit Content: Language, Conventions, Culture

Language Forms

- numbers and percentages (Lesson 1)
- subject-verb agreement (Lesson 1)
- expressions of quantity (Lesson 1)
- comparative and superlative expressions (Lessons 1 and 5)
- demographics vocabulary (Lesson 1)
- past and present tense verb forms (Lessons 2, 3, 4 and 5)
- simple versus complex sentence structures (Lesson 2)
- place names (Lesson 2)
- descriptive vocabulary (Lessons 2, 3 and 5)
- first-person narration (Lesson 3 and 5)
- infinitival clauses (Lessons 4 and 5)
- American dream vocabulary (Lessons 4 and 5)

Conventions

- pie charts and graphs (Lesson 1)
- bolding and color font (Lesson 1)
- relationship between image and text (Lessons 1, 4 and 5)

- points on a map (Lesson 2)
- photo captioning (Lessons 2 and 4)
- simple and complex sentences (Lesson 2)
- multimedia digital stories (Lessons 3 and 5)
- dream statement and motivation (Lesson 4)

Cultural Products, Practices, and Perspectives

- demographic and historical information about immigration in the United States (Lesson 1)
- Ellis Island (Lesson 2)
- concept of the "melting pot" (Lesson 2)
- personal stories (Lessons 2, 3, 4 and 5); digital stories (Lesson 3)
- concept of the American dream (Lessons 4 and 5)

Unit Assessment Plan

Formative Assessments:

- Homework (10% of overall unit grade; assesses learning objective 1)
- In-class participation (20% of overall unit grade; assesses learning objectives 1, 2, 3, and 4)
- Quizzes (5% of overall unit grade; assesses learning objective 1)

Summative Assessments:

- Interview of a family member/friend (20% of overall unit grade; assesses learning objectives 1, 2, and 3)
- American dream statement (20% of overall unit grade; assesses learning objectives 2, 3, and 4)
- Digital story (25% of overall unit grade; assesses learning objectives 2 and 4)

Unit Implementation Plan

1. Lesson 1—Overview of Immigration in the United States: Information about immigration/immigrants in the United States, including demographics and historical trends (three days; targets learning objective 1)
2. Lesson 2—Ellis Island: A historical look at the significance of Ellis Island as the arrival point of immigrants to the United States, including personal immigration stories and a critical look at the concept of the "melting pot" (five days; targets learning objectives 1 and 2)
3. Lesson 3—Who Are Immigrants to the United States?: Profiles of immigrants from different parts of the world, their experiences, their views of the United States (five days; targets learning objectives 2 and 3)
4. Lesson 4—The American Dream: Understanding and critiquing the concept of the American dream from multiple perspectives (five days; targets learning objectives 2, 3, and 4)

5. Lesson 5—Digital Storytelling Project: Creation of personal stories based on students' experiences and perspectives as immigrants to the United States or children of immigrants to the United States. Topics to address include country of origin, experiences and views about life in the United States, and definition of the American dream (four days; targets learning objectives 2 and 4)

B

Literacies-Based Lesson Plan

THIS SAMPLE LESSON PLAN is provided in an abbreviated format here. The complete lesson, which is presented using the planning template referenced throughout the book and which includes all handouts and links to target language texts, is available on the companion website (https://carla.umn.edu/literacies/book/).

Lesson Title: The American Dream

Learning Context

- Language: English as a second language
- Level: US high school; intermediate-level course
- Duration: five class periods (sixty minutes each)

Lesson Learning Objectives

At the end of this lesson students will be able to . . .

1. Define key features of the American dream using vocabulary presented in written and visual texts
2. Express their own American dream and its motivation using infinitival clauses and past tense verb forms orally and in writing
3. Employ images/photos to support their written or spoken text
4. Orally discuss relationships between text, captions, and images in texts addressing the American dream

Lesson Content

Texts

- "What Americans Think of the American Dream" (Lesson 4; The Center for a New American Dream, 2014)
- "American Dreams" (I. Brown 2016)

Language Forms

- Vocabulary: personal freedom, basic needs, potential and possibilities, affluence, sacrifice, equality
- Grammar: infinitival clauses (My American dream is + [infinitive] OR [clause]; I want to [infinitive]); past tense narration

Conventions

- Images to convey meanings, photos and captions, dream statement, motivation for dream

Cultural Products, Practices, and Perspectives

- The American dream

Instructional Sequence

Stage 1: Preparing to Interact with Texts

1. Students bring an image that represents their reasons or hopes for coming to the United States (or those of a family member or friend). In class, the teacher shares an example, accompanied by images to represent that reason. In groups of three or four, students share their images and the reasons or hopes they represent and compile a list of reasons and hopes of immigrants. Each group reports back to the class, with the teacher creating a whole class list and tally. (Experiencing; Day 1)
2. The teacher introduces the phrase "the American dream" and asks groups to brainstorm words they associate with this concept based on their experiences. Then students share ideas as a whole class. The teacher may prompt students to move beyond the what (What are the dreams?) to the how (How are they realized?). (Experiencing; Day 1)
3. Students work in small groups to create a concept map, diagramming relationships between the various concepts named in the previous steps. After mapping their elements, students identify images that might represent each concept. (Conceptualizing; Day 1)
4. Small groups draft a definition of "the American dream" to share with the class. (Conceptualizing; Day 1)

Stage 2: Building Global Comprehension

1. The teacher introduces the infographic "What Americans Think of the American Dream." With only the images displayed, students are first asked to describe what they see and predict what aspect of the American dream each image portrays. The teacher then reveals the labels associated with each image, and students compare them with their predictions: Do they match? If not, how might the image be changed to better reflect the label? The teacher defines unfamiliar vocabulary as the class collaboratively works through this. (Conceptualizing and Analyzing; Day 2)

2. Students read the infographic and react to its content in small groups: What concepts are reflected in your definition of the American dream? What surprises you? Students are invited to revise the definitions crafted during Day 1. (Experiencing and Analyzing; Day 2)
3. The teacher presents the statement: "The American dream is the same for all." Students are asked to move to a corner of the room that aligns with their level of agreement: strongly agree, agree, disagree, strongly disagree. In their corners, groups identify evidence to support their viewpoint and/or identify factors that might influence an individual's American dream. (Analyzing; Day 2)
4. The teacher introduces the "American Dreams" piece from the *New York Times* (*NYT*), overviewing the motivation for and process of creating the collection. As a class, students identify the audience and author(s) of the collection as presented in the *NYT* and predict content and tone (prereading activities in the handout). (Analyzing; Day 2)
5. The teacher draws student attention to the entry for Skylar Kergil. Students individually read this entry and regroup as a whole class to collectively identify details about Skylar, Skylar's dream, which of the ideas from the American dream infographic encompasses Skylar's dream, why this dream is important to Skylar, and what Skylar had to do to achieve his dream. (Experiencing; Day 2)

Stage 3: Understanding Meaningful Details

1. As homework, students complete the first part of a jigsaw activity and become experts on two texts from the *NYT* "American Dreams" piece. They complete a handout in which they note the following details for each text: author's identity, the author's dream, the dream's category, why it's important, and how the dream was or will be accomplished. (Experiencing; homework in preparation for Day 3)
2. In class, students form an expert group with peers who read the same texts to ensure comprehension by all in group. (Experiencing; Day 3)

Stage 4: Making Form-Meaning Connections

1. The teacher directs students' attention to how individual texts are written. Through an instructional conversation, they first identify the components of each text: author's name and location, dream statement(s), motivation, photograph with caption, photo of handwritten text. In small groups students then discuss what each component contributes to the text's overall meaning and why it is needed. After a whole class debrief, students discuss issues related to layout: Why is the layout consistent through the entire text? Why are both handwritten and typeset texts included? (Conceptualizing; Day 3)
2. The teacher leads the class in identifying the specific linguistic forms used in Skylar's text to express his dream and its motivation. Students then work in their expert group to underline the dream statement and its motivation for their assigned texts. Next, they determine whether the same linguistic

forms are used as in Skylar's text. If not, they identify which forms are used instead. The teacher circulates to check and support student work. Finally, the class compiles a list of ways to express a dream and its motivation. (Conceptualizing; Day 3)

Stage 5: Analyzing and Contextualizing Textual Meaning

1. To complete the jigsaw activity, students form home groups that include an expert for each text. Together they share the content from the texts and record it in the summary table on their handout. They then look for patterns across texts, using the discussion questions on the handout to guide their work: What American dream categories are most common? Do the dreams in these texts confirm or differ from the survey findings depicted in the infographic? Why do you think the author of the *NYT* essay chose to include these individuals/texts from the more than three hundred stories collected? What can you conclude about the American dream? Teacher conducts a whole-class follow-up conversation. (Analyzing; Day 3)

Stage 6: Applying Knowledge

1. Students reflect and brainstorm about their dreams and aspirations for the future. What do they hope for themselves? Why do they dream that? What in their personal history has led them to that dream? (Experiencing and Analyzing; homework in preparation for Day 4)
2. Students draft their own American dream text to be included as part of the larger "American Dreams" project. Their text must include images and text, either spoken or written, and include a dream statement, its motivation, and language forms studied in the lesson. (Applying; Day 4)
3. Students share texts in small groups and decide what categories their dreams could be classified into and how their dreams align with those from the 2014 project. As a group, they collaboratively reflect on the relationships between text and images, dreams and motivations, and the role of the American dream in society. (Experiencing, Conceptualizing, and Analyzing; Day 5)

C

Sample Applying Rubric (adapted from CARLA, forthcoming)

	Exceeds expectations	Meets expectations	Does not meet expectations
Content knowledge: Does the student show sufficient mastery of the major nonlinguistic concepts, data, and/or other factual information in this unit?	Provides an extremely clear, accurate, and detailed representation of content. Effectively synthesizes various information sources and ideas.	Provides a clear, accurate, and somewhat detailed representation of content. Reports information without synthesizing ideas.	Provides an unclear, inaccurate, or superficial representation of content. Omits or misrepresents critical details.
Language control: To what extent does student language use contribute to effective communication of the message?	Strong use (range and accuracy) of targeted unit vocabulary. Few errors using targeted unit grammar. Accurate use of targeted conventions and mechanics of the product's genre (e.g., spelling, formatting, punctuation, capitalization, pronunciation).	Good use (range and accuracy) of targeted unit vocabulary. Some errors using targeted unit grammar. Mostly accurate use of targeted conventions and mechanics of the product's genre.	Basic or limited use of targeted unit vocabulary. Errors using targeted unit grammar, conventions, or mechanics impede communication.
Task appropriateness: To what extent are the discourse or organizational features reflective of the purpose and context of the task?	All discourse and organizational features (e.g., paragraph structure, turn taking, transition words, headings, layout, chronology) are appropriate to the purpose, context, and audience.	Most discourse and organizational features are appropriate to the purpose, context, and audience.	Discourse and organizational features do not support fulfillment of the task.
Task completion: Does the student fulfill the requirements of the assessment?	Excellent completion of the task. All instructions and task requirements are fully addressed.	Acceptable completion of the task. Some instructions or task requirements are not fully addressed.	Unacceptable completion of the task. Many instructions or task requirements are minimally addressed or not addressed at all.

Glossary of Key Terms

THIS GLOSSARY CONTAINS THE concepts introduced and defined throughout the book. Some of these concepts are also included in CARLA's Literacies Glossary, linked on this book's companion website (https://carla.umn.edu/literacies/book).

analyzing: Learning by connecting the content of texts to social, cultural, and historical contexts; questioning the meaning, importance, and consequences of textual content; critically reflecting on textual content and its relationship to one's own culture, perspectives, and learning. One of the four knowledge processes of multiliteracies pedagogy.

applying: Learning by using new knowledge, skills, and understandings and by producing language in creative ways. One of the four knowledge processes of multiliteracies pedagogy.

assessment: The general processes of gathering information about a student's learning and measuring their level of knowledge or skills.

Available Designs: Patterns and conventions of representation in a text, including language, conventions, and cultural content. Referred to more generally as textual features.

backward design: Three-stage model of curricular planning that includes (1) identifying desired results (goals, objectives, content), (2) determining acceptable evidence (assessment plan, individual assessments), and (3) planning learning experiences (instructional activities).

breadth of understanding: Demonstrating knowledge in innovative or nontraditional ways across multiple modes (e.g., written, visual, audio, gestural), thereby preparing learners to engage with diverse peoples and contexts outside of the classroom context.

cohesion relationships: Activity type in which students focus on devices (e.g., words, phrases) that make paragraphs or texts cohere, with the purpose of understanding how these devices contribute to the overall meaning of the text.

collaborative drafting: Activity type that involves the whole class or small groups of students working together to create a text.

communication: Understanding and interpreting written and spoken language on varied topics, communicating in meaningful and appropriate ways, taking audience and context into account. One of the five Cs of the World-Readiness Standards, revised by Kern (2003) to incorporate literacies principles (see chapter 1).

communicative competence: The ability to use language appropriately to carry out specific functions in different social situations.

communicative language teaching: A pedagogical approach that places communication and the development of students' communicative competence at the center of instruction.

communities: Participating in multilingual communities at home and around the world for personal enjoyment and enrichment; relating to past and present worlds outside of our immediate community through textual interaction; examining the ways that language is used to capture and express ideas and experiences within those communities. One of the five Cs of the World-Readiness Standards, revised by Kern (2003) to incorporate literacies principles (see chapter 1).

comparisons: Understanding the nature of language and culture through comparisons of the language and culture studied and one's own. One of the five Cs of the World-Readiness Standards, revised by Kern (2003) to incorporate literacies principles (see chapter 1).

conceptualizing: Learning how language forms, conventions, organization, and other features of texts work to convey meaning; unpacking texts, practicing skills and knowledge, and explicitly learning about textual features helps learners participate more fully in communication. One of the four knowledge processes of multiliteracies pedagogy.

connections: Strengthening knowledge of other disciplines through language study—art, music, film studies, history, and so forth; acquiring information and recognizing viewpoints available through the language and its cultures. One of the five Cs of the World-Readiness Standards, revised by Kern (2003) to incorporate literacies principles (see chapter 1).

conventions: One type of textual feature; the accepted ways of using different meaning-making systems (e.g., language, sounds, images, gestures) to communicate messages in different text types.

counterbalance: Attributing complementary status to both language learning and learning of academic or cultural content such that neither takes on a disproportionate role in the curriculum.

creation: Applying the language forms and cultural knowledge learned from a text to create something new.

critical focus questions: Activity type that raises students' awareness of the significance of the language and ideas in a text and their effect on a reader, listener, or viewer. Questions focus on the why and how of a text rather than on the who, what, where, and when.

critical pedagogies: Ways of teaching that equip students with the skills necessary to interrogate the knowledge they receive and create.

cultural content: One type of textual feature; includes the products, practices, and perspectives represented in a text, the meanings attributed to them, and the relationships among them.

cultural perspectives: The values, beliefs, attitudes, and philosophical perspectives of a society.

cultural practices: Patterns of social interactions and behaviors (e.g., holiday traditions, meals).

cultural products: The tangible (e.g., books, films) or intangible (e.g., rituals, laws) creations of a particular culture.

cultures: Understanding relationships between the social practices, cultural products, and perspectives of people in the foreign culture. One of the five Cs of the World-Readiness Standards, revised by Kern (2003) to incorporate literacies principles (see chapter 1).

curriculum: An educational sequence that creates connections among units of instruction (e.g., series of courses or thematic course segments) to enhance learning; takes into consideration learning objectives, content, assessment practices, and instructional approach.

declarative knowledge: Knowing the facts (e.g., language, conventions, cultural content) from a lesson, unit, or course.

depth of understanding: Demonstrating knowledge in ways that are consistent with the ideas, genres, language forms, and skills students have encountered throughout a unit or lesson.

diagnostic assessment: Occurs prior to the onset of instruction and allows teachers to identify what students already know or what they can already do.

dialogue journals: Activity type in which student and teacher exchange thoughts in informal written or oral journal entries.

digital social annotated reading (DSAR): An online tool that allows learners to synchronously and asynchronously construct and revise their interpretation of texts with other students.

digital storytelling: A multimodal composition through which students tell a fictional or true story using video, image, and/or audio; a type of performance-based assessment.

essential questions: Open-ended questions around a topic or theme that provoke inquiry and deep thought, encourage students to consider multiple viewpoints and question assumptions, connect to prior learning and experiences, and promote transfer of learning to other contexts.

evaluation: The analysis, interpretation, or judgment of information collected from assessment; assigning a value (e.g., meets expectations, exceeds expectations) to student performance.

experiencing: Learning through immersion in texts, activities, and social situations; expressing thoughts, reactions, opinions, and feelings and gaining global comprehension about familiar or new experiences, objects, ideas, situations, perspectives, and ways of communicating. Does not involve deep reflection or analysis. One of the four knowledge processes of multiliteracies pedagogy.

experiencing the known: Activities in which students discuss their worlds using familiar patterns of communication and bring their cultural backgrounds, identities, and interests into the classroom.

experiencing the new: Activities that expose students to ideas, information, or situations outside or beyond their reality.

fishbowl: Activity type that provides opportunities for multiple perspectives on a topic addressed in a text-based lesson. Students alternate being inside of the fishbowl (answering questions, sharing perspectives) and outside of the fishbowl (asking questions, listening to ideas presented).

foreign language literacies: The ability to interpret and transform target language texts, engage with texts of different modalities and genres, connect language and culture, and recognize the centrality of language in understanding diverse societies and perspectives.

formal discourses: Communication characterized by formal or public exchanges that are central to participation in various societal contexts; formal discourse genres are typically encountered at school or work and include poetry, political debates, book reviews, TED talks, and the like.

formative assessment: Serves to monitor student learning during a lesson or unit and provide information about progress toward learning objectives; feedback from formative assessments helps students to identify areas of struggle or gaps in learning and allows teachers to address problems in real time.

genre: Text types that possess particular patterns that are culturally situated and that users expect, understand, apply, and adapt.

genre reformulation: Activity type in which learners transform one genre into another genre (e.g., turning a travel brochure into a promotional video).

grading: The reporting of assessment or evaluation results to stakeholders (e.g., students, parents, administrators); student performance represented as a number, letter, or something else that is meaningful to these stakeholders.

informal discourses: Communication characterized by informal or personal exchanges on topics of common knowledge; informal discourse genres are usually encountered in the home and include personal narratives, cartoons, picture stories, diary entries, and the like.

instructional conversations: Teacher-led classroom discussions with the purpose of improving students' proficiency and their ability to think in complex ways about textual content. Include open-ended questions, exchange of ideas, and responsive feedback similar to everyday, noninstructional conversations.

Integrated Performance Assessment (IPA): Engages learners in three different tasks across three communicative modes—interpretive, interpersonal, and presentational—around a common topic or theme and includes a feedback loop; a type of performance-based assessment.

interpersonal communication: Two-way interaction and meaning negotiation in spoken, written, or signed conversations. When students interact in this mode, they explore and negotiate relationships, shared assumptions, conventions, imagination, creativity, and emotions that are grounded in their understandings of the texts they interpret.

interpretation: Understanding the gist or surface-level facts as well as critically examining cultural messages and viewpoints and the way language is used to express those messages and viewpoints.

interpretive communication: Allows a reader, listener, or viewer to construct meaning (e.g., understand, interpret, analyze) from written, audio, audiovisual, digital, or visual texts. Engaging with texts in this way includes establishing literal understanding of basic information, making inferences, and analyzing cultural products, practices, and perspectives embedded in texts. Because this is a one-way communication mode, there is no possibility of meaning negotiation.

knowledge processes: Four nonsequential, nonhierarchical activity types that compose multiliteracies pedagogy, promote students' foreign language literacies development, and engage them in meaning design.

language: One type of textual feature; the linguistic content of texts, including grammatical forms, vocabulary, pronunciation, prosody, spelling, metaphors and idiomatic phrases, pronoun referents, simple and complex sentences, and so on.

language-content integration: Language learning through academic or cultural content. Language and content are seen as complementary, with the instructional focus shifting between the two depending on learning objectives, student needs, and so on to enhance the learning of both.

learning objectives: Brief statements articulating what students will know and be able to do at the end of a learning sequence (e.g., lesson, unit, course, program) to reach a curriculum's overarching goal(s).

literacy: The ability to read and write.

meaning design: Identifying, understanding, and analyzing patterns in the ways ideas are presented in texts and incorporating those patterns into one's linguistic and communicative repertoire; has linguistic, sociocultural, and cognitive dimensions.

multiliteracies pedagogy: An instructional approach that applies the concept of foreign language literacies in classroom instruction; prioritizes meaningful communication around target language texts and the language forms used to express ideas within those texts.

multimodal/multimodality: The combination of written, audio, visual, or digital modes in a text.

performance-based assessments: Allow learners to showcase knowledge and skills gained throughout a lesson, unit, or course; require learners to use language meaningfully and creatively.

personal action plan: Activity type in which learners turn an idea gleaned from a text into action by identifying a goal, the steps and resources needed to carry it out, and possible barriers to achieving the goal.

portfolios: A collection of student-selected work over time that provides evidence of learning and a reflection on the learning process; a type of performance-based assessment.

presentational communication: Sharing information and ideas to an (often) distant audience in order to inform, explain, persuade, or narrate on various topics. Learners also demonstrate awareness of communicative conventions relevant to the text type they are presenting. There is no opportunity for meaning negotiation during oral or written presentational tasks.

procedural knowledge: Knowing how to apply what has been learned in a lesson, unit, or course.

reader's theater: Group activity in which students perform a written text using their multiple voices to create and reflect their understanding. Students collaboratively segment the original text and read or perform it aloud with different voices.

scaffolding: Guided assistance by a peer or more capable other that focuses learners' attention on a task, draws their attention to essential ideas or features, and keeps them motivated; is multifaceted and can relate to the structure of individual activities, the structure of a lesson, or the strategies a teacher uses to lead students through an activity or lesson.

story maps: A flexible activity type that supports learners' comprehension of a text as they visually map key story events by locating them in time or space.

story retelling: Activity type in which students rewrite a text from a different point of view, such as that of a different character, narrator, time period, or culture, using language forms and conventions learned through textual interpretation activities.

substitutions: Activity type in which students swap out one linguistic feature for another, similar feature; allows students to understand language use as a series of choices between forms that communicate different meanings rather than as an arbitrary set of rules.

summative assessment: Serves to evaluate student learning against a standard or benchmark (e.g., a rubric) at the close of a lesson or unit; seeks to determine whether students have met learning objectives.

target language text: A socially and culturally situated text created for some real-world purpose other than language learning.

text: Any concrete, observable product that communicates meaning; can be written, audio, audiovisual, visual, digital, or multimodal.

text complexity: Determined based on a text's form (e.g., levels of meaning, organization, language forms, clarity) and readability, as well as reader- and task-based factors, including motivation, background knowledge, and purpose.

textual features: The interrelated building blocks, or meaning-making resources, of target language texts that reflect a text creator's thinking and decision-making; include language, conventions, and cultural content. Also called Available Designs in multiliteracies parlance.

3-2-1 activity: Activity type that asks learners to summarize and analyze the knowledge they have gained from target language texts and to identify areas of misunderstanding. The content of the 3, 2, and 1 varies, but often includes three summary sentences, two new ideas learned, and one question.

References

Adair-Hauck, Bonnie, Eileen W. Glisan, Keiko Koda, Elvira Swender, and Paul Sandrock. 2006. "The Integrated Performance Assessment (IPA): Connecting Assessment to Instruction and Learning." *Foreign Language Annals* 39, no. 3: 359–82. https://doi.org/10.1111/j.1944-9720.2006.tb02894.x.

Adair-Hauck, Bonnie, Eileen W. Glisan, and Francis J. Troyan. 2013. *Implementing Integrated Performance Assessment*. Alexandria, VA: ACTFL.

Allen, Heather W. 2011. "Embracing Literacy-Based Teaching: A Longitudinal Study of the Conceptual Development of Novice Foreign Language Teachers." In *Research on Second Language Teacher Education: A Sociocultural Perspective on Professional Development*, edited by Karen E. Johnson and Paula R. Golombek, 86–101. New York: Routledge.

Allen, Heather W., and Beatrice Dupuy. 2013. "Evolving Notions of Literacy-Based Foreign Language Teaching: A Qualitative Study of Graduate Student Instructors." In *Educating the Future Foreign Language Professoriate for the 21st Century*, edited by Heather W. Allen and Hiram H. Maxim, 171–91. Boston: Heinle. http://hdl.handle.net/10125/69702.

Allen, Heather W., and Lauren Goodspeed. 2018. "Textual Borrowing and Perspective-Taking: A Genre-Based Approach to L2 Writing." *L2 Journal* 10, no. 2: 87–110. https://doi.org/10.5070/L210235331.

Allen, Heather W., and Kate Paesani. 2010. "Exploring the Feasibility of a Pedagogy of Multiliteracies in Introductory Foreign Language Courses." *L2 Journal* 2, no. 1: 119–42. https://doi.org/10.5070/L2219064.

———. 2022. "Genre Instruction, Textual Borrowing, and Foreign Language Writing: Graduate Teaching Assistant Perspectives and Practices." *Language Teaching Research* 26, no. 4: 755–76. https://doi.org/10.1177/1362168820911194.

American Association of Teachers of Arabic (AATA). 2020. "Arabic Manuscripts." Accessed January 24, 2022. https://aataweb.org/manuscripts.

American Association of Teachers of French (AATF). 2019. "Curated Resources." Accessed January 24, 2022. https://frenchteachers.org/resources/curated-resources/.

American Council on the Teaching of Foreign Languages (ACTFL). 2012. *ACTFL Proficiency Guidelines 2021*. Accessed January 24, 2022. https://www.actfl.org/sites/default/files/guidelines/ACTFLProficiencyGuidelines2012.pdf.

———. n.d. "Facilitate Target Language Use." Accessed January 24, 2022. https://www.actfl.org/resources/guiding-principles-language-learning/target-language.

American Immigration Council. 2017. "What Immigration Means to the United States." Infographic. The Immigrant Learning Center. https://www.immigrationresearch.org/node/2509.

Anderson, Lorin W., and David R. Krathwohl, eds. 2001. *A Taxonomy for Learning, Teaching, and Assessing: A Revision of Bloom's Taxonomy of Educational Objectives*. New York: Addison Wesley Longman Inc.

Andrews, Stephen. 2007. *Teacher Language Awareness*. Cambridge: Cambridge University Press. https://doi.org/10.1017/CBO9780511497643.

Angay-Crowder, Tuba, Jayoung Choi, and Youngjoo Yi. 2013. "Putting Multiliteracies into Practice: Digital Storytelling for Multilingual Adolescents in a Summer Program." *TESL Canada Journal* 30, no. 2: 36–45. https://doi.org/10.18806/tesl.v30i2.1140.

Annenberg Learner. n.d.a. "French: Interpreting La Belle et la Bete." Teaching Foreign Languages K–12: A Library of Classroom Practices. Accessed February 16, 2022. https://www.learner.org/series/teaching-foreign-languages-k-12-a-library-of-classroom-practices/french-interpreting-la-belle-et-la-bete/.

Annenberg Learner. n.d.b. "View & Analyze the Video." Teaching Foreign Languages K–12: A Library of Classroom Practices. Accessed February 16, 2022. https://www.learner.org/series/teaching-foreign-languages-k-12-a-library-of-classroom-practices/spanish-interpreting-literature/view-analyze-video/.

Anstey, Michèle, and Geoff Bull. 2018. *Foundations of Multiliteracies: Reading, Writing and Talking in the 21st Century*. London: Routledge. https://doi.org/10.4324/9781315114194.

Armstrong, Patricia. 2010. "Bloom's Taxonomy." Center for Teaching, Vanderbilt University. Accessed January 24, 2022. https://cft.vanderbilt.edu/guides-sub-pages/blooms-taxonomy/.

Barnes-Karol, Gwendolyn, and Maggie A. Broner. 2010. "Using Images as Springboards to Teach Cultural Perspectives in Light of the Ideals of the MLA Report." *Foreign Language Annals* 43, no. 3: 422–45. https://doi.org/10.1111/j.1944-9720.2010.01091.x.

Benjamin, John, Devon Donohue-Bergeler, Katrin Fuchs, and Alexander Lorenz. n.d. "Alles offen: Öffentliche verkehrsmittel und weltoffenheit." FLLITE. Accessed February 16, 2022. Creative Commons License (CC BY-SA). https://drive.google.com/file/d/0Byg7PyauMJRSMGMxUHh3c0gxTFk/view.

Bhooth, Abdullah Mohammad, Hazita Azman, and Kemboja Ismail. 2015. "Investigating the Reading Practices of EFL Yemeni Students Using the Learning by Design Framework." *TESOL Journal* 6, no. 3: 418–46. https://doi.org/10.1002/tesj.148.

Bigelow, Martha. 2010. "Learning to Plan for a Focus on Form in CBI: The Role of Teacher Knowledge and Teaching Context." In *World Language Teacher Education: Transitions and Challenges in the 21st Century*, edited by Jacqueline F. Davis, 35–56. Greenwich, CT: Information Age Publishing.

Blau, Eileen K. 1982. "The Effect of Syntax on Readability for ESL Students in Puerto Rico." *TESOL Quarterly* 16, no. 4: 517–26. https://doi.org/10.2307/3586469.

Bloom, Benjamin S., ed. 1956. *Taxonomy of Educational Objectives. Handbook I: Cognitive Domain*. New York: David McKay Company.

Bloom's Taxonomy. n.d. "Helpful Graphic Organisers." Accessed February 15, 2022. https://bloomstaxonomy2013.weebly.com/helpful-graphic-organisers.html.

Blyth, Carl S. 2014. "Exploring the Affordances of Digital Social Reading for L2 Literacy: The Case of eComma." In *Digital Literacies in Foreign and Second Language Education*, edited by Janel Pettes Guikema and Lawrence Williams, 201–26. San Marcos, TX: Computer Assisted Language Instruction Consortium (CALICO).

Brosnan, D., K. Brown, and S. Hood. 1984. *Reading in Context: Developing the Reading Strategies of Adult ESL Learners*. Adelaide: National Curriculum Resource Center.

Brown, Ian. 2016. "American Dreams." *New York Times*, July 2, 2016. Accessed January 24, 2022. https://www.nytimes.com/interactive/2016/07/01/opinion/sunday/american-dreams.html.

Brown, Ian, Lori Lockyer, and Peter Caputi. 2010. "Multiliteracies and Assessment Practice." In *Multiliteracies in Motion: Current Theory and Practice*, edited by David R. Cole and Darren L. Pullen, 191–206. New York: Routledge. https://doi.org/10.4324/9780203864036.

Brown, Lucien, Noriko Iwasaki, and Keunyoung Lee. 2016. "Implementing Multiliteracies in the Korean Classroom through Visual Media." In *Multiliteracies in World Language Education*, edited by Yuri Kumagai, Ana López-Sánchez, and Sujane Wu, 158–81. New York: Routledge.

Bull, Geoff, and Michèle Anstey. 2010. "Using the Principles of Multiliteracies to Inform Pedagogical Change." In *Multiliteracies in Motion: Current Theory and Practice*, edited by David R. Cole and Darren L. Pullen, 141–59. New York: Routledge. https://doi.org/10.4324/9780203864036.

———. 2019. *Elaborating Multiliteracies through Multimodal Texts: Changing Classroom Practices and Developing Teacher Pedagogies*. London: Routledge.

Burgess, Julianne, and Jennifer Rowsell. 2020. "Transcultural-Affective Flows and Multimodal Engagements: Reimagining Pedagogy and Assessment with Adult Language Learners." *Language and Education* 34, no. 2: 173–91. https://doi.org/10.1080/09500782.2020.1720226.

Burke, Anne, and Shawnee Hardware. 2015. "Honouring ESL Students' Lived Experiences in School Learning with Multiliteracies Pedagogy." *Language, Culture and Curriculum* 28, no. 2: 143–57. https://doi.org/10.1080/07908318.2015.1027214.

Byrnes, Heidi. 1998. "Constructing Curricula in Collegiate Foreign Language Departments." In *Learning Foreign and Second Languages: Perspectives in Research and Scholarship*, edited by Heidi Byrnes, 262–95. New York: Modern Language Association of America.

———. 2001. "Articulating Foreign Language Programs: The Need for New, Curricular Bases." In *Foreign Language Program Articulation: Current Practice and Future Prospects*, edited by Carolyn Gascoigne Lally, 63–77. Westport, Connecticut: Bergin & Garvey.

———, ed. 2006. "Perspectives." *Modern Language Journal* 90, no. 2: 244–66. https://doi.org/10.1111/j.1540-4781.2006.00395_1.x.

Byrnes, Heidi, Cori Crane, Hiram H. Maxim, and Katherine A. Sprang. 2006. "Taking Text to Task: Issues and Choices in Curriculum Construction." *International Journal of Applied Linguistics* 152, no. 1: 85–109. https://doi.org/10.2143/ITL.152.0.2017864.

Byrnes, Heidi, Hiram H. Maxim, and John M. Norris. 2010. "Realizing Advanced Foreign Language Writing Developing in Collegiate Education: Curricular Design, Pedagogy, Assessment." *Modern Language Journal* 94, Supplement 1: 1–235. https://doi.org/10.1111/j.1540-4781.2010.01136.x.

Cammarata, Laurent, and Diane J. Tedick. 2012. "Balancing Content and Language in Instruction: The Experience of Immersion Teachers." *Modern Language Journal* 96, no. 2: 251–69. https://doi.org/10.1111/j.1540-4781.2012.01330.x.

Canagarajah, Suresh. 2014. "In Search of a New Paradigm for Teaching English as an International Language." *TESOL Journal* 5, no. 44: 767–85. https://doi.org/10.1002/tesj.166.

Center for Advanced Research on Language Acquisition (CARLA). 2021a. "Literacies Glossary." Regents of the University of Minnesota. Accessed March 17, 2022. https://carla.umn.edu/literacies/glossary.html.

———. 2021b. "Literacies Infographics." Regents of the University of Minnesota. Accessed March 17, 2022. https://carla.umn.edu/literacies/infographic.html.

———. 2021c. "Literacies in Language Education." Regents of the University of Minnesota. Accessed March 17, 2022. https://carla.umn.edu/literacies/.

———. 2021d. "Target Language Text Resources." Regents of the University of Minnesota. Accessed January 24, 2022. https://carla.umn.edu/literacies/textresources.html.

———. Forthcoming. "Action-Oriented Assessment Rubric." Regents of the University of Minnesota.

———. n.d.a. "Analyzing Texts." Content-Based Second Language Instruction (CoBaLLT). Last modified January 5, 2021. https://carla.umn.edu/cobaltt/modules/curriculum/ta_form.html.

———. n.d.b. "Resources for Assessment-Related Topics." Regents of the University of Minnesota. Last modified August 26, 2020. https://carla.umn.edu/assessment/vac/resources/index.html.

———. n.d.c. "Teacher-Developed Standards-Based Integrated Performance Assessment (IPA) & Unit Overview: Virtual Assessment Center." Regents of the University of Minnesota. Accessed January 24, 2022. https://carla.umn.edu/assessment/vac/CreateUnit/documents/CARLA.IPA.HealthyBreakfast.pdf.

Center for a New American Dream. 2014. "What Americans Think of the American Dream." Infographic. New Dream. Accessed January 24, 2022. https://newdream.org/resources/poll-2014.

Chi, Feng-Ming. 2012. "Constructing Gender Identities through Responses to Female-Centered Texts." *Language and Education* 26, no. 5: 423–34. http://dx.doi.org/10.1080/09500782.2012.655283.

Choi, Jayoung. 2015. "A Heritage Language Learner's Literacy Practices in a Korean Language Course in a US University: From a Multiliteracies Perspective." *Journal of Language and Literacy Education* 11, no. 2: 116–33.

Choi, Jayoung, and Youngjoo Yi. 2016. "Teachers' Integration of Multimodality into Classroom Practices for English Language Learners." *TESOL Journal* 7, no. 2: 304–27. https://doi.org/10.1002/tesj.204.

Chun, Christian W. 2009. "Critical Literacies and Graphic Novels for English-Language Learners: Teaching Maus." *Journal of Adolescent & Adult Literacy* 53, no. 2: 144–53. https://doi.org/10.1598/JAAL.53.2.5.

Clementi, Donna, and Laura Terrill. 2013. "The Keys to Planning for Learning: Effective Curriculum, Unit, and Lesson Design." American Council on the Teaching of Foreign Languages. Accessed January 24, 2022. https://www.actfl.org/resources/store/books/the-keys-planning-learning-resources.

Cloonan, Anne. 2010. *Multiliteracies, Multimodality, and Teacher Professional Learning*. Champaign, IL: Common Ground Research Networks. https://doi.org/10.18848/978-1-86335-713-5/CGP.

Common Core State Standards Initiative. 2021. "Measuring Text Complexity: Three Factors." Accessed January 24, 2022. http://www.corestandards.org/ELA-Literacy/standard-10-range-quality-complexity/measuring-text-complexity-three-factors/.

The Comprehensible Classroom. 2018. "Is This Novel Really Level 1? Understand the Factors That Contribute to Text Complexity." Accessed January 24, 2022. https://comprehensibleclassroom.com/2018/05/16/is-this-text-really-level-1-which-factors-contribute-to-text-complexity/.

Cope, Bill, and Mary Kalantzis. 2009. "'Multiliteracies': New Literacies, New Learning." *Pedagogies: An International Journal* 4, no. 3: 164–94. https://doi.org/10.1080/15544800903076044.

———. 2015. "The Things You Do to Know: An Introduction to the Pedagogy of Multiliteracies." In *A Pedagogy of Multiliteracies: Learning by Design*, edited by Bill Cope and Mary Kalantzis, 1–36. London: Palgrave Macmillan. https://doi.org/10.1057/9781137539724.

Crafton, Linda K., Penny Silvers, and Mary Brennan. 2009. "Creating a Critical Multiliteracies Curriculum: Repositioning Art in the Early Childhood Classroom." In *Making Meaning: Educating the Young Child*, vol. 2, edited by Marilyn Narey, 31–51. New York: Springer. https://doi.org/10.1007/978-0-387-87539-2_3.

Davin, Kristin J., Francis J. Troyan, Richard Donato, and Ashley Hellman. 2011. "Research on the Integrated Performance Assessment in an Early Foreign Language Learning Program." *Foreign Language Annals* 44, no. 4: 605–25. https://doi.org/10.1111/j.1944-9720.2011.01153.x.

Day, Richard D. 2004. "A Critical Look at Authentic Materials." *Journal of Asia TEFL* 1, no. 1: 101–14.

Delett, Jennifer S., Sarah Barnhardt, and Jennifer A. Kevorkian. 2001. "A Framework for Portfolio Assessment in the Language Classroom." *Foreign Language Annals* 34, no. 6: 559–68. https://doi.org/10.1111/j.1944-9720.2001.tb02103.x.

Department of German. 2011a. "Curriculum." Georgetown University. Accessed January 25, 2022. https://german.georgetown.edu/undergraduate/curriculum/.

Department of German. 2011b. "Curriculum Project." Georgetown University. Accessed January 25, 2022. https://german.georgetown.edu/curriculumproject/.

Donato, Richard, and Bonnie Adair-Hauck. 1994. "PACE: A Model to Focus on Form." Paper presented at the American Council on the Teaching of Foreign Languages Conference, San Antonio, TX.

Donato, Richard, and Frank B. Brooks. 2004. "Literary Discussions and Advanced Speaking Functions: Researching the (Dis)connection." *Foreign Language Annals* 37, no. 2: 183–99. https://doi.org/10.1111/j.1944-9720.2004.tb02192.x.

Dotson, Erika K. 2010. "The Effects of Deductive and Guided Inductive Approaches on the Learning of Grammar in an Advanced College French Curse." PhD diss., Emory University, Atlanta, GA.

Dumitru, Daniela. 2019. "Creating Meaning: The Importance of Arts, Humanities, and Culture for Critical Thinking Development." *Studies in Higher Education* 44, no. 5: 870–79. https://doi.org/10.1080/03075079.2019.1586345.

Dupuy, Beatrice, and Heather W. Allen. 2012. "Appropriating Conceptual and Pedagogical Tools of Literacy: A Qualitative Study of Two Novice Foreign Language Teaching Assistants." In *Working Theories for Teaching Assistant and International Teaching Assistant Development*, edited by Greta Gorsuch, 275–315. Stillwater, OK: New Forums Press.

Education Queensland. 2004. *New Basics: The Why, What, How, and When of Rich Tasks*. Queensland Government.

Ellis, Rod, and Natsuko Shintani. 2013. *Exploring Language Pedagogy through Second Language Acquisition Research.* London: Routledge. https://doi.org/10.4324/9780203796580.

Ennser-Kananen, Johanna. 2016. "A Pedagogy of Pain: New Directions for World Language Education." *Modern Language Journal* 100, no. 2: 556–64. https://doi.org/10.1111/modl.1_12337.

Ferris, Dana, and John S. Hedgcock. 1998. *Teaching ESL Composition: Purpose, Process, and Practice.* Mahwah, NJ: Lawrence Erlbaum.

Fterniati, Anna. 2010. "Literacy Pedagogy and Multiliteracies in Greek Elementary School Language Arts." *International Journal of Learning* 17, no. 3: 319–50.

Fukunaga, Natsuki. 2006. "'Those Anime Students': Foreign Language Literacy Development through Japanese Popular Culture." *Journal of Adolescent and Adult Literacy* 50, no. 3: 206–22. https://doi.org/10.1598/JAAL.50.3.5.

Gee, James Paul. 2015. *Social Linguistics and Literacies: Ideology in Discourses.* 5th ed. London: Routledge. https://doi.org/10.4324/9781315722511.

Gilmore, Alex. 2007. "Authentic Materials and Authenticity in Foreign Language Learning." *Language Teaching* 40, no. 2: 97–118. https://doi.org/10.1017/S0261444807004144.

Glisan, Eileen W., and Richard Donato. 2017. *Enacting the Work of Language Instruction: High-Leverage Teaching Practices.* Vol. 1. Alexandria, VA: ACTFL.

———. 2021. *Enacting the Work of Language Instruction: High-Leverage Teaching Practices.* Vol. 2. Alexandria, VA: ACTFL.

Glisan, Eileen W., Daniel Uribe, and Bonnie Adair-Hauck. 2007. "Research on Integrated Performance Assessment at the Post-Secondary Level: Student Performance across the Modes of Communication." *Canadian Modern Language Review* 64, no. 1: 39–68. https://doi.org/10.3138/cmlr.64.1.039.

Glynn, Cassandra, and Beth Wassell. 2022. "Rethinking Our Introduction: Calling out Ourselves and Calling in Our Field." In *Transforming World Language Teaching and Teacher Education for Equity and Justice: Pushing Boundaries in US Contexts,* edited by Beth Wassell and Cassandra Glynn, 1–19. Bristol, UK: Multilingual Matters. https://doi.org/10.21832/9781788926522-004.

Glynn, Cassandra, Pamela Wesely, and Beth Wassell. 2018. *Words and Actions: Teaching Languages through the Lens of Social Justice.* 2nd ed. Alexandria, VA: ACTFL.

Godwin-Jones, Robert. 2012. "Digital Video Revisited: Storytelling, Conferencing, Remixing." *Language Learning & Technology* 16, no. 1: 1–9. http://dx.doi.org/10125/44268.

Goodspeed, Lauren, Mandy Menke, Kate Paesani, and Helena Ruf. 2021. "Bringing Social Justice into Language Classes: Templates to Guide Instructional Planning." Paper presented at the CARLA Presentation Series, Minneapolis, MN. Accessed January 31, 2022. https://carla.umn.edu/presentations/recordings.html.

Graves, Kathleen. 1999. *Designing Language Courses: A Guide for Teachers.* Boston: Heinle.

Grim, Frédérique. 2008. "The Integration of Focus-on-Form Instruction within Culture-Enriched Lessons." *Foreign Language Annals* 41, no. 2: 321–46. https://doi.org/10.1111/j.1944-9720.2008.tb03295.x.

Gurzynski-Weiss, Laura, and Melissa Baralt. 2014. "Exploring Learner Perception and Use of Task-Based Interactional Feedback in FTF and CMC Modes." *Studies in Second Language Acquisition* 36, no. 1: 1–37. https://doi.org/10.1017/S0272263113000363.

———. 2015. "A Closer Look at Learner Responses to Feedback and Their Effect on Noticing in Face-to-Face and Computer-Mediated Task-Based Interaction." *Applied Psycholinguistics* 36, no. 6: 1393–420. https://doi.org/10.1017/S0142716414000320.

Hackman, Heather W. 2005. "Five Essential Components for Social Justice Education." *Equity & Excellence in Education* 38, no. 2: 103–9. https://doi.org/10.1080/10665680590935034.

Haight, Carrie E., Carol Herron, and Steven P. Cole. 2007. "The Effect of Deductive and Guided Inductive Instructional Approaches on the Learning of Grammar in the Elementary Foreign Language Classroom." *Foreign Language Annals* 40, no. 2: 288–310. https://doi.org/10.1111/j.1944-9720.2007.tb03202.x.

Hall, Joan Kelly. 2001. *Methods for Teaching Foreign Languages: Creating a Community of Learners in the Classroom.* Upper Saddle River, NJ: Prentice Hall.

Halliday, Michael A. K., and Ruqaiya Hasan. 1976. *Cohesion in English*. London: Routledge. https://doi.org/10.4324/9781315836010.

Hawkins, Roger. 2001. *Second Language Syntax: A Generative Introduction*. Oxford: Wiley Blackwell.

Heineke, Amy J., and Jay McTighe. 2018. *Using Understanding by Design in the Culturally and Linguistically Diverse Classroom*. Alexandria, VA: ASCD.

Herron, Carol, and Michael Tomasello. 1992. "Acquiring Grammatical Structures by Guided Induction." *French Review* 65, no. 5: 708–18.

Hilton, Annette, Kim Nichols, and Christina Gitsaki. 2010. "Multiliteracies in Secondary Chemistry: A Model for Using Digital Technologies to Scaffold the Development of Students' Chemical Literacy." In *Multiliteracies and Technology Enhanced Education: Social Practice and the Global Classroom*, edited by Darren L. Pullen and David R. Cole, 186–208. Hershey, PA: IGI Global. https://doi.org/10.4018/978-1-60566-673-0.

Honeyfield, John. 1977. "Simplification." *TESOL Quarterly* 11, no. 4: 431–40. https://doi.org/10.2307/3585739.

Hsiaomei, Tsai. n.d. "How Does a Caterpillar Become a Butterfly?" Accessed January 26, 2022. Creative Commons License (CC BY-SA 4.0). https://drive.google.com/file/d/0Byg7PyauMJRSbmxGampCOG1STok/edit.

Hyland, Ken, and Fiona Hyland. 2006. "Feedback on Second Language Students' Writing." *Language Teaching* 39, no. 2: 83–101. https://doi.org/10.1017/S0261444806003399.

Immigration History Research Center. n.d. "Immigrant Stories." University of Minnesota. Accessed February 25, 2022. https://immigrantstories.umn.edu/.

"Interactive Tour of Ellis Island." n.d. Scholastic. Accessed February 24, 2022. http://teacher.scholastic.com/activities/immigration/tour/index.htm.

Jacobs, George M., and Thomas S. C. Farrell. 2003. "Understanding and Implementing the CLT (Communicative Language Teaching) Paradigm." *RELC Journal* 34, no. 1: 5–30. https://doi.org/10.1177/003368820303400102.

Jacobs, Gloria E. 2013. "Designing Assessments: A Multiliteracies Approach." *Journal of Adolescent and Adult Literacy* 56, no. 8: 623–26. https://doi.org/10.1002/JAAL.189.

Janks, Hilary. 2005. "Language and the Design of Texts." *English Teaching: Practice and Critique* 4, no. 3: 97–110.

Johnson, Karen E., and Paula R. Golombek. 2020. "Informing and Transforming Language Teacher Education Pedagogy." *Language Teaching Research* 24, no. 1: 116–27. https://doi.org/10.1177/1362168818777539.

Joutsenlahti, Jorma, and Pirjo Kulju. 2017. "Multimodal Languaging as a Pedagogical Model: A Case Study of the Concept of Division in School Mathematics." *Education Sciences* 7, no. 1: 1–9. https://doi.org/10.3390/educsci7010009.

Kalantzis, Mary, and Bill Cope. 2016a. "Analytical and Applied Learning." YouTube video, 6:47, February 1, 2016. https://newlearningonline.com/literacies/chapter-3/analytical-and-applied-learning.

———. 2016b. "Experiential and Conceptual Learning." YouTube video, 6:37, February 1, 2016. https://newlearningonline.com/literacies/chapter-3/experiential-and-conceptual-learning.

———. 2021a. "Analysing Critically (Glossary)." Works & Days. Accessed January 26, 2022. https://newlearningonline.com/learning-by-design/glossary/analysing-critically.

———. 2021b. "Analysing Critically (The Knowledge Process)." Works & Days. Accessed February 16, 2022. https://newlearningonline.com/learning-by-design/the-knowledge-processes/analysing-critically.

———. 2021c. "Analysing Functionally." Works & Days. Accessed February 16, 2022. https://newlearningonline.com/learning-by-design/the-knowledge-processes/analysing.

———. 2021d. "Applying Appropriately." Works & Days. Accessed January 26, 2022. https://newlearningonline.com/learning-by-design/glossary/applying-appropriately.

———. 2021e. "Applying Creatively." Works & Days. Accessed January 26, 2022. https://newlearningonline.com/learning-by-design/glossary/applying-creatively.

———. 2021f. "Assessment." Works & Days. Accessed February 15, 2022. https://newlearningonline.com/learning-by-design/assessment.

———. 2021g. "Conceptualising by Naming." Works & Days. Accessed February 15, 2022. https://newlearningonline.com/learning-by-design/the-knowledge-processes/conceptualising.

———. 2021h. "Conceptualising by Theorizing." Works & Days. Accessed February 15, 2022. https://newlearningonline.com/learning-by-design/the-knowledge-processes/conceptualising-by-theorising.

———. 2021i. "Experiencing the Known." Works & Days. Accessed February 15, 2022. https://newlearningonline.com/learning-by-design/the-knowledge-processes/activities.

———. 2021j. "Experiencing the New." Works & Days. Accessed February 14, 2022. https://newlearningonline.com/learning-by-design/glossary/experiencing-the-new.

———. 2021k. "Glossary." Works and Days. Accessed January 26, 2022. https://newlearningonline.com/learning-by-design/glossary.

———. 2021l. "Pedagogy." Works & Days. Accessed February 14, 2022. https://newlearningonline.com/learning-by-design/pedagogy.

Kalantzis, Mary, Bill Cope, Eveline Chan, and Leanne Dalley-Trim. 2016. *Literacies*. 2nd ed. Cambridge: Cambridge University Press. https://doi.org/10.1017/9781316442821.

Kearney, Erin. 2014. "Addressing Culture in Introductory Levels of World Language Teaching: Insights from Research in Pre-K to Post-Secondary Classrooms." *New York State Association of Foreign Language Teachers* 64, no. 2: 17–38.

Kearney, Erin, and So-Yeon Ahn. 2013a. "Awakening to World Languages: Intercultural Awareness in Very Young Learners." *Learning Languages* 18, no. 2: 44–48.

———. 2013b. "Preschool World Language Learners' Engagement with Language: What Are the Possibilities?" *Language Awareness* 23, no. 4: 319–33. https://doi.org/10.1080/09658416.2013.804831.

Kennedy, Laura M., Rae L. Oviatt, and Peter I. De Costa. 2019. "Refugee Youth's Identity Expressions and Multimodal Literacy Practices in a Third Space." *Journal of Research in Childhood Education* 33, no. 1: 56–70. https://doi.org/10.1080/02568543.2018.1531446.

Kern, Richard. 2000. *Literacy and Language Teaching*. Oxford: Oxford University Press.

———. 2003. "Literacy and Advanced Foreign Language Learning: Rethinking the Curriculum." In *Advanced Foreign Language Learning: A Challenge to College Programs*, edited by Heidi Byrnes and Hiram H. Maxim, 19–35. Boston: Heinle. http://hdl.handle.net/10125/69596.

———. 2015. *Language, Literacy, and Technology*. Cambridge: Cambridge University Press. https://doi.org/10.1017/CBO9781139567701.

Kim, Mi Song, and Xiaotong Xing. 2019. "Appropriation of Affordances of Multiliteracies for Chinese Literacy Teaching in Canada." *Research and Practice in Technology Enhanced Learning* 14, no. 1: 1–14. https://doi.org/10.1186/s41039-019-0095-2.

Kintsch, Walter, and Teun A. van Dijk. 1978. "Toward a Model of Text Comprehension and Production." *Psychological Review* 85, no. 5: 363–94. https://doi.org/10.1037/0033-295X.85.5.363.

Kramsch, Claire. 1997. "The Privilege of the Nonnative Speaker." *Publications of the Modern Language Association of America* 112, no. 3: 359–69. https://doi.org/10.1632/S0030812900060673.

———. 2006. "From Communicative Competence to Symbolic Competence." *Modern Language Journal* 90, no. 2: 249–52. https://doi.org/10.1111/j.1540-4781.2006.00395_3.x.

Krashen, Stephen. 1981. *Second Language Acquisition and Second Language Learning*. Oxford: Pergamon Press.

Kress, Gunther. 2010. *Multimodality: A Social Semiotic Approach to Contemporary Communication*. London: Routledge. https://doi.org/10.4324/9780203970034.

Kress, Gunther, and Theo van Leeuwen. 2006. *Reading Images: The Grammar of Visual Design*. 2nd ed. London: Routledge.

Kucer, Stephen B. 2014. *Dimensions of Literacy: A Conceptual Base for Teaching Reading and Writing in School Settings*. 4th ed. New York: Routledge. https://doi.org/10.4324/9780203428405.

Kumagai, Yuri, Keiko Konoeda, Miyuki Nishimata (Fukai), and Shinji Sato. 2016. "Fostering Multimodal Literacies in the Japanese Language Classroom: Digital Video Projects." In *Multiliteracies in World Language Education*, edited by Yuri Kumagai, Ana López-Sánchez, and Sujane Wu, 135–57. New York: Routledge.

Kumagai, Yuri, Ana López-Sánchez, and Sujane Wu, eds. 2016. *Multiliteracies in World Language Education*. New York: Routledge. https://doi.org/10.4324/9781315736143.

Lacorte, Manel. 2018. "Multiliteracies Pedagogy and Heritage Language Teacher Education: A Model for Professional Development." In *Multiliteracies Pedagogy and Language Learning: Teaching Spanish to Heritage Speakers*, edited by Gabriela C. Zapata and Manel Lacorte, 197–225. Cham, Switzerland: Palgrave Macmillian. https://doi.org/10.1007/978-3-319-63103-5_8.

Ladage, Rutu. 2015. "21 Grumpy Cat Memes to Instantly Make You Grumpy However Happy You Are!" *India.com*, November 30, 2015. https://www.india.com/news/21-grumpy-cat-memes-to-instantly-make-you-grumpy-however-happy-you-are-746432/.

Lantolf, James P. 2000. "Second Language Learning as a Mediated Process." *Language Teaching* 33, no. 2: 79–96. https://doi.org/10.1017/S0261444800015329.

Lawson, Hazel, Lyn Layton, Juliet Goldbart, Penny Lacey, and Carol Miller. 2012. "Conceptualisations of Literacy and Literacy Practices for Children with Severe Learning Difficulties." *Literacy* 46, no. 2: 101–8. https://doi.org/10.1111/j.1741-4369.2011.00603.x.

Learning for Justice. 2021. "Social Justice Standards." Accessed January 26, 2022. https://www.learningforjustice.org/frameworks/social-justice-standards.

Leier, Vera. 2018. "Using Instagram in a Tertiary German Language Course: Students' Perceptions and Approaches." *New Zealand Language Teacher* 44: 77–90.

Levine, Glenn S., Charlotte Melin, Corinne Crane, Monika Chavez, and Thomas A. Lovik. 2008. "The Language Program Director in Curricular and Departmental Reform." *Profession*, no. 1: 240–54.

Liamkina, Olga. 2008. "Teaching Grammatical Meaning to Advanced Learners: A Cognitive Semantic Perspective." In *The Longitudinal Study of Advanced L2 Capacities*, edited by Lourdes Ortega and Heidi Byrnes, 161–81. New York: Routledge. https://doi.org/10.4324/9780203871652.

Little, David, Sean Devitt, and David Singleton. 1989. *Learning Foreign Languages from Authentic Texts: Theory and Practice*. Dublin: Authentik.

Littlewood, William. 2011. "Communicative Language Teaching: An Expanding Concept for a Changing World." In *Handbook of Research in Second Language Teaching and Learning*, vol. 2, edited by Eli Hinkel, 541–57. New York: Routledge.

Long, Michael H. 1981. "Input, Interaction, and Second Language Acquisition." *Annals of the New York Academy of Sciences* 379, no. 1: 259–78. https://doi.org/10.1111/j.1749-6632.1981.tb42014.x.

———. 1996. "The Role of the Linguistic Environment in Second Language Acquisition." In *Handbook of Second Language Acquisition*, edited by William C. Ritchie and Tej K. Bhatia, 413–68. San Diego: Academic Press.

López-Sánchez, Ana. 2014. "Hacia una pedagogía para la multialfabetización: El diseño de una unidad didáctica inspirada en las propuestas del New London Group." *Hispania* 97, no. 2: 281–97. https://doi.org/10.1353/hpn.2014.0060.

———. 2016. "Redesigning the Intermediate Level of the Spanish Curriculum through a Multiliteracies Lens." In *Multiliteracies in World Language Education*, edited by Yuri Kumagai, Ana López-Sánchez, and Sujane Wu, 58–80. New York: Routledge.

Losada Rivas, Jhon Jairo, and David Alfonso Suaza Cardozo. 2018. "Video-Mediated Listening and Multiliteracies." *Colombian Applied Linguistics Journal* 20, no. 1: 11–24. https://doi.org/10.14483/22487085.12349.

Luks, Joanna. 2013a. "Un portrait chinois: Le littéraire dans le quotidien: Resources for a Transdisciplinary Approach to Reading/Writing at the First and Second Year Levels of College French." Accessed February 16, 2022. Creative Commons License (CC BY). https://docs.google.com/document/d/1z-Dd7kKMnrLbYaBoC75k42Nk_8yyi-gAo04Nnw1RQgk/edit.

———. 2013b. "What's in a name? Le littéraire dans le quotidien: Resources for a Transdisciplinary Approach to Reading/Writing at the First and Second Year Levels of College French." Accessed February 15, 2022. Creative Commons License (CC BY). https://docs.google.com/document/d/1Dit7mWCRmGoRvUHM32WXk3euMdRfD6c7Xsl6cNbUJwE/edit.

———. 2018. "2018 COERLL Webinar—Techniques for Digital Social Reading." YouTube video, 51:48, April 11, 2018. https://www.coerll.utexas.edu/coerll/social-reading-webinar.

Lundstrom, Kristi, and Wendy Baker. 2009. "To Give Is Better Than to Receive: The Benefits of Peer Review to the Reviewer's Own Writing." *Journal of Second Language Writing* 18, no. 1: 30–43. https://doi.org/10.1016/j.jslw.2008.06.002.

Lyster, Roy. 2007. *Learning and Teaching Languages through Content: A Counterbalanced Approach*. Amsterdam: John Benjamins. https://doi.org/10.1075/lllt.18.

Mackey, Alison, and Jaemyung Goo. 2007. "Interaction Research in SLA: A Meta-Analysis and Research Synthesis." In *Conversational Interaction in Second Language Acquisition*, edited by Alison Mackey, 407–52. Oxford: Oxford University Press.

Martel, Jason. 2013. "Saying our Final Goodbyes to the Grammatical Syllabus: A Curricular Imperative." *French Review* 86, no. 6: 1122–33. https://doi.org/10.1353/tfr.2013.0106.

———. 2022. *Moving beyond the Grammatical Syllabus: Practical Strategies for Content-Based Curriculum Design*. New York: Routledge. https://doi.org/10.4324/9781003017424.

Martin, James R. 2009. "Genre and Language Learning: A Social Semiotic Perspective." *Linguistics and Education* 20, no. 1: 10–21. https://doi.org/10.1016/j.linged.2009.01.003.

Maxim, Hiram H. 2002. "A Study into the Feasibility and Effects of Reading Extended Authentic Discourse in the Beginning German Language Classroom." *Modern Language Journal* 86, no. 1: 20–35. https://doi.org/10.1111/1540-4781.00134.

———. 2006. "Integrating Textual Thinking into the Introductory College-Level Foreign Language Classroom." *Modern Language Journal* 90, no. 1: 19–32. https://doi.org/10.1111/j.1540-4781.2006.00382.x.

———. 2009. "An Essay on the Role of Language in Collegiate Foreign Language Programmatic Reform." *Die Unterrichtspraxis/Teaching German* 42, no. 2: 123–29. https://doi.org/10.1111/j.1756-1221.2009.00046.x.

———. 2014. "Curricular Integration and Faculty Development: Teaching Language-Based Content across the Foreign Language Curriculum." In *Transforming Postsecondary Foreign Language Teaching in the United States*, edited by Janet K. Swaffar and Per Urlaub, 79–101. New York: Springer. https://doi.org/10.1007/978-94-017-9159-5_4.

Maxim, Hiram H., Peter Höyng, Marianne Lancaster, Caroline Schaumann, and Maximilian Aue. 2013. "Overcoming Curricular Bifurcation: A Departmental Approach to Curriculum Reform." *Die Unterrichtspraxis/Teaching German* 46, no. 1: 1–26. https://doi.org/10.1111/tger.10126.

McKay, Marlene E. 2008. "Readers Theater—Take Another Look—It's More Than Fluency Instruction." *LEARNing Landscapes* 2, no. 1: 131–44. https://doi.org/10.36510/learnland.v2i1.280.

McLaren, Peter. 2003. *Life in Schools: An Introduction to Critical Pedagogy in the Foundations of Education*. 4th ed. London: Longman.

McTighe and Associates Consulting (MAC). n.d. "Resources." Accessed February 15, 2022. https://jaymctighe.com/resources.

Mehrpour, Saeed, and Abdolmehdi Riazi. 2004. "The Impact of Text Length on EFL Students' Reading Comprehension." *Asian EFL Journal* 6, no. 3: 72–90.

Menke, Mandy R. 2018. "Literacy-Based Curricula in University Foreign Language Instruction: Perceptions from Non-Tenure-Track Faculty." *L2 Journal* 10, no. 2: 111–33. https://doi.org/10.5070/L210235280.

Menke, Mandy R., and Liz Lake. 2017. "Student and Instructor Perceptions of an Integrated Performance Assessment." Paper presented at the Central States Council on the Teaching of Foreign Languages, Chicago, IL.

Menke, Mandy R., and Kate Paesani. 2019. "Analysing Foreign Language Instructional Materials through the Lens of the Multiliteracies Framework." *Language, Culture and Curriculum* 32, no. 1: 34–49. https://doi.org/10.1080/07908318.2018.1461898.

———. 2021. "Understanding Teacher Discourse around Multiliteracies Pedagogy." In *Pathways to Paradigm Change: Critical Examinations of Prevailing Discourses and Ideologies in Second Language Education*, edited by Beatrice Dupuy and Kristen Michelson, 83–107. Boston: Cengage. http://hdl.handle.net/10125/69793.

Michelson, Kristen. 2018. "Teaching Culture as a Relational Process through a Multiliteracies-Based Global Simulation." *Language, Culture and Curriculum* 31, no. 1: 1–20. https://doi.org/10.1080/07908318.2017.1338295.

———. 2019. "Global Simulation as a Mediating Tool for Teaching and Learning Language and Culture as Discourse." *Foreign Language Annals* 52, no. 2: 284–313. https://doi.org/10.1111/flan.12392.

Michelson, Kristen, and Beatrice Dupuy. 2014. "Multi-Storied Lives: Global Simulation as an Approach to Developing Multiliteracies in an Intermediate French Course." *L2 Journal* 6, no. 1: 21–49. https://doi.org/10.5070/L26119613.

———. 2018. "Teacher Learning under Co-Construction: Affordances of Digital Social Annotated Reading." *Apprentissage des langues et systèmes d'information et de communication* 21. https://doi.org/10.4000/alsic.3344.

Mills, Kathy A. 2006. "Critical Framing in a Pedagogy of Multiliteracies." In *Voices, Vibes, Visions: Hearing the Voices, Feeling the Vibes, Capturing the Visions: Proceedings of the AATE/ALEA National Conference*, edited by Jennifer Rennie, 1–15. Australian Association for Teaching English/Australian Literacy Educators Association.

Modern Language Association Ad Hoc Committee on Foreign Languages. 2007. "Foreign Languages and Higher Education: New Structures for a Changed World." *Profession*: 234–45.

Morrow, K. 1977. "Authentic Texts and ESP." In *English for Specific Purposes*, edited by Susan Holden, 13–17. London: Modern English Publications.

Morton, Tom. 2016. "Conceptualizing and Investigating Teachers' Knowledge for Integrating Content and Language in Content-Based Instruction." *Journal of Immersion and Content-Based Language Education* 4, no. 2: 144–67. https://doi.org/10.1075/jicb.4.2.01mor.

National Academies of Sciences, Engineering, and Medicine. n.d. "Ten Things You Probably Didn't Know about Immigrants." Infographic. The National Academies Press. Accessed January 24, 2022. https://www.nap.edu/visualizations/integration-of-immigrants/.

National Standards Collaborative Board (NSCB). 2015. *World-Readiness Standards for Learning Languages*. 4th ed. Alexandria, VA: ACTFL.

Nauman, Gretchen. 2011. "Synthesizing the Academic and the Everyday." In *Research on Second Language Teacher Education: A Sociocultural Perspective on Professional Development*, edited by Karen E. Johnson and Paula R. Golombek, 102–17. New York: Routledge. https://doi.org/10.4324/9780203844991.

———. 2014. "Paths to New Conceptualizations of Literacy in Chinese EFL Teachers." PhD diss., Pennsylvania State University, State College, PA.

New London Group. 1996. "A Pedagogy of Multiliteracies: Designing Social Futures." *Harvard Educational Review* 66, no. 1: 60–92. https://doi.org/10.17763/haer.66.1.17370n67v22j160u.

Nieto, Sonia. 2010. *Language, Culture, and Teaching: Critical Perspectives*. Vol. 2. New York: Routledge. https://doi.org/10.4324/9780203872284.

Nunan, David. 2017. "The Integrated Syllabus: Content, Tasks, and Projects." In *The Content-Based Classroom: New Perspectives on Integrating Language and Content*, 2nd ed., edited by Marguerite Ann Snow and Donna M. Brinton, 124–36. University of Michigan Press. https://doi.org/10.3998/mpub.8198148.

Oh, Sun-Young. 2001. "Two Types of Input Modification and EFL Reading Comprehension: Simplification versus Elaboration." *TESOL Quarterly* 35, no. 1: 69–96. https://doi.org/10.2307/3587860.

Ornstein, Allan C. 1994. "The Textbook-Driven Curriculum." *Peabody Journal of Education* 69, no. 3: 70–85. https://doi.org/10.1080/01619569409538778.

Paesani, Kate. 2013. "A Literacy-Based Approach to Foreign Language Teacher Development." In *Educating the Future Foreign Language Professoriate for the 21st Century*, edited by Heater W. Allen and Hiram H. Maxim, 60–81. Boston: Heinle. http://hdl.handle.net/10125/69697.

———. 2015. "Student Perceptions of Multiliteracies-Oriented and Traditional Grammar Activities: A Mixed-Methods Case Study." *Konin Language Studies* 3, no. 1: 31–55.

———. 2016. "Investigating Connections among Reading, Writing, and Language Development: A Multiliteracies Perspective." *Reading in a Foreign Language* 28, no. 2: 266–89. http://hdl.handle.net/10125/66902.

———. 2017. "Redesigning an Introductory Language Curriculum: A Backward Design Approach." *L2 Journal* 9, no. 1: 1–20. https://doi.org/10.5070/L29130408.

Paesani, Kate, and Heather W. Allen. 2020. "Teacher Development and Multiliteracies Pedagogy: Challenges and Opportunities for Postsecondary Language Programs." *Second Language Research & Practice* 1, no. 1: 124–38. http://hdl.handle.net/10125/69844.

Paesani, Kate, Heather W. Allen, and Beatrice Dupuy. 2016. *A Multiliteracies Framework for Collegiate Foreign Language Teaching*. Boston: Pearson.

Paesani, Kate, and Mandy R. Menke. 2019. "Using Teacher Voices to Inform Professional Development." Paper presented at the 11th International Language Teacher Educator Conference, Minneapolis, MN.

Parra, María Luisa, Araceli Otero, Rosa Flores, and Marguerite Lavalleé. 2018. "Designing a Comprehensive Curriculum for Advanced Spanish Heritage Learners: Contributions from the Multiliteracies Framework." In *Multiliteracies Pedagogy and Language Learning: Teaching Spanish to Heritage Speakers*, edited by Gabriela C. Zapata and Manel Lacorte, 27–66. Cham, Switzerland: Palgrave Macmillan. http://doi.org/10.1007/978-3-319-63103-5_2.

Pirbhai-Illich, Fatima, K. C. Nat Turner, and Theresa Y. Austin. 2009. "Using Digital Technologies to Address Aboriginal Adolescents' Education: An Alternative School Intervention." *Multicultural Education and Technology Journal* 3, no. 2: 144–62. https://doi.org/10.1108/17504970910967573.

Porter, Catherine. 2009. "The MLA Recommendations: Can We Get There from Here?" *ADFL Bulletin* 41, no. 1: 16–23. https://doi.org/10.1632/adfl.41.1.16.

Porter, Don, and Jon Roberts. 1981. "Authentic Listening Activities." *ELT Journal* 36, no. 1: 37–47. https://doi.org/10.1093/elt/36.1.37.

Porto, Melina. 2018. "Does Education for Intercultural Citizenship Lead to Language Learning?" *Language, Culture and Curriculum* 32, no. 1: 16–33. https://doi.org/10.1080/07908318.2017.1421642.

Randolph, Linwood J., Jr., and Stacey Margarita Johnson. 2017. "Social Justice in the Classroom: A Call to Action." *Dimension* 99: 9–31.

Ready, Carol. n.d. "La globalización de comida." FLLITE. Accessed January 28, 2022. https://drive.google.com/file/d/0Byg7PyauMJRSSC1wQTBEWmY1SGc/view?resourcekey=0-V-RtPk3H90JV-1QWMs9S4A.

Reagan, Timothy G., and Terry A. Osborn. 2021. *World Language Education as Critical Pedagogy: The Promise of Social Justice*. New York: Routledge. https://doi.org/10.4324/9781003029267.

Redmann, Jennifer. 2005a. "An Interactive Reading Journal for All Levels of the Foreign Language Curriculum." *Foreign Language Annals* 38, no. 4: 484–93. https://doi.org/10.1111/j.1944-9720.2005.tb02515.x.

———. 2005b. "*Stationenlernen*: A student-centered approach to working with foreign language texts." *Die Unterrichtspraxis* 38, no. 2: 135–42. https://doi.org/10.1111/j.1756-1221.2005.tb00051.x.

Reyes-Torres, Agustín, and Matilde Portalés Raga. 2020. "Multimodal Approach to Foster the Multiliteracies Pedagogy in the Teaching of EFL through Picturebooks: *The Snow Lion*." *Atlantis: Journal of the Spanish Association of Anglo-American Studies* 42, no. 1: 94–119. https://doi.org/10.28914/Atlantis-2020-42.1.06.

Richards, Jack C. 2006. *Communicative Language Teaching Today*. New York: Cambridge University Press.

———. 2013. "Curriculum Approaches in Language Teaching: Forward, Central, and Backward Design." *RELC Journal* 44, no. 1: 5–33. https://doi.org/10.1177/0033688212473293.

Richards, Jack C., and Theodore S. Rodgers. 2014. *Approaches and Methods in Language Teaching*. 3rd ed. Cambridge: Cambridge University Press.

Rilliard, Marylise. 2021. "Becoming a Legitimate L2 Speaker: The Role of Non-Traditional Speaker Models." *Second Language Research & Practice* 2, no. 1: 65–80. http://hdl.handle.net/10125/69858.

Robin, Bernard R. 2006. "The Educational Uses of Digital Storytelling." In *Proceedings of Society for Information Technology and Teacher Education International Conference*, edited by Caroline M. Crawford, Roger Carlsen, Karen McFerrin, Jerry Price, Roberta Weber, and Dee Anna Willis, 709–16. Waynesville, NC: Association for the Advancement of Computing in Education (AACE).

Rogers, Carmen V., and Frank W. Medley, Jr. 1988. "Language with a Purpose: Using Authentic Materials in the Foreign Language Classroom." *Foreign Language Annals* 21, no. 5: 467–78. https://doi.org/10.1111/j.1944-9720.1988.tb01098.x.

Ross, Diana, vocalist. 1975. "Do You Know Where You're Going To." Track 1 on *Mahogany (Original Motion Picture Soundtrack)*. Motown.

Rowland, Luke, Nick Canning, David Faulhaber, Will Lingle, and Andrew Redgrave. 2014. "A Multiliteracies Approach to Materials Analysis." *Language, Culture and Curriculum* 27, no. 2: 136–50. https://doi.org/10.1080/07908318.2014.927883.

Ryshina-Pankova, Marianna. 2010. "Towards Mastering the Discourses of Reasoning: Using Grammatical Metaphor at Advanced Levels of FL Acquisition." *Modern Language Journal* 94, no. 2: 181–97. https://doi.org/10.1111/j.1540-4781.2010.01016.x.

———. 2013. "Connecting Languaging and Knowing through Genre: Exemplifying the Link in a Curricular Progression." In *Traditions and Transitions: German Curricula*, edited by John L. Plews and Barbara Schmenk, 227–51. Waterloo: Wilfrid Laurier University Press.

———. 2016. "Scaffolding Advanced Literacy Abilities in the FL Classroom: Implementing a Genre-Driven Content-Based Approach." In *Content-Based Foreign Language Teaching: Curriculum and Pedagogy for Developing Advanced Thinking and Literacy Skills*, edited by Laurent Cammarata, 51–70. New York: Routledge. https://doi.org/10.4324/9780203850497.

Sandrock, Paul. 2010. *The Keys to Assessing Language Performance*. Alexandria, VA: ACTFL.

Saudelli, Mary Gene, and Jennifer Rowsell. 2013. "Walking the Talk: Towards a Notion of Multiliteracies in Literacy Teacher Education." In *Literacy Teacher Educators: Preparing Teachers for a Changing World*, edited by Clare M. Kosnik, Jennifer Rowsell, Peter Williamson, Rob Simon, and Clive Beck, 35–47. Rotterdam; Boston: Sense Publishers. https://doi.org/10.1007/978-94-6209-200-6_4.

Schmerbeck, Nicola, and Felecia Lucht, F. 2017. "Creating Meaning through Multimodality: Multiliteracies Assessment and Photo Projects for Online Portfolios." *Die Unterrichtspraxis/Teaching German* 50, no. 1: 32–44. https://doi.org/10.1111/tger.12020.

Shor, Ira. 1992. *Empowering Education: Critical Teaching for Social Change*. University of Chicago: Chicago Press.

Shrum, Judith L., and Eileen W. Glisan. 2016. *Teacher's Handbook: Contextualized Language Instruction*. 5th ed. Boston: Cengage.

Simonsen, Russell. 2019. "An Analysis of the Problematic Discourse Surrounding 'Authentic Texts.'" *Hispania* 102, no. 2: 245–58. https://doi.org/10.1353/hpn.2019.0045.

Stoller, Fredricka L., and William Grabe. 1997. "A Six-T's Approach to Content-Based Instruction." In *The Content-Based Classroom: Perspectives on Integrating Language and Content*, edited by Marguerite Ann Snow and Donna M. Brinton, 78–94. White Plains, NY: Addison Wesley Longman.

Swaffar, Janet K. 1985. "Reading Authentic Texts in a Foreign Language: A Cognitive Model." *Modern Language Journal* 69, no. 1: 15–34. https://doi.org/10.1111/j.1540-4781.1985.tb02521.x.

———. 2006. "Terminology and Its Discontents: Some Caveats about Communicative Competence." *Modern Language Journal* 90, no. 2: 246–49. https://doi.org/10.1111/j.1540-4781.2006.00395_2.x.

———. 2014. "From Language to Literacy: The Evolving Concepts of Foreign Language Teaching at American Colleges and Universities Since 1945." In *Transforming Postsecondary Foreign Language Teaching in the United States*, edited by Janet K. Swaffar and Per Urlaub, 19–54. Dordrecht, Netherlands: Springer. https://doi.org/10.1007/978-94-017-9159-5_2.

Swaffar, Judith K., and Katherine Arens. 2005. *Remapping the Foreign Language Curriculum: An Approach through Multiple Literacies*. New York: Modern Language Association of America.

Swaffar, Judith K., Katherine Arens, and Heidi Byrnes. 1991. *Reading for Meaning: An Integrated Approach to Language Learning*. Englewood Cliffs, NJ: Prentice Hall.

Swain, Merrill. 1985. "Communicative Competence: Some Roles of Comprehensible Input and Comprehensible Output in Its Development." In *Input in Second Language Acquisition*, edited by Susan M. Gass and Carolyn G. Madden, 235–53. Rowley, MA: Newbury House.

Tan, Lynde, Jeanette Bopry, and Libo Guo. 2010. "Portraits of New Literacies in Two Singapore Classrooms." *RELC Journal* 41, no. 1: 5–17. https://doi.org/10.1177/0033688210343864.

Tan, Lynde, Katina Zammit, Jacqueline D'warte, and Anne Gearside. 2020. "Assessing Multimodal Literacies in Practice: A Critical Review of Its Implementations in Educational Settings." *Language and Education* 34, no. 2: 97–114. https://doi.org/10.1080/09500782.2019.1708926.

Tanner, Fran A. 1993. *Readers Theater Fundamentals*. 2nd ed. Clark Publishing.

Tarone, Elaine. 2009. "Equipping Teachers to Be Language Explorers: Exploring Language in the Classroom." In *Bridging Contexts Making Connections: Selected Papers from the Fifth International Conference on*

Language Teacher Education, edited by Michael E. Anderson and Anne Lazaraton, 7–21. Minneapolis: CARLA.

Tedick, Diane J., and Roy Lyster. 2020. *Scaffolding Language Development in Immersion and Dual Language Classrooms*. London: Routledge. https://doi.org/10.4324/9780429428319.

Thoms, Joshua J., Ko-Yin Sung, and Frederick Poole. 2017. "Investigating the Linguistic and Pedagogical Affordances of an L2 Open Reading Environment via eComma: An Exploratory Study in a Chinese Language Course." *System*, no. 69: 38–53. https://doi.org/10.1016/j.system.2017.08.003.

Todhunter, Susan. 2007. "Instructional Conversations in a High School Spanish Class." *Foreign Language Annals* 40, no. 4: 604–21. https://doi.org/10.1111/j.1944-9720.2007.tb02883.x.

Troyan, Francis J. 2016. "Learning to Mean in Spanish Writing: A Case Study of a Genre-Based Pedagogy for Standards-Based Writing Instruction." *Foreign Language Annals* 49, no. 2: 317–35. https://doi.org/10.1111/flan.12192.

Turpin, Kristen M. 2019. "Training Foreign Language Learners to Be Peer Responders: A Multiliteracies Approach." *L2 Journal* 11, no. 1: 35–60. https://doi.org/10.5070/L211140673.

United States Department of Homeland Security. 2017. "The US Immigration System." Infographic. Homeland Security. Accessed January 24, 2022. https://www.dhs.gov/immigration-statistics/visualization/2017.

United States Department of Homeland Security. n.d. "Explore Immigration Data." Infographic. Scholastic Inc. Accessed January 25, 2022. http://teacher.scholastic.com/activities/immigration/immigration_data/index.htm.

University of California, Berkeley. n.d. "Design Effective Assessments." Berkeley Center for Teaching and Learning. Accessed February 15, 2022. https://teaching.berkeley.edu/resources/course-design-guide/design-effective-assessments.

Unsworth, Len. 2014. "Multimodal Reading Comprehension: Curriculum Expectations and Large-Scale Literacy Testing Practices." *Pedagogies: An International Journal* 9, no. 1: 26–44. https://doi.org/10.1080/1554480X.2014.878968.

VanPatten, Bill. 1993. "Grammar Teaching for the Acquisition-Rich Classroom." *Foreign Language Annals* 26, no. 4: 435–50. https://doi.org/10.1111/j.1944-9720.1993.tb01179.x.

Vygotsky, Lev S. 1978. *Mind in Society: The Development of Higher Psychological Processes*. Cambridge, MA: Harvard University Press.

Wardhaugh, Ronald. 1999. *Proper English: Myths and Misunderstandings about Language*. Malden, MA: Blackwell.

Warford, Mark K., and William L. White. 2012. "Reconnecting Proficiency, Literacy, and Culture: From Theory to Practice." *Foreign Language Annals* 45, no. 3: 400–14. https://doi.org/10.1111/j.1944-9720.2012.01200.x.

Warner, Chantelle, and Beatrice Dupuy. 2018. "Moving to Multiliteracies in Foreign Language Teaching: Past and Present Perspectives . . . and Beyond." *Foreign Language Annals* 51, no. 1: 116–28. https://doi.org/10.1111/flan.12316.

Warren, Mackenzie, and Claudia Winkler. 2016. "Developing Multiliteracies through Genre in the Beginner German Classroom." In *Multiliteracies in World Language Education*, edited by Yuri Kumagai, Ana López-Sánchez, and Sujane Wu, 29–57. New York: Routledge.

White, Lydia. 2003. *Second Language Acquisition and Universal Grammar*. Cambridge: Cambridge University Press. https://doi.org/10.1017/CBO9780511815065.

Wiggins, Grant P., and Jay McTighe. 2005. *Understanding by Design*. 2nd ed. Alexandria, VA: ASCD.

WikiEducator. 2010. "OER Life Cycle." Accessed January 29, 2022. https://wikieducator/OER_Handbook/educator.

Wink, Joan. 2000. *Critical Pedagogy: Notes from the Real World*. 2nd ed. New York: Longman.

Wood, David, Jerome S. Bruner, and Gail Ross. 1976. "The Role of Tutoring in Problem-Solving." *Journal of Child Psychology and Psychiatry in Applied Disciplines* 17, no. 2: 89–100. https://doi.org/10.1111/j.1469-7610.1976.tb00381.x.

Wyatt-Smith, Claire, and Kay Kimber. 2009. "Working Multimodally: Challenges for Assessment." *English Teaching: Practice and Critique* 8, no. 3: 70–90.

Yale University. 2017. "Bloom's Taxonomy." Yale Poorvu Center for Teaching and Learning. Accessed January 29, 2022. https://poorvucenter.yale.edu/BloomsTaxonomy.

Yáñez Prieto, Maria del Carmen. 2010. "Authentic Instruction in Literary Worlds: Learning the Stylistics of Concept-Based Grammar." *Language and Literature* 19, no. 1: 59–75. https://doi.org/10.1177/0963947009356723.

———. 2015. "Sense and Subjectivity: Teaching Literature from a Sociolinguistic Perspective." *Language and Sociocultural Theory* 1, no. 2: 179–203. https://doi.org/10.1558/lst.v1i2.179.

Yano, Yasukata, Michael H. Long, and Steven Ross. 1994. "The Effects of Simplified and Elaborated Texts on Foreign Language Reading Comprehension." *Language Learning* 44, no. 2: 189–219. https://doi.org/10.1111/j.1467-1770.1994.tb01100.x.

Yasuda, Sachiko. 2011. "Genre-Based Tasks in Foreign Language Writing: Developing Writers' Genre Awareness, Linguistic Knowledge, and Writing Competence." *Journal of Second Language Writing* 20, no. 2: 111–33. https://doi.org/10.1016/j.jslw.2011.03.001.

Yi, Youngjoo, and Jayoung Choi. 2015. "Teachers' Views of Multimodal Practices in K–12 Classrooms: Voices from Teachers in the United States." *TESOL Quarterly* 49, no. 4: 838–47. https://doi.org/10.1002/tesq.219.

Young, Dolly Jesusita. 1993. "Processing Strategies of Foreign Language Readers: Authentic and Edited Input." *Foreign Language Annals* 26, no. 4: 451–68. https://doi.org/10.1111/j.1944-9720.1993.tb01180.x.

Yu, Shulin, and Icy Lee. 2016. "Peer Feedback in Second Language Writing." *Language Teaching* 49, no. 4: 461–93. https://doi.org/10.1017/S0261444816000161.

Zapata, Gabriela C. 2016. "University Students' Perceptions of Integrated Performance Assessments and the Connection between Classroom Learning and Assessment." *Foreign Language Annals* 49, no. 1: 93–104. https://doi.org/10.1111/flan.12176.

———. 2018. "The Role of Digital, *Learning by Design* Instructional Materials in the Development of Spanish Heritage Learners' Literacy Skills." In *Multiliteracies Pedagogy and Language Learning: Teaching Spanish to Heritage Speakers*, edited by Gabriela C. Zapata and Manel Lacorte, 67–106. Cham, Switzerland: Palgrave Macmillan. https://doi.org/10.1007/978-3-319-63103-5_3.

Zapata, Gabriela C., and Alessandra Ribota. 2021. "The Instructional Benefits of Identity Texts and Learning by Design for Learner Motivation in Required Second Language Classes." *Pedagogies: An International Journal* 16, no. 1: 1–18. https://doi.org/10.1080/1554480X.2020.1738937.

Zhou, Jiming, Ke Zhao, and Phillip Dawson. 2020. "How First-Year Students Perceive and Experience Assessment of Academic Literacies." *Assessment and Evaluation in Higher Education* 45, no. 2: 266–78. https://doi.org/10.1080/02602938.2019.1637513.

Ziegler, Nicole. 2016. "Synchronous Computer-Mediated Communication and Interaction: A Meta-Analysis." *Studies in Second Language Acquisition* 38, no. 3: 553–86. https://doi.org/10.1017/S027226311500025X.

Zygouris-Coe, Vicky, Matthew B. Wiggins, and Lourdes H. Smith. 2004. "Engaging Students with Text: The 3-2-1 Strategy." *Reading Teacher* 58, no. 4: 381–84. https://doi.org/10.1598/RT.58.4.8.

Zyzik, Eve, and Charlene Polio. 2008. "Incidental Focus on Form in Spanish Literature Courses." *Modern Language Journal* 92, no. 1: 50–73. https://doi.org/10.1111/j.1540-4781.2008.00686.x.

———. 2017. *Authentic Materials Myths: Applying Second Language Research to Classroom Teaching*. Ann Arbor, MI: University of Michigan Press. https://doi.org/10.3998/mpub.7892433.

Index

About the Authors

Kate Paesani (PhD, Indiana University) is director of the Center for Advanced Research on Language Acquisition (CARLA) and associate professor of French at the University of Minnesota. Her research interests include multiliteracies pedagogy, text-based curriculum and instruction, and teacher development. She began adopting a literacies orientation to language education in the mid 2000s and has numerous publications on the topic, including the coauthored book *A Multiliteracies Framework for Collegiate Foreign Language Teaching* (2016). Her current research explores teachers' cognition and identity construction as they apply multiliteracies and social justice pedagogies, a collaborative project stemming from CARLA's Social Justice in Language Education initiative.

Mandy Menke (PhD, University of Minnesota) examines the acquisition of Spanish as a second language as well as topics related to foreign language teaching. Her work spans the linguistic subdisciplines of phonology, syntax, and pragmatics and encompasses teachers and learners in K–12 language immersion programs and postsecondary foreign language contexts. She is the coauthor of *Language and Learning Disabilities in Immersion Education: Educators' Top Questions and Research-Based, Practitioner-Informed Responses* (2010) and the coeditor of *Evolving Perspective on Advancedness: Research from Second Language Spanish* (2021). She is an associate professor of Hispanic linguistics at the University of Minnesota, where she directs the Spanish and Portuguese language programs. Working and learning with other language educators—language immersion teachers, graduate instructors, preservice teacher candidates, and in-service secondary and postsecondary teachers—is one of her favorite professional activities.